Murder in the Model City

Murder in the Model City

The Black Panthers, Yale, and the Redemption of a Killer

PAUL BASS AND DOUGLAS W. RAE

BASIC
BOOKS

A Member of the Perseus Books Group
New York

Published by Basic Books
A Member of the Perseus Books Group

Designed by Trish Wilkinson
Set in 11-point Goudy by the Perseus Books Group

A catalog-in-publication record for this book is available from the Library of Congress.
ISBN 10: 0-465-06902-9
ISBN 13: 978-0465-06902-6

06 07 08 09/ 10 9 8 7 6 5 4 3 2 1

Contents

PART III

To Carole and Ellen

Prologue

The First New Haven Pig Trial

NEW HAVEN HAD no Black Panthers back in 1641. Sadly for one George Spencer, New Haven had Puritans, another band of fiery, besieged rebels who arrived in the brand-new colony determined to create an ideal society. The Puritans, like the Black Panthers centuries later, had a ten-point program, called the Ten Commandments.

George Spencer didn't read the ten-point program unless ordered to. Spencer was poor, unskilled, rootless, a nobody in New Haven. He spent his days shoveling manure and tending the pigs on Henry Browning's farm two blocks north of the colony's central Green, by the intersection of what would one day become Hillhouse Avenue and Grove Street. If people took notice of George Spencer, they remarked on his pearly eye. Spencer occasionally ran afoul of the authorities. One time he stole a rowboat. Another time he mocked the Sabbath.

The latter was an unwise offense to commit in New Haven Colony in 1641. The Puritans, fundamentalist Christians who interpreted the Bible literally, were on constant lookout for signs from God. The Puritans had founded New Haven five years earlier, after their religious zealotry led to their being hounded out of Massachusetts Bay Colony. The Puritans put down new roots and started building a community whose only basis for law would be found in scripture.

In February 1641, the Almighty appeared to one Goodwife Wakeman, the wife of a planter. Goodwife Wakeman had come across an odd creature in the possession of George Spencer's boss—a stillborn piglet. The piglet had a deformed nose, mouth, and chin. And yet, Goodwife Wakeman revealed, those features were "not unlike a child's." The same with the creature's neck and ears. The piglet was hairless, its skin reddish, also, it was remarked on, like a child's.

The piglet's head, as reported in the New Haven Colony Records, was "most straing. . . . In the bottome of the foreheade w[hi]ch was like a childes, a thing of flesh grew forth and hung downe, itt was hollow, and like a mans instrum[en]t of gen[e]ration."

Strangest of all, right below this member-like membrane, the piglet had but one eye—an occluded eye.

Goodwife Wakeman's mind flashed on another lowly creature in town with a pearly eye. She had a vision. "Some hand of God appeared in an impr[e]ssion upon Goodwife Wakemans speritt, sadly expecting, though she knew nott why, some strange accident in thatt sows pigging, and a strange impr[e]ssion was also upon many thatt saw the monster, (therein guided by the neare resemblance of the eye,) that one George Spencer, late servant to the said Henry Browning, had beene actor in unnatureall and abominable fithynes w[i]th the sow."

In other words, the Lord, through Goodwife Wakeman, accused George Spencer of consorting with a pig, fathering the piglet. Bestiality, not surprisingly, violated the written laws of Puritan New Haven, found in Chapter 18 of the Book of Leviticus. The law spelled out the penalty: death.

An inquest commenced. The authorities imprisoned George Spencer in a little block house near the colony meeting hall. There he remained confined for close to a year, as a parade of worthies took turns engaging him in conversation about his supposed deed. Sometimes he denied it; other times, according to the records, he confessed, to the visitors or to other prisoners. Under interrogation by leading citizens, including the feared schoolmaster Ezekiel Cheever, Spencer broke down. He concocted detailed accounts of an early-evening tryst with the sow, the whiteness of whose eye lured him into Satan's grasp.

Hauled before a court, Spencer infuriated the notables by denying, then admitting, then denying again the dreadful tale. As time progressed, the Puritans worked themselves into a fury, drowning any doubts about the likelihood of the scenario in a quest for divinely authorized retribution and communal purgation.

The execution was set for April 8, 1642. The gallows stood by the so-called Oyster-shell field by the waterfront. Both parties to this putative fornication were slated for execution. Awaiting his fate on the gallows, Spencer watched the offending sow run through with a sword.

The time arrived for his final message to the crowd, a full confession and testament to the Lord scripted by the colony fathers. But Spencer opened with yet another denial. So his executioners applied a little persuasion—"the halter being fastened to the gallowes, and fitted to his neck, and being tolde it was an ill time now to p[ro]voke God when he was falling into his hands." Spencer found his voice. He "justified the sentence as righteous, and fully confessed the beastiality in all the circumstances." Then he was put to death.

Timeline

APRIL 8, 1642: George Spencer, a rootless farmhand, is executed in New Haven Colony. A band of fiery, besieged zealots known as Puritans condemned Spencer to death on charges of having an unnatural relationship with a pig.

DEC. 10, 1924: J. Edgar Hoover is named the Federal Bureau of Investigation's first director, embarking on a fight against Communists and advocates of Negro rights.

AUG. 28, 1963: Martin Luther King Jr. delivers his "I Have a Dream Speech" before hundreds of thousands of civil rights advocates at the March on Washington.

JULY 2, 1964: President Lyndon Johnson signs the Civil Rights Act.

FEB. 21, 1965: Rival black Muslims assassinate Malcolm X in Harlem.

OCTOBER 1966: In Oakland, California, Huey Newton and Bobby Seale form the Black Panther Party for Self-Defense.

APRIL 4, 1968: Martin Luther King Jr. is assassinated. Riots follow in cities across the country.

NOV. 5, 1968: Richard M. Nixon is elected president.

JAN. 17, 1969: Rival black radicals murder Black Panthers John Huggins and Alprentice "Bunchy" Carter in L.A.

MAY 20, 1969: Alex Rackley, a rootless nineteen-year-old from Florida, is executed. Black Panthers in New Haven condemned Rackley to death on charges of being an undercover "pig."

Dec. 4, 1969:   Chicago police, working in tandem with the FBI, shoot Panther leader Fred Hampton to death in his sleep.

May 1, 1970:   President Nixon dispatches National Guard troops to New Haven to confront radicals protesting the murder trial of Bobby Seale and Ericka Huggins.

May 2, 1972:   FBI Director J. Edgar Hoover dies.

April 26, 1974: A committee led by U.S. Senator Frank Church releases a report exposing massive illegal attacks on radical groups carried out by the FBI.

Aug. 9, 1974:   President Nixon resigns because of the Watergate scandal.

2004:   America's state and federal prison population tops 1.4 million, seven times as many as in 1970. Over 12 percent of African-American males between the ages of twenty-five and twenty-nine are behind bars.

Part I

CHAPTER 1

Trigger Man

"Truth be told, there were no heroes."
—WARREN KIMBRO

ON THE NIGHT of Tuesday, May 20, 1969, four men sped north from New Haven, Connecticut, in a borrowed Buick Riviera. All belonged to the revolutionary Black Panther Party.

Warren Kimbro sat nervously in the front passenger seat, directing the driver through ghetto streets, away from the campus of Yale University, looking to find a patch of privacy. Warren, a tall, sinewy figure, was normally quick with his tongue, loose, funny. Yet he was scared silent by the power sitting behind him in the Buick that night. That power was named George Sams. Maybe it was the pistol Sams always waved around. Maybe it was the threats Sams barked, the herky-jerky intensity of his stocky body. Maybe it was because Sams was part of a team, including a national leader named Landon Williams, flown in from the Panthers' California headquarters to whip East Coast chapters into shape.

Landon Williams and George Sams evoked the paranoia that dogged the Panthers throughout their history: anyone, at any moment, could find himself accused of collaboration with the FBI or local police. Such collaboration was a capital offense.

Earlier, at Panther headquarters in downtown New Haven, Sams had said, "I'm going for a ride. Come with me." Loyalty was spelled "Sure thing."

In the front seat, as they traveled north, Warren was hyped up. Sparked by caffeine, by a speed pill, an electric current jangled Warren's nerves. Warren didn't know exactly where he would lead the driver, beyond searching, at Sams's orders, for a secluded spot. But he knew they were headed to some kind of hell. Something's going to happen, Kimbro thought to himself. He tried not to think about specifics, although it didn't require much imagination.

For the three days leading up to May 20, imported Panthers Landon Williams and George Sams had commandeered Warren Kimbro's three-story townhouse apartment in the mixed-income Ethan Gardens complex on Orchard Street in New Haven's Dwight neighborhood. The apartment doubled as New Haven Panther headquarters. Sams oversaw a kangaroo trial, interrogation, torture, and confinement there of a suspected FBI informant named Alex Rackley. Now Rackley was to be transported from the house.

It was around midnight when the orders were issued: Alex Rackley needed to be taken away, driven to the bus station.

Someone suggested taking Warren's Mustang.

No, someone else said. The police will recognize it.

Would that be a problem for a trip to the bus station? The question went unanswered.

Instead, a call went to Kelly Moye, a hanger-on around thirty years old, who made deliveries for a package store. Moye showed up at Panther meetings and always seemed eager to lend the party money or offer a meal. Would Brother Kelly lend the Panthers his car now for an important mission?

Sure thing, Moye said.

Moye hung up the phone and dialed another number—Nick Pastore's number. Nick Pastore ran the intelligence division of the New Haven police department. He paid Moye to spy on the Panthers. Moye enjoyed the Panther meetings. He especially enjoyed watching Ericka Huggins, the tall, slender, frizzy-haired firebrand who spoke so eloquently, who was followed around in public like the pied piper by adoring Yale students.

Moye reported the request to borrow his car. Nick Pastore advised Moye to go ahead and lend it. Nick had a hunch that something big was happening on Orchard Street; he told Moye that a Panther from New York was being held there and was about to be transported. "Go over and see what is happening," Nick said.

Within minutes, Moye showed up outside Ethan Gardens in his two-door green Buick Riviera. George Sams stood by the curb waiting for him. When Moye emerged from the Buick, Sams stuck a gun to his head.

"I want to use your car," Sams said.

"Hey, look," Moye said, "you can *take* the car."

Moye handed over the keys. Another Panther drove him home. No one asked why Kelly Moye was so prompt, so accommodating, because people helped the Black Panthers all the time. They pitched in for the cause the instant they were summoned. That was how a revolution worked.

BACK IN THE Panther apartment, Warren changed into dark clothes. He went upstairs to put on black dungarees, a Navy mock turtleneck, plus a black knit cap. Then he entered the bedroom usually occupied by his seven-year-old daughter, who was now sharing a room with her brother. Alex Rackley, a tall, simple-seeming Floridian, lay strapped to the child's bed. Rackley had been there three days since his interrogation. He lay in his own urine and feces. Warren joined other Panthers in untying Rackley. Some Panther women cleaned Rackley up, dressed him, and then returned to the kitchen downstairs.

A wire-hanger noose hung visibly around Rackley's neck. That wouldn't do. The men looked around for something to throw over it; they found a Nehru jacket belonging to one of the party members. That would do.

Raised to his feet, Rackley teetered. He wanted to sit down. Instead, the men clambered down the stairs and pushed Rackley through the kitchen, to the back door—out of sight, they hoped, of the police.

From her perch by the kitchen counter, Ericka Huggins, the highest-ranking female Panther in town, watched Sams and Warren walk Rackley out the door. Sams brandished the .45 automatic as he held Rackley's arms, which were tied together with ropes. Rackley didn't resist.

On the way out, someone handed Warren a pill and a cup of coffee. "This'll keep you awake," he said. Warren needed a jolt. He had barely slept for days amid all the nonstop activity in the house and on the street, not to mention the climate of paranoia.

Kelly Moye's car was parked on Orchard Street. Sams steered Rackley to the back seat, then sat beside him. Warren sat in front, where he would direct the ride. He assumed that some of the other cars on the block had undercover agents in them; the police and FBI spent enough time on the block to have their mail forwarded.

"Right on," one of the Panthers called to the departing carload of party brothers. "All power to the people."

"Right on!"

Off they went. Sams started rolling a joint.

Alex Rackley spoke up. Don't do that, George, he said. The cops might be watching.

The comment caught Sams by surprise. "You're right, Alex," he said. Sams stopped rolling the joint.

Sitting up front, Warren directed the driver, Lonnie McLucas, toward the highway. Warren had traveled far in the short, intense space of a year. In May 1968 he held a job as a youth worker in a social program run by the city. He could talk troubled kids out of fights and into school or jobs while working the back channels of power—in City Hall, schools, the court system—to help them. Intellectually curious and personable, he tried to touch the lives of most everyone he encountered, from all walks of life; Warren was a beloved son of the city. He also had a short fuse. When outrage hit, he spoke his mind, and he could turn violent. From the day he entered kindergarten, to his encounters with churchgoers and black-marketeers on the block where he grew up, Warren had one foot on a path to success and one foot in a pile of trouble. He straddled a world of accommodation and one increasingly in conflict.

Now, in May 1969, Warren belonged to an outlaw political movement that preached, and sometimes practiced, violent revolution. The Black Panther Party had come to New Haven just five months earlier; Warren was their prized local conscript.

Founded in Oakland in 1966 by Huey Newton and Bobby Seale, the Panthers carried loaded guns and told white America that they were ready to shoot when necessary. The party combined socialist ideology with street credibility. Oakland's police force, recruited in part from the Deep South, openly brutalized black citizens, whether law-abiding or not. In response, the Panthers formed armed neighborhood "self-defense" patrols. The party drew middle-class, intellectual idealists inspired by Algerian writer Frantz Fanon. His *Wretched of the Earth* inspired Third World liberation movements; advocates of Black Power increasingly came to see this work as relevant to the United States. The Panthers held classes on Fanon's book and talked about sharing its ideas with the "baddest" characters on urban American street corners. Like Malcolm X right before his death, they hoped to tie an American rebellion to the spirit and program of liberation movements in the Third World. In a world where India, Kenya, Congo, Cuba, and other downtrodden societies could throw colonial masters out of power, why not aim for revolutionary change?

The Panthers' ten-point party platform claimed "the power to determine the destiny of our Black Community." It sought full employment, "an end to the robbery by the capitalist of our Black and oppressed communities," better housing, "education for our people . . . that teaches us our true history and our role in the present-day society," universal military exemptions for black Americans, and "an immediate end to police brutality and murder of black people." The platform also called for a blanket amnesty for all black prison inmates, as well as juries composed of true "peers" for black defendants. It concluded with a proposal for "a United Nations-supervised plebiscite to be held throughout the black colony in which only black colonial subjects will be allowed to participate for the purpose of determining the will of the black people as to their national destiny."

The Black Panther Party also drew heavily upon working-class blacks without intellectual, or moral, pretensions. Some of these were street thugs and rapists who couldn't care less about dialectical materialism but loved the idea of shooting cops. Some, like leaders Huey Newton and Eldridge Cleaver, managed to combine intellectual prowess with an unmistakable edge of violence. Seen from the heights of America's white establishment, the Panthers were small, ragtag, and hardly a match for one major agency of law enforcement, namely, the FBI. But, as FBI director J. Edgar Hoover understood perfectly, one cannot be a great hero without a dangerous enemy. The FBI did everything it could to dramatize the dangerous revolutionary powers of Pantherdom. The Panthers cooperated with braggadocio of their own. Wherever the Panthers went, conflict, rabble-rousing, and challenges to established authority followed. So the New Haven police—who, in conjunction with local FBI agents, were commanded to wipe out the Black Panther Party by any means necessary—watched every move of Warren and his comrades.

INDEED, UNDERCOVER POLICE watched the Panther car pull away from Warren's apartment complex with Alex Rackley. They followed—at first. Warren led the Buick's driver onto the highway northbound on Interstate 91, aimed toward nothing more specific than darkness and seclusion.

At some point, the officers disappeared. They would eventually claim they lost the car.

According to a later affidavit by Nick Pastore, he received a call from a "reliable" informant he had "known for at least five years." The informant reported that Kelly Moye's car "would be used, or was about to be used, to transport a person who was about to be murdered, to an unknown destination."

Even the police chief, Jim Ahern, had advance notice of an event worth watching. Ahern was in the nearby Hill neighborhood eating dinner at Leon's, one of New Haven's finest Italian restaurants. In his book *Police in Trouble*, Ahern would offer his version of the police's reaction, with a bevy of supporting actors and extra vehicles, a version strikingly at odds with the mountain of details that would emerge later from the case. According to Ahern:

My portable police radio told the story.

The phone rang. Something was happening at Panther headquarters; there was a great deal of activity. But we decided there was still not probable cause for arrests. We agreed, however, that more unmarked cars should be brought into position. The call went out, and they were on the way.

But before they could arrive, the gathering at Panther headquarters suddenly broke. Knowing that they were being watched, the Panthers split up into four cars and left in different directions. The radio was crowded with noise as our men sorted the cars out. Three were followed. In the confusion, the fourth slipped away.

That car had to be stopped. We put out an all-points bulletin on it for suspicion of kidnapping.

Yet the car "somehow" managed to elude the police twenty miles up the highway, according to Ahern.

Ahern may not have been fully forthcoming about how much police officials actually knew in advance about the activity at Panther headquarters. There has never been any other evidence to suggest the Panthers had four cars leaving the scene. Ahern downplayed the existence of probable cause for arrests—or, at the very least, a visit—before the crew in Kelly Moye's car took off.

"As a result of this information," Ahern wrote, the local police did eventually stop the Buick. But they wouldn't "find" it until hours later, around 4 A.M. By that time the car would be back in New Haven, back in Kelly Moye's possession.

IN THE BACK SEAT of Moye's car, George Sams informed Alex Rackley that he was being kicked out of the party. Sams also assured Rackley that, despite orders to kill him, he would be allowed to flee to freedom.

Warren directed the driver to exit the highway onto State Route 66, then onto a two-lane road winding through the sleepy hamlet of Middlefield. Warren saw a sign for Powder Ridge, a ski resort quiet in the off-season. The car twisted down through woodlands into the floodplain of the Coginchaug River. The headlights revealed a long stretch of darkness; the driver stopped the car by a low bridge off Middlefield's deserted Route 157.

Sams ordered everyone out. The four men walked into the woods. The moon shone, but they could barely see beneath all the trees. They crunched their way through skunk cabbage and dead branches, weaving past the trunks of swamp maples to the bank of the Coginchaug.

Alex Rackley passively hobbled alongside them. Rackley was thirteen days shy of his twentieth birthday. Clothesline bound his wrists. The makeshift noose around his neck jutted out beneath the Nehru jacket. Second-degree burns stung his chest and thighs. The burns came from pots of boiled water poured over Rackley's body during the torture session; they had festered over the subsequent three days Rackley spent tied up. Now Rackley's bare feet sank into a deepening layer of muck as the four traversed the marsh grass by the river.

Sams ordered the group to the edge of the open water. He told Rackley freedom was at hand: "You're gonna take a boat. You can take the boat to New York or Florida."

Sams reassured Rackley again, then warned him: While you wait for the boat to come get you, stay in the woods. Sams suggested that the woods might be crawling with Minutemen, members of a violent white supremacist group active in the area.

Thank you, Rackley said. No one asked: What kind of boat could sail the Coginchaug River? Perhaps a canoe. Certainly not a vessel capable of reaching New York, much less Florida.

Sams turned to Warren. He placed a .45 automatic in Warren's palm. "Here, Brother Warren," Sams said. "Ice him. Orders from National."

Warren gripped the .45. He knew how to handle the gun from his Air Force days in Korea. He waded toward Alex Rackley through the ankle-deep muck. He aimed at the back of Rackley's head and pulled the trigger. Rackley collapsed into the water. Sams took back the gun and handed it to McLucas. On Sams's order, McLucas kicked around in the marsh until he found Rackley's body. He shot an insurance bullet into his chest. As they turned to leave, Rackley's executioners abandoned his body for dead. According to later expert testimony, Rackley's heart may have continued beating—he may not have breathed his final gasp for four more hours.

Deep down, Warren knew Rackley was no FBI agent, no spy. If Warren wanted to, he could have stood up to the man in charge, the way he had refused to follow orders from the bosses at his last job with the New Haven antipoverty agency, Community Progress, Inc. Why didn't he stand up to Sams? Fear. Yes, Warren had held the gun, but he still had the sense that the Black Panther Party stood behind these orders. They could kill him instead of Rackley. His son and daughter were asleep back in the townhouse apartment. Something could happen to them, too.

THE THREE SURVIVING Panthers trudged back to the car. McLucas turned the wheel toward New Haven. They got lost on the twisting rural roads. Before they hit the highway, Sams threw bullets out the window. He preferred to return without any unused bullets; he wanted to impress the Panthers that this was a big job requiring lots of ammo.

Sams was hyped up when the three returned to headquarters. One coat-hanger-collared member of their party was conspicuously missing. Several other Panthers, night owls, remained awake, drinking coffee in the kitchen. Although there was no mention of what exactly had happened, it seemed clear that the returning warriors had been up to some mission of consequence.

Warren scrubbed his hands right away. He was wiped out. He wanted to sleep.

While most of New Haven slumbered, the Panther apartment buzzed with people not yet ready to go to bed. Joints were rolled and passed around. Warren, ever mindful of his wardrobe, washed off his muddy shoes. He cleaned the .45 and returned it to the coffee table drawer in the living room, where the party had been keeping it.

Loretta Luckes, a twenty-two-year-old aspiring Panther, was still awake. Sams ordered her and some others to clean up Alex Rackley's room. She'd performed a similar job days before, in the blood-stained basement after Rackley's interrogation. Sams terrified her, the way he waved the .45 around, the way he declared that he would kill his mother if he ran into her again, the way he vowed to take some "pigs" with him if they ever arrested him.

Once the cleanup was completed, Sams focused on Luckes. He ordered her to put on music. She chose some records. Displeased with the selections, Sams slapped her. Then Sams demanded that she recite the Black Panther Party's ten-point platform. Luckes tried; she stumbled. Sams put a gun to her head. She was headed for expulsion from the party, he informed her. She had no way of knowing that, when it came time to pull a trigger, at least earlier that night, Sams hadn't done it; he had others do the job.

George Sams ran about the apartment high on the aftermath of battle. "Brother Warren," he exclaimed, "is a true revolutionary!"

WARREN KIMBRO KNEW he was no hero that night. He didn't grasp the full significance of his act, of just how many casualties he left behind when he pulled the trigger. All he knew at this point was that a young man lost his life. Another casualty that night in the swamp was truth. Along with Alex Rackley's corpse, the facts were left behind to decompose in the Coginchaug River, devalued, abused, ultimately forgotten in America's domestic war over race, poverty, and the right to dissent.

"A lot of educated people are going to have to be convinced the facts are irrelevant!" protest leader Tom Hayden would soon yell into a microphone when he joined other radicals in protesting the arrests of Black Panthers in Alex Rackley's murder. Indeed, it may have seemed that the facts were irrelevant to everyone touched by the murder. Everyone, it seemed, was lying when it came to the Rackley case and the protests it provoked: the president, the FBI, the New Haven police, the man who pulled the trigger, the Black Panthers, the white radicals who swooped to their cause. No one had use for the facts.

Still, the facts mattered. They would prove central to the story of how Alex Rackley ended up dead in a swamp and to the subsequent trial that put the criminal justice system's travails on national display. The facts would prove central to the story of how America lost its innocence at the end of the sixties—how, in the course of a decade, a nation on the path to greater civil rights and opportunities for its most disenfranchised citizens jerked violently backward and chose to lock up huge portions of ghettos rather than seek solutions. An idealistic youth-powered movement that helped stop a war and rewrite civil rights laws succumbed to fratricide and exhaustion. The facts were relevant to how liberalism became a dirty word in the country and how questioning people in power became un-American.

CHAPTER 2

Busted

MAY 21, 1969, was a good day for a ride, the air clear, spring in blossom. John Mroczka started up his Triumph motorcycle and drove around the winding open roads of Connecticut's Middlesex County. Mroczka, a tool-and-die maker, had eight hours or so before the midnight shift at the local Pratt & Whitney jet-engine plant. Three weeks earlier he had returned home from a two-year tour in Vietnam. Mroczka was a local boy, still single at twenty-two, five-foot-ten, down to 135 pounds. He was no revolutionary; indeed Mroczka had no political views to speak of. The passions consuming so many others of his generation seemed alien. His own passions involved his Triumph and his fishing rod.

Mroczka swept on his Triumph along the quiet roads of Middlefield. He passed Route 157 near his favorite fishing spot. It was off a deserted stretch of country road, beneath a tiny bridge overlooking the Coginchaug River. The state stocked that spot with trout each year. Mroczka decided to make a quick detour. He didn't have his rod with him. He wanted to check, anyway, to see if the trout had arrived.

He parked his Triumph and crossed the street. Before he got to the bridge, he spotted what looked like a mannequin half submerged in the river.

He walked over to inspect it. The mouth was open; flies buzzed around the body.

This was no mannequin. This was a corpse.

He noticed rope around the corpse's wrists. He couldn't tell whether the rope was tied or just hanging. He didn't know what to think, what to do. He didn't yet realize how nervous he was. The scarecrow-like figure had on a jacket, blue striped trousers, a green shirt, no shoes.

Mroczka ran back to his Triumph. He rode to a deli up the road. It was between 4:30 and 5 P.M. His face white with shock, he told the woman behind the counter about the body. The state police were called. State Trooper William Leonard was the first to show up at the deli. Mroczka got back on the Triumph to lead him to the fishing spot.

Trooper Leonard didn't call in the report over the radio; he wanted to avoid alerting other law enforcement agencies just yet. Instead, he left two volunteer firemen behind with the body and took Mroczka to a gas station, where Leonard called from a phone booth. Then it was back to the Coginchaug. More troopers had arrived.

Waiting around for the coroner to arrive and declare the body dead—this would take hours—Mroczka had to repeat his story, word for word, six different times, to different troopers.

In between he heard them speculating about the victim. The victim had blue pants on. Some thought he was an escapee from the prison in Haddam.

Then the coroner arrived. "He has a bullet hole in his ear," one of the troopers reported to the group. "There's another one in his chest."

After the coroner made his official declaration of death, the cops found a handwritten note inside a pocket of the jacket draped around the body. The note was addressed to "Chairman Bobby."

"Someone called from Oregon," the note read. "There have been bombings at the University of Oregon. Called to your mother's house. They said it would be best if you did not come to Oregon at all. There have been threats to murder you. The brother in Oregon, who is head of the Party there, says there have been bombings, but they have calmed down. No danger . . ."

The note was signed, "Ericka."

National Panther chairman Bobby Seale had been in the news earlier in the week when he delivered a fiery speech on Yale University's campus in New Haven. He had left town early Tuesday morning, just before the Oregon call came in to Warren Kimbro's apartment. Ericka Huggins dispatched some Panthers to the airport with the note, but they arrived too late to deliver it to Seale.

Around 8 P.M., Steve Ahern, chief of detectives of New Haven's police department, received a call at his home about a "male Negro body" found in Middlesex Country, shot in the head. He returned right to work at police headquarters, a block east of the city's seventeenth-century Green. Ahern, the head of the detectives, brother of the chief, as well as the mastermind of the department's illegal wiretapping operation, knew he'd be working through the night.

A call followed from a state cop at Middlesex Hospital with the news about the "Chairman Bobby" note. Ahern ordered his men to call in street informants. Soon he was in a room in the first-floor detective bureau with Nick Pastore and Sergeant Vincent DeRosa, talking with a woman whose information had helped them make successful busts in the past. The woman was close to the Panthers, including Warren Kimbro. She told the cops about the torture of a "Brother Alex" at the apartment. She described a trial tape-recorded in the presence of Warren and Ericka and some tough guy named "Sam."

Around 9 o'clock, the FBI arrived with fingerprints of the victim. They matched the prints of an Alex Rackley who had a record of two minor arrests in Florida. Ahern called cops in Florida and confirmed the prints.

Police in Bridgeport, a twenty-five-minute drive west, rounded up a woman named Frances Carter and brought her to New Haven. She identified herself as secretary of the New Haven chapter. She admitted she had seen the torture victim held at Warren Kimbro's apartment.

Steve Ahern shoved a color Polaroid of Alex Rackley's devastated corpse under Carter's nose. "Isn't that the man?!" he yelled from close range. "Isn't that the man?"

Yes, it was. She talked until midnight. She would remember being badgered by ten to twenty cops at a time hovering over her. "Everybody's dead!" they told her. Instantly she flashed on her sister Peggy and Peggy's kids. "Where's Peggy? What did you do with Peggy? I've got to have a phone. I got to call Peggy!"

The interrogation proceeded with threats of her ending up in an electric chair. Sweating, her head pounding, Carter passed out. Right before losing consciousness, she remembers the one policewoman in the room whispering to her, "Peggy's fine."

MEANWHILE, NICK PASTORE was collecting details from his own informants—the location of the guns and the identities of the Panthers the
cops might find at Warren's apartment when, as it now appeared likely,
they would bust through the door. A shoe-leather cop straight out of an
O. Henry story, Nick knew criminals personally, from the neighborhood.
Rather than pull a gun on them, he'd just as soon share a drink before
putting on the cuffs. No one in New Haven had a deeper reservoir of informants than Nick. The intelligence operation he oversaw was the
envy of the local FBI. Nick liked many of the people he arrested, too.
But he didn't like the Panthers. In Nick's view, this was a war between
cops and cop-killers, between the mob and the law. He had no doubt
which side he stood on.

As the police planned a raid on Warren's Ethan Gardens apartment,
the party went on with its business. Warren arranged for the purchase of
three snub-nosed .38s from a black-market dealer working inside the
Colt factory in Hartford. He gave Lonnie McLucas $105, the keys to his
Mustang, and the directions, and then sent him off to collect the guns.

Midnight approached, the raid set. Steve Ahern gathered his detectives to discuss the details. He assigned some to arrest the people downstairs and others to go upstairs. Female officers would handle the women.
Nick would head to the basement; he knew that Alex Rackley's torture
had taken place there and would be looking for rope and other evidence
to tie the apartment to the Rackley torture and therefore the murder.

The police needed to tell the Panthers right away why they'd come—
because of the killing. They had to show they meant business.

"There are children in there," Ahern added. So be careful. No shots if
they could help it.

IT WAS AN early night for the Panthers. By 12:30 A.M., most of the household was asleep. The women scattered around the living room; a handful
held babies. Warren lay on the floor beside a rifle. His young son, Germano, and daughter, Veronica, shared a bed in Germano's room. (Veronica still didn't have her own bed back. Other Panther children had
moved in after Rackley's departure.)

A crash shattered the dark stillness. Down fell the front door. Sergeant
DeRosa would later claim that he did knock first. If he did, no one heard
him. Apparently DeRosa hadn't known the front door was unlocked.

Swarming in, officers moved in every direction, stepping over the women on pallets. They overturned flour bins and ransacked the premises.

"You're all under arrest!" Steve Ahern announced.

Warren awoke to a snub-nosed .38 in his face wielded by DeRosa. The gun shook in his hand; he had the hammer of the gun cocked. "Don't move!" he barked.

Beside him, Detective Billy White lunged for Warren's rifle. Billy White and Warren had known each other for years. They once worked together in a New Haven antipoverty program, and Warren had also coached White's younger brother in little league football. They'd always gotten along. Like many others in New Haven, White couldn't understand the radical turn Warren's life had taken, but he still liked him.

"Warren," White told him, "you're under arrest." White was too young to panic or to worry about retaliation. He wasn't angry, especially not at Warren. This was business. Warren did what Warren had to do. White did what he had to do.

"Black Power!" Warren called out. He followed revolutionary protocol: Don't let the pigs scare you. More to the point, never give them the satisfaction of knowing that you're about to urinate in your pants. Still, it wasn't Billy White who scared him. Warren understood that his friend was just doing his job. He worried more about men like DeRosa and the other armed soldiers scouring the place and handcuffing people. Warren and the Panthers were caught by surprise, outgunned, and at the complete mercy of their enemies.

One officer went straight upstairs to Warren's bedroom. He quickly returned downstairs announcing that he'd found the murder weapon. Warren was surprised because he had been sure George Sams had taken the gun with him. He had no idea it was still in the house. Yet the police seemed to know exactly where to look. An informant had told Nick Pastore where to find the gun.

Warren's wife, Sylvia, had emerged from the shower, about to get ready for work the next morning at her job at a drug treatment center, when a black cop stormed up the stairs and pointed his gun at her. Sylvia recognized him; she was his son's godmother. The officer instantly recognized the only partially dressed Sylvia. He turned away, embarrassed. Frightened as much for her children as for herself, Sylvia realized she didn't even know who was sleeping in which room. Sylvia and Warren didn't sleep together;

their marriage had been crumbling ever since the Panthers took over her husband's life. Sylvia had no time for this band of revolutionaries who invaded her home—especially Ericka Huggins. People told Sylvia that Warren and Ericka were an item. Warren denied it, but Sylvia could tell.

A female officer came up the stairs and placed Panther-hating Sylvia under arrest. Unlike Warren, Sylvia was not scared. She was humiliated. The cop watched her get dressed. Then she escorted Sylvia out the door to the police station.

Germano and Veronica awoke to lights flashing in their eyes. Germano instinctively rolled onto his sister. They stared at gun barrels. There was talk of searching them. Then Germano and Veronica heard someone say, "These are just kids."

The kids were shepherded downstairs. Germano and Veronica saw their dad handcuffed behind his back, his face toward the floor, a lit cigarette in his mouth. The smoke swirled into his eyes. The ash grew longer; nobody noticed. The image would sear Veronica's memory for years to come, the nightmare's sharpest mental photograph. Veronica had never seen her dad in a position like that before. She was terrified. She wondered if the ash would start a fire when it fell onto the carpet.

"Can you loosen the handcuffs? They're too tight," the kids heard Warren ask his tormentors.

"The handcuffs are too tight!" Veronica piped up. "The smoke is in his eyes."

Germano wondered: Where is the shoot-out? He had heard tales of Panther-cop shoot-outs in other cities. Friends in Ethan Gardens showed him where their family cut holes in the wall of their apartment to climb up to a skylight; there the parents kept a lookout and a cache of guns in case the cops came. Now the real confrontation was happening, and it was one sided.

Germano and Veronica were ushered outside into a squad car. They were taken four blocks north to Sylvia's mother's house on Dickerman Street. Veronica couldn't sleep. She wondered where her parents were being taken. She was petrified about what would happen to them, to all of them.

Back at Ethan Gardens, everyone was rounded up. Investigators stayed another four hours digging for every shred of evidence. They'd return over the next few days. The inside of the three-floor apartment, part of a ballyhooed government-financed experiment in mixed-income housing, was reduced practically to rubble, with walls torn apart, furniture upended, household items thrown around the floor.

The police didn't find everyone. One of the ringleaders, George Sams, managed to disappear right before the police raid. Warren had no inkling of Sams's whereabouts. He was spotted shortly afterward in Chicago.

WHILE THE POLICE rummaged through Warren's apartment, the phone woke Betty Kimbro Osborne. One of Warren's neighbors was calling. Something's happening at Ethan Gardens, the caller said. Your brother Warren's house has been raided by the cops.

Betty hung up. She handed the phone to her husband, Ernie Osborne. Both were close to Warren, so close that they named their son after him. Both worked for New Haven antipoverty programs. Warren's radical turn to "Panthermania," as Betty called it, frustrated them, but they remained loyal.

Ernie made the call to the apartment. He was stunned to hear the voice on the other end.

"Steve? *Steve?*"

Ernie recognized that the voice on the other end belonged to Police Inspector Steve Ahern. Ernie knew Ahern from Ernie's job running the Hill neighborhood office for the city's redevelopment agency; the two worked together to prevent summer riots in the neighborhood.

Now, though, Ahern didn't acknowledge Ernie. Saying nothing at all, he hung up the phone.

Betty and Ernie threw on clothes. They rushed downtown. By the time they arrived on Court Street, Warren was already in the fire department headquarters, where the police intelligence division had a third-floor lockup for interrogating prisoners. Ernie and Betty were not allowed in.

Warren was shuttled into one of the cages in the lockup. He was ordered to strip. Then they handed him what for the sartorially conscious Warren constituted an ultimate insult: shabby clothes. His new uniform consisted of a baggy shirt, damp oversized khaki pants, too-small sneakers. They took fingerprints and fingernail scrapings. Warren didn't remember being read his Miranda rights.

In straggled George Edwards, another local Panther. Edwards was a short, wiry, dramatic activist under continual surveillance by the FBI.

George Sams didn't trust Edwards, either, because Edwards had refused to torture Alex Rackley in the Ethan Gardens basement. He had ordered Edwards beaten, too. After his beating, Edwards left the apartment and went into hiding from the Panthers. The night of Alex Rackley's murder, the Panthers sought Edwards to deliver the same brand of justice to him. After clearing out the Panther headquarters, the cops had gone over to Edwards's apartment on Hazel Street and arrested him too.

A FRIENDLY VOICE broke through the corridor.

"Hey, give Warren a cigarette! I know Warren from St. John's. He's a nice guy."

It was Nick Pastore. Nick approached the door of Warren's cage. "Warren," Nick told him, "we know you did the shooting."

"I know nothing," Warren retorted. He thought to himself: Could they really know that already? Or was this just Nicky Pastore doing his thing? Nick could be rough if he felt the occasion merited it; some cops in that very station that night seemed to relish any opportunity to bark at people or throw them around. But Nick understood, instinctively, that you usually didn't have to badger people to get information. In fact, in his experience, that usually backfired. Treating people respectfully often broke barriers, earned their trust, and—put simply—was just a nicer way to treat people.

Warren had almost convinced himself he hadn't shot anyone. The Panther worldview he had heard so many times slipped out from between his lips like a subliminal tape recording: It doesn't matter who pulled the trigger. Cops are always the villains. They always frame black people. They make violence inevitable. They commit the crimes. They did this.

After all, the cops knew everything that went on. They could have stopped the Rackley torture, Warren was convinced. They could have stormed in and freed Alex Rackley whenever they wanted. They could have stopped the car on the way to Middlefield. *They wanted this to happen.* Maybe one of their infiltrators, one of their agents provocateurs, had even hatched the plot in the first place.

Sylvia, too, didn't know what to think. She spent hours in a cell answering questions from Nick Pastore. He showed her photographs. He played her the brutal tape of Alex Rackley's interrogation; he asked her to identify voices. She told Nick all she knew. Finally, she was allowed to leave.

THE POLICE WEREN'T going to wrest a confession from Warren, not tonight. Shackled at his ankles, handcuffed, outfitted in his floppy rags, Warren was escorted from the cage downstairs onto Court Street.

A crowd had gathered on the sidewalk in the pre-dawn, illuminated like extras on a movie set by the overhead streetlights. News of the bust had shot along telephone wires to radicals across the slumbering city. The crowd watched as more than a half-dozen Panthers were hauled into custody. Unbeknownst to the police, the anonymous crowd included one of the Panthers they hoped to have in handcuffs, Lonnie McLucas. He had come back from the mission to Hartford empty-handed; Warren's contact double-crossed him. He took McLucas's money and failed to produce the three snub-nosed .38s. All of a sudden, McLucas was not so worried about his failure to secure the guns. He was consumed by the need to flee for his freedom, maybe even for his life. He slipped out of the crowd, out of New Haven, and on to Salt Lake City.

For Warren, the next stop was the police station across the street. He was brought to the lockup there. Dawn was on its way. Warren stayed awake awaiting arraignment and an uncertain future.

The next morning Warren, worn out, still in his shabby getup, went to the circuit court to appear before a judge. He knew the prosecutor, Phil Mancini; Warren had discussed clients' cases with Mancini when Warren was a worker at a program called the Residential Youth Center. Now Mancini looked at Warren and shook his head. He presented the charges against Warren. As usual with felony cases, this one was bound over to the state courthouse on Elm Street. Warren wouldn't end up appearing there until the following week. So it was off to the state lockup on Whalley Avenue. After a convulsive half day, Warren would land in one spot and stay there.

CHAPTER 3

Burial of a Footnote

The bust, and Rackley's death, made national news. "8 Black Panthers Seized in Torture-Murder Case," reported the *New York Times*. The daily *New Haven Register* ran the story that same afternoon, hours after the New Haven police finished their first four-hour scouring of Warren Kimbro's apartment. The paper plastered the headline across the front page: "8 Panthers Held in Murder Plot." All the mug shots made it to the paper on time. The disheveled faces of the suspects looked more like a motley rogue's gallery than a battalion of revolutionaries.

The *Register* had biographical details about each suspect and already knew all about the "kangaroo trial" and torture that took place in the apartment days before the murder. The police had reported that the manhunt for other suspects and the commitment of law enforcement agents would extend nationwide. Among the missing were George Sams and several national Panther leaders who had skipped town hours before the bust.

As for Rackley, the *Register* had only this to say: "Alex Rackley, 24 [*sic*], of New York City and formerly of Jacksonville, Fla., reportedly had been a member of the Black Panther party in New York for better than six months." The paper also claimed, falsely, that he had been brought to New Haven against his will.

In the hundreds of newspaper articles, public speeches and court documents to come, little of substance would ever be said about the victim. Even his age was unclear: His death certificate showed him less than two weeks shy of his twentieth birthday. For decades, other papers and subsequent books and articles would repeat the *Register's* mistaken twenty-four-year-old figure. (The *Hartford Courant* put Rackley's age at thirty-five.) Rather than look into his past, the Panthers, the cops, and a generation of reporters and writers would merely attach bits of hearsay to the narrative surrounding Rackley's footnote-referenced name.

The real Alex Rackley was born in Jacksonville on June 2, 1949. Jacksonville was still a backward north Florida community in the late '60s, more like an Old South town than a civil rights–era city in transition. An Associated Press dispatch referred to Jacksonville as "the major Florida city most deeply rooted in the old-style Dixie politics." Ruling whites kept blacks out of the better jobs, out of the First Baptist Church, which ran the city, out of public debates. A decade and a half after the Supreme Court's *Brown v. Board of Education* decision, years after the sit-ins at the Greensboro Woolworth's lunch counter and the 1964 federal Civil Rights Act, Jacksonville's sewage plant still had signs defiantly marking separate white and black employee lunch rooms. The right-wing daily papers didn't write much about blacks unless they committed crimes. ("City police arrested a giant Negro as he calmly ate a boxed chicken dinner shortly after his girl friend had been stabbed to death, officers said," read the lead of one such story in the *Jacksonville Journal* in January 1968.) Black people appeared on the front page in April 1968, when they rioted in the aftermath of Martin Luther King's assassination. The riot's trigger was the drive-by shooting by a group of whites of a black man a year older than Alex. In decrying the black looting and violence, the *Jacksonville Journal* downplayed the shooting and didn't mention the King assassination. (A black weekly, the *Star*, printed the victim's photo and noted the riot's link to King.)

Alex was the first of eight children fathered by a variety of men. His mother, Parlee, was a strong woman—large and outspoken. She set boundaries and disciplined her children—when she was around. A cook, she sometimes worked at an exclusive Jacksonville club. The job just as often took her north, where she cooked for rich people for months at a time or longer. Those northern jobs paid more, plus Parlee enjoyed the travel. She left her parents, Isaac and Rosalie, in charge of the children and sent money home as often as she could.

Alex grew up on a crowded block surrounded by poultry plants, slaughterhouses, and a dog pound. The neighborhood, known as Mixontown, may have smelled like dead chickens, but the people had jobs. Grandfather Isaac raised chickens; the Rackleys ate a lot of chicken. Twenty or more Rackleys at a time shared the three-bedroom house on Watts Street—brothers, sisters, aunts, uncles, grandparents bumping into each other all day, sleeping in bunk beds.

With such a crowded house, the Rackley kids tended to spend time outdoors. Alex and other kids on the block would play stickball, football, marbles. Alex liked sports, liked dancing and music, though he wasn't a standout in any of these pursuits. While not particularly interested in school, he did love clothes. Hoping to become a tailor, he enrolled in Stanton Vocational after junior high, but he dropped out before very long. He sometimes had luck at dice, which once helped pay for a double-breasted suit. What would later become known as the "Superfly" look was coming in, and Alex took to it. He parted his Afro on the side. He had his two front teeth capped; he'd chipped them in elementary school when Freddie, the brother closest to him in age, accidentally tripped him on the way home.

Alex took up karate at seventeen and became a black belt. Karate came in handy. One day, with no key, Alex found he could knock down a locked door at his house. And though he wasn't known for starting fights, he got into his share of neighborhood scraps; he wanted to look out for himself and his younger siblings. He looked out for Parlee, too. Despite her long absences, he and his mother were close. One time Parlee's boyfriend appeared ready to strike her. Alex jumped him first and prevented him from attacking. Alex was muscular, around six-one, 175 pounds.

Still, he didn't leave much of a mark beyond his own block. When the FBI tried to track down information on him, they found little. The FBI noted that he had brown hair and eyes, a scar over his left eyebrow, and two misdemeanor arrests on his record, both in the first part of 1968, one for "vagrancy and loitering" on Jacksonville Beach and another for "disorderly conduct—gambling." Alex bounced around jobs. He pumped gas for a while, working the night shift. One night his younger brother Wayne heard him come home and ask Parlee for a gun; people kept robbing him at the station, and he was fed up with it.

In 1968, Alex turned nineteen. Parlee was up in New York cooking. He headed north to join his mom, since nothing much was developing for him in Jacksonville. And that was about all the family ever heard from him again. He sent one snapshot home of himself in his new Super-fly duds. No hint of politics, no talk of revolution.

Drinking and using drugs, jobless, homeless, Alex walked around New York City barefoot after staying briefly with Parlee. He stumbled onto the Panthers through friends he knew from Jacksonville. He started crashing at communal Panther pads. He hung around Panther headquarters in New York, always eager to help. He sold Panther newspapers. He attended political education classes; inevitably, he'd fail the exams. "Listen, brother," ranking Panthers told him. "You need more political education." Rackley's claim to a black belt was perhaps his only distinction. As the chapter's "karate instructor," he taught martial arts to other Panthers at the Panther office in Harlem. He struck New York Panthers like Shirley Wolterding as "unsophisticated, like a baby, a child . . . very, very naïve . . . almost like an eager puppy." Gene Roberts, an undercover cop posing as a chapter member, learned little about Rackley during Rackley's time in New York; Rackley said nothing about his past except to claim, falsely, that he'd been a member of the notorious Blackstone Rangers street gang in Chicago. Roberts was trained not to press people on their personal stories. He figured Rackley for a hanger-on, a nonentity in the Panther universe. Rackley's marginality left him as something of a mystery.

Everybody distrusted everyone else in Panther chapters. Everyone believed that the offices were crawling with spies. Pantherdom had become a hall of mirrors: anyone might be a spy, and few seemed totally trustworthy. The FBI and the New York police red squad relied on two kinds of helpers. The first kind were their own spies, posing as real Panthers. The second kind were loyal Panthers whom the FBI had "bad-jacketed" by inserting false rumors of *dis*loyalty. Like everyone else, Rackley could with equal credibility have been either or neither of these in the eyes of his comrades. And like practically everyone else, he was wondered about when he wasn't around, though not, apparently, more than anyone else. On March 11, in a conversation secretly recorded by a police infiltrator, one member expressed doubts about Rackley's party loyalty. As was so often true of the heavily infiltrated party, it is impossible to know which speakers were genuine Panthers and which were agents provocateurs charged with creating suspicion. The New York Panthers were consumed with detecting the informers among them. According to the police infiltrator, they allegedly discussed killing an unidentified suspected undercover agent, then blaming the murder on the FBI.

That paranoia was ratcheted even higher after an April 1 police bust. Twenty-one Panthers were arrested on charges of having planned to blow up department stores and landmarks like the Botanical Garden and the Statue of Liberty. It would never become clear, even at trial, if such a plan ever really existed, or if it had, whether it came from the imaginations of undercover law enforcement seeking to incite law-breaking by the Panthers.

The top priority in the Black Panther Party increasingly became weeding out informers. Earlier goals such as "serving the people" took a lesser priority. The party's national office sent leaders of its military wing to the East Coast to investigate and instill discipline. The heavies, including enforcers Landon Williams and George Sams, took control. Sams called himself "Crazy George" and "Nigger George." He had been in fights and trouble with the law since his childhood bouncing around foster homes and mental hospitals in the South, then New York City and Michigan. The Panthers once kicked him out of the party for stabbing another Panther. Party leaders reinstated him only when nationalist leader Stokely Carmichael, whom Sams served as a bodyguard, intervened on his behalf. Sams was known in Panther circles around the country as the wild man who swung into town and made threats, beat people, harassed women, and left internecine fights in his wake. A dark-skinned stocky man with a big Afro, Sams made up for his shorter-than-average height—no more than five foot eight—with a permanent air of menace. He kept two or three pistols inside his brown trench coat; he clattered when he walked. He bounced with nervous energy, always moving, twitching, glaring at people as though daring them to challenge him.

Sams particularly seemed to enjoy meting out discipline in the Harlem office that April. One time Alex Rackley walked into the office with his hair braided. Sams exploded: Rackley was guilty of "disrespecting the people." Hair braiding, apparently, constituted "cultural nationalism."

Needless to say, the Panthers abhorred cultural nationalism. Besides, Sams declared, Rackley looked like a pickaninny. Sams beat Rackley on the spot. Then he ordered him to run around the block.

Rackley hung on because he had nowhere else to go. On Saturday, May 17, he begged Sams—on his knees, his hands clasped in prayer—and the other leaders to allow him to accompany them on a trip to New Haven. It seemed he was desperate to be part of the group no matter how much abuse he took. "*Please*, sister," he begged one of the local chapter officers, Rose Mary Byrd. "Please let me go."

Rackley won a seat in one of the two cars to New Haven. Once there, he hung out with the crowd, while leaders met privately to plan discipline as well as the appearance in town, two days later, of Bobby Seale.

From the moment they arrived at local Panther headquarters at Ethan Gardens in New Haven, the visiting leaders, Landon Williams and George Sams, whispered to Warren Kimbro and Ericka Huggins about Alex Rackley. They told Warren and Ericka to watch Alex Rackley: he might be a spy.

Rackley's identity may have been confused with that of Alex McKiever, one of the Panthers indicted in the New York bombing-conspiracy case. That Alex, former president of the Afro-American History Club at New York's Benjamin Franklin High School, fled the country before the police could arrest him. The Panthers suspected him of being a police agent. And, for some reason, one leader decided that Alex McKiever and Alex Rackley must be the same person; the Panthers involved would later identify Rackley that way. In reality, the Alexes occupied different echelons in Pantherdom; McKiever served on New York's elite security team before the bust and was responsible for the safety of high-ranking Panthers visiting town. He was close to Eldridge Cleaver.

Alex Rackley didn't realize he was under suspicion in New Haven. He settled into the Orchard Street apartment, eager, as usual, to help. He and Warren rolled up posters for the upcoming Bobby Seale event. Meanwhile, George Sams and Landon Williams took charge. Sams called Warren and Ericka to the side and issued an order: one of the women should seduce Rackley, then determine if he was an informer. The assignment went to fifteen-year-old Maude Francis. Sams handed Francis a speed pill to stay awake. Rackley willingly succumbed to the girl's entreaties.

In the aftermath, Francis popped the question. No, Rackley told her, he was no spy.

Whether or not Maude Francis believed Alex Rackley's answer about not being a spy, suspicion in the house remained strong. Sams would claim years later that even he didn't believe Alex Rackley was a spy. But his job was to find out for sure.

One Sunday morning, Ericka came downstairs to find Rackley dozing on the couch in the living room. Ericka was a commanding presence in the Panther apartment, a natural leader. She walked tall and spoke with confidence. Beneath her sometimes hippie-sounding, idealistic patter burned a ferocity that flashed bright and hard whenever she perceived a threat. Dozing Alex looked like a threat—to revolutionary comportment, perhaps. Wake up! Ericka demanded. She threw a book at him. The thud of *Selected Military Writings* by Mao Tse-tung startled Rackley awake.

Ordered to read, Rackley raised the book—upside down. He scanned the letters.

Rackley told Ericka that he couldn't read, and then proceeded to say how he wished he could read, how he wished the Panthers in New York had given him more help. Enraged, Ericka lectured Rackley that he should have asked the sisters.

Warren was coming downstairs with George Sams. They'd heard the last exchange. To an outsider, the scene may have seemed bizarre. But inside Panther headquarters, every hour of the day was revolution time, every encounter, no matter how small, an opportunity to foster an atmosphere of toughness. Sometimes that involved picking out scapegoats. The timid, like Alex Rackley, made for handy scapegoats.

"If you can't read," Sams asked Rackley, "what are you doing with the military works of Mao?"

"Stand up!" Sams barked. He accused Rackley of lying.

Sams directed someone to get the "Panther stick." The "stick" was a fraternity hazing paddle Warren had picked up. People called it the "Panther stick," and until now it had been merely a decorative threat.

Rackley tried to resist. He lunged at Sams, kicked Warren, kicked Ericka. Blood spurted from Rackley's head from the paddling.

"Where are you from?" Sams demanded.

"Jacksonville, Florida."

Sams then informed Rackley that he was hereby expelled from the Black Panther Party for "lying to the sister." He was *not* to show his face at any other chapter offices, either. Where did he want to go now?

"New York."

Call the bus station, Sams ordered Warren. Find out what it costs to get there.

Warren called. Sams put out money for Rackley. Rackley left the apartment—and remained right outside, sitting. He returned, said he needed his coat. He couldn't find the coat. Everyone started looking for the coat. No one could find the coat.

Hmmm, maybe Rackley had no coat. Anyone remember Brother Alex coming in with a coat?

"Brother," George Sams said, "I don't really think you want to leave. And I think you are the pig."

Sams ordered Rackley, Warren, and Lonnie McLucas into the basement. Warren had never finished the basement since moving into Ethan Gardens. The walls were mostly concrete; one had partial sheetrock. Incandescent lights on the ceiling illuminated a concrete floor bare except for boxes and a combination desk-chair low to the ground. Warren had originally planned for his kids to use the desk for their homework.

The group fashioned a noose around Rackley's neck and threw it over a joist; McLucas held the rope and told Rackley to read. Again he insisted that he could not read.

"Brother," declared Sams, "this calls for more discipline." Warren and the others took turns whacking at Rackley with the Panther stick.

Then they stood Rackley's limp body, paddled a good fifteen times on the buttocks alone, back up. The order resumed: Read! Desperate, Rackley muttered words. It sounded as if it might have been reading, or it might have been a mixture of recognized written syllables with remembered recitations of cant.

To Sams, it was proof of perfidy. Clearly, Rackley could read. "We are going to tie him up and get some information from the brother."

Rackley landed in the desk-chair. Warren and the others bound Rackley to the chair by his arms and legs and around the waist.

"Get some hot water," Sams directed. Upstairs, women started boiling water. Meanwhile, Sams ordered Warren to gag Rackley with a towel. When the water boiled, Panthers brought it downstairs. Sams poured the boiling water over Rackley's back, over his shoulders. First one pot, then a second. Then a third. Then a fourth.

OK, Rackley cried through the towel gagging his mouth, his head bobbing, OK! He was ready to talk.

Upstairs, Warren's children, Germano and Veronica, saw people carrying the pots of water downstairs. The kids could hear the cracks of beatings. They heard Alex Rackley's pitiful screams. Veronica's stomach twisted. Germano tried to peek down the stairs, figure out who was doing what to whom. "We need to get these kids out of here," he heard someone say. Sylvia took them away.

In the basement, Sams once again poured the boiling water over Rackley's back and shoulders.

A tape recorder was brought into the room. A party member who worked at the phone company had donated it to the party. The proceedings would be preserved as evidence for party officials. Ericka was called downstairs. For Ericka, for Warren, this felt crazy. The whole scene was careening out of control. And yet they had to watch out. Who knew who would be accused next? Who could be revealed as the next "pig"? Sams was from National. Disobey him, and, indeed, the next butt in that chair could be yours.

Besides, who knew for sure about Alex Rackley? It might all *sound* ridiculous. But spies *were* everywhere, endangering the revolution, endangering lives. It didn't take much, in that house, in that party, in those paranoid times, to convince yourself of just about anything.

In spite of any misgivings, Ericka and Warren soon glided into the roles as interrogators. Not a hint of hesitation, or doubt, could be detected in Ericka's voice as Sams (waving his pistol toward her, she would later claim) had her introduce the proceedings on tape.

"Ericka Huggins," she announced, "member of the New Haven Chapter Black Panther Party, political education instructor. On May 17th at approximately 10 o'clock, Brother Alex from New York was sleeping in the office, that is, a house that we use as an office, and I kicked him and said, 'Motherfucker, wake up, because we don't sleep in the office and we relate to reading or getting out!'

"And so Brother Alex picked up a book, *Selected Military Writings* of Mao Tse-tung, and began to read. I was talking to Brother George and Warren, and George looked over at Alex and said, 'Brother, I thought you couldn't read. You told me you couldn't read before? What you read-ing?' And so the brother said, 'I can't read.'. . ."

"So then the brother got some discipline, you know, in the areas of the nose and mouth, and the brother began to show cowardly tenden-cies, began to whimper and moan."

Ericka hesitated. A conversation ensued in the background. Then she resumed, coached on her next lines.

"Right. After he would not, you know, say if he could read, we were puzzled because he picked up the newspaper saying he could not read, and the first person, the first word that he deciphered was McCall, you know, a relatively big word for an illiterate person. So we decided he was a motherfucking phony, that he was lying, and that if he lied to us, he lied to other party members and to the people.

"So they, George began to give him other disciplinary . . . things. Like, you know, a stick was taken to the brother, you see, because he was acting like a coward, acting like a non-Panther. And, as I said before, he was lying. We asked him again and again if he could read, and he said no, he couldn't read, so that, you know, he received discipline for a while.

"During the time he grabbed George and tried to fight back and was kicking, kicked Warren, kicked me, you know. Discombobulated the whole office and began to cry real tears.

"We then stood him up in the middle of the floor and asked him what his name was, if he was a Panther, if he wanted to be a Panther, how long he had been in the party. And he answered, 'I've been in the party eight months.' This is a disgrace to the people's revolutionary struggle!"

Rackley at this point apparently tried to get up from his seat, as though he still had a means of escape.

"Sit down, motherfucker!" Ericka scolded him. "Be still."

Ericka related for the record how the Panthers had started posing questions "with a little coercive force," how "the answers came after a few buckets of water." So they had their proof: "He is an informer. Oh, he knows all the informers."

"Name names, nigger!" Warren barked, after Ericka completed her in-troduction. Warren continued for a bit, then deferred to George Sams, who handled most of the formal interrogation. Warren inserted himself occasionally with interjections like, "*Are you a pig?!*"

Rackley struggled in the chair for comfort and for words. Amid his blinding pain, Sams demanded that he name "pigs" infiltrating the New York party. Rackley started singing for his life, a disjointed melody of all the names and settings he could summon from his memory.

"Well, there's Janet, Akbar. . . . Let's see, James. Let's see, Bright. . . . They've been saying," Rackley stammered on, "that Janet, Janet, if Janet could get put in jail, she was going to get out in a month. Because she had to stay in there for a month, then she be got out."

Tales followed of pigs paying off brothers who informed on other brothers. None of the interrogators asked: How could Rackley know all this?

"I, there's the telephone in the office is bugged, and the one next door in the restaurant—you can hear when the brothers . . . sometimes you can hear what the brothers in the restaurant is saying by dialing three-nine-one. Only all the telephones theys pick up the lever and dial, and you hear them talking to the pig. And the pigs know when you pick up the receiver—they think, you know, they heard information, they'll cut you off."

"Do you have to put a dime in the phone, too?"

"Sometimes," Rackley offered.

More tales of conversations, of informers, of a visit to a brother's house that the cops had raided. Why hadn't he told the party all this before? "I was, I was scared, brother. I was scared because the brothers there was talking about shooting me."

There was more. One time, en route to buying some "rugi" (marijuana), Rackley happened upon some turncoats walking right into the Twenty-Eighth Precinct house, it appeared.

Wait. The precinct house was down by 23rd Street. Rackley lived on 128th street. The Panther office was between 122nd and 121st. What was he doing all the way down there?

Another Panther in the room butted in to help Rackley out. "He says he going to get some rugi."

No one could understand why he had to travel one hundred blocks to buy weed.

The captive did his best to explain.

"Yeah. Because he doesn't like to sell rugi unless I'm standing in the door," Rackley offered. "Like, I went over there to get some rugi because the same, the same brothers that asked me where I copped the rugi from last night—you know, I had copped for them and the brothers, and they got, you know. . . . We was in there talking about rugi, so I went on in there, and I bought an ounce of rugi from him. I went back to the, I went back, I left the outside office and went in the office and started, and started, and started talking to the brothers and the sisters. You know, the pig class. And they started—the topic was liberalism. . . ."

Rackley had found his voice. The stories poured forth, punctuated by more beatings and boiling water poured from replenished pots. At the merciful end of Rackley's travail, Sams, Warren, Lonnie McLucas, Ericka, and the rest of the girls and young women followed Rackley upstairs to the second floor. He had a cold shower. The women cleaned Rackley's wounds, covered them with bandages. He was bleeding, battered, in obvious, deep pain, scarred from his head all down his body. Second-degree burns covered his chest and thighs. For days, members rotated on duty guarding Rackley as he lay wallowing in his waste in Veronica's bedroom.

"The New Haven Police Department had received information that members of the New Haven Black Panther party had kidnapped a New York Panther and were holding him in the Orchard Street apartment of Warren Kimbro that was functioning as party headquarters," Ahern would claim in his 1972 book, *Police in Trouble*. "We did not have enough information to make arrests, but we had the apartment under surveillance." According to Nick Pastore, the cops knew an interrogation, but not "torture," took place. The cops tried to learn more, according to Nick, but were unable for once, it seemed, to piece together a story.

When Bobby Seale arrived in town the next afternoon with other national party leaders in tow, the Panthers kept him away from Ethan Gardens. They hunkered with him at Ericka's apartment in the Hill neighborhood. Warren did take some of the other visitors to the apartment to listen to the interrogation tape.

During the subsequent pig-in-a-bed tour at Ethan Gardens for the party dignitaries, Alex Rackley spoke up.

"Is Chairman Bobby," he asked June Hilliard, one of the leaders from California, "going to have me killed?"

June Hilliard had more important matters to worry about. "I'm not concerned about you," Hilliard told Rackley. "You're a pig."

And that was the last known discussion about Alex Rackley's fate until the following night, when George Sams's murder party drove to the swamp.

Alex Rackley's murder made the *New York Times*. It didn't make either daily newspaper in his hometown of Jacksonville, Florida. A couple of days later the papers did run a one-paragraph death notice. It offered no hint of how Jacksonville's native son died. It mentioned merely that he "passed in Middletown, Connecticut" (close enough—one town over from Middlefield) and that he "had been living in Middletown for the past two years."

Parlee Rackley, who had returned to Jacksonville from New York, learned the news from the police. She didn't know what to think. The Black Panthers? Since when was her son involved with the Black Panthers? Alex's sisters and brothers would remember little about the subsequent events, besides Parlee's visible despair. A few details of the murder trickled their way; they'd never get anywhere near a complete story. The Rackleys had a hard time imagining Alex as an informer. Freddie, the brother who was breaking high-hurdle records at Eugene Butler High School, was the closest to Alex in age. It hurt him to watch his mother grieve, to see her cry, so much that he stayed away from the funeral. He and his siblings would remember the family having to wait two weeks to bury Alex; they were told that the authorities sent the wrong body the first time.

Wayne, born three years after Alex, and Velva, ten years Alex's junior, accompanied Parlee to the funeral. The event drew a sparse crowd. Wayne would remember no one crying except Parlee and her children. He cried because his mother cried.

CHAPTER 4

Jailhouse Days

Even if Alex Rackley's murder didn't create much of a stir in his hometown, it sure *was* big news among FBI bureau chiefs. Suspected accomplices were on the run; they could be anywhere. FBI Director J. Edgar Hoover's men now had a justification to raid Panther offices in Chicago and Detroit, which they hastened to do. Raids would follow on Panther offices in Indianapolis, San Diego, Philadelphia, and Los Angeles. Somehow, whenever the pretext involved a tip about George Sams's whereabouts, Sams managed to escape just before the G-men busted down the door, upturned the furniture, and made off with weapons or documents. His string of escapes convinced some of his former party colleagues that he was not only crazy, but a government agent, a charge he denied.

Warren Kimbro was stuck in the old state jail on New Haven's Whalley Avenue. Its tiny metal cells reeked of human waste and frustration. Warren's cell had a small can in which he could urinate or defecate overnight. Prisoners took their cans to a toilet the next morning. In spite of such indignity, he remained determined to maintain his revolutionary facade. He saw himself as a political prisoner. The corrections pigs wouldn't make him crack. A visit from the Panthers' lawyers, the flamboyant William Kuntsler and Gerald Lefcourt, offered little comfort: he considered them showboats, phonies.

Warren's old support base was almost entirely gone. His employers at Community Progress Inc. announced—with embarrassing tardiness—that they were officially suspending him. In fact, he had stopped coming to work months earlier. He had attacked his bosses in public for selling out the community. He had spent his days organizing for the Panthers instead. He'd even gone so far as to tell a reporter a month earlier, "CPI is paternalism, which is capitalism. The agency says to poor people, you first abide by my rules. Its aim is to co-opt reform, to fit into the mainstream, not to rock the boat. . . . I cannot work for CPI. I can never again work for the pig power structure." Until his arrest for murder, the agency had allowed him technically to remain on medical leave. His status now went far beyond the reach of medicine.

A week after his arrest, Warren returned to court along with five other Panthers. This time they were taken to the marble state superior court on Elm Street, where major crimes were heard. They were to be arraigned on charges of murder, conspiracy to commit murder, kidnapping, conspiracy to commit kidnapping, and unlawful detainment. The state's prosecutor, Arnold Markle, shook his head when Warren came upstairs from the detention area to Courtroom A. Markle, like Phil Mancini, had previously worked with Warren to help young people. "You were really helping kids," Markle said with disgust.

WHEN ERICKA HUGGINS showed up to be arraigned on charges including aiding and abetting murder and kidnapping resulting in death, she recognized the lawyer who would represent her. A few years back, Catherine Roraback had accompanied Ericka's husband, John, to a court date for his arrest in a protest.

Roraback saw the sheriffs escort Ericka in. She didn't remember meeting Ericka before. Ericka stopped right behind Roraback's back.

"Oh my God," Ericka said.

"What's the matter?" Roraback asked her, alarmed.

"*It's all men.*"

Roraback looked at the judge, at the sheriffs, at the other attorneys, at the court stenographers, at the news reporters. Yep, all men. On a superficial level, Roraback knew that, of course. She had practiced in that courtroom for twenty years. She knew that women rarely if ever took part in daily court combat, but until Ericka made the observation, she had never really thought about it.

Roraback had been representing radicals in Connecticut since the 1950s, when Connecticut Communists went to jail under the Smith Act for "conspiring" to advocate the overthrow of the U.S. government—not even advocating it, merely associating with others of similar beliefs who had the potential to advocate it. Catherine Roraback was also a prototypical feminist, a graduate of Mount Holyoke College, and the only female criminal defense lawyer practicing in New Haven, if not all of Connecticut. In 1965 she convinced the U.S. Supreme Court to overturn Connecticut's ban on disseminating birth-control information, a precursor for the *Roe v. Wade* decision on abortion.

Roraback was descended from privileged Yankee stock; her grandfather was a state supreme court justice, her great uncle a powerful state Republican leader and chief of Connecticut Light and Power Company, her father a Congregationalist minister. From her start in private practice, Roraback defended pacifists, Communists, political outsiders caught in the web of overreaching law enforcement. That earned her a reputation as a Red, or, in the eyes of people like prosecutor Markle, un-American. In truth, she was a true Connecticut Yankee, devoted to upholding the constitutional freedoms in the cases that mattered most—the ones with wildly unpopular defendants.

BACK AT THE Whalley Avenue jail, Warren looked for advice from a childhood friend who happened to be in the same cellblock—Eddie Devlin. Warren and Eddie knew each other from St. John's Elementary School. They got in trouble together in Sister Margaret's first-grade classroom. As an adult, Devlin got in even more trouble than Warren, pursuing a career in organized crime. Even behind bars, in New Haven, it seemed, everybody knew each other. Devlin was surprised to find his old pal in the recreation area inside the jail.

"Warren," he said, "if I knew you were gonna be killing people, I could have paid you a couple of thousand dollars!"

"Don't think so much of this guy," one guard warned Warren about Devlin. "He's responsible for a lot of people being dead."

Perhaps. But Devlin could also provide valuable advice about the rules of survival behind bars—whom to trust, whom to avoid. Devlin offered to keep Warren in cigarettes, valuable currency behind bars. And Devlin promised Warren protection from Devlin's bank-robbing buddies: "No one's gonna fuck with you. Don't worry about it."

The first week of June, the feds caught up in Denver with two fugitive Panthers wanted in the Rackley case. They tracked down Lonnie McLucas in Salt Lake City. Local and state police flew to Utah to join federal agents in interrogating McLucas at the Salt Lake County jail, before his extradition to Connecticut. The news traveled among cops and lawyers. Returning from a court appearance, Eddie Devlin brought Warren the news: they picked up a Panther in Salt Lake City. The marshals are all saying he pinned the whole murder on Warren.

"You know you've already been fingered," Devlin told Warren. "If you want to escape, I can have a car for you."

"Eddie," Warren said, "I'm afraid if I escape, they'll shoot me. They'll kill me."

"I just hope," Devlin responded, "you have a good lawyer."

Warren's instinctual reasons for sitting out the escape were soon borne out. He had noticed that every morning, as the inmates passed through a tunnel connecting their cells to the mess hall, one inmate would slip into a laundry room. While the inmate sawed off bars to a window, someone else would bring his food.

The morning arrived: Warren saw ten or twelve of the guys slip into the laundry room and through the window. He wondered why some of the escapees, who faced minor charges, would put their pending legal liberty at stake.

Warren and the others returned to their cells. Suddenly sirens rang out. Warren overheard the guards narrating events: "The little old ladies [in the surrounding neighborhood] are complaining. . . ." "The guys are going over the fence!"

As part of the escape, in order to confuse the guards, one of the inmates mixed up the information on a board that kept track of which prisoners belonged in which cells. So even though Warren was in his assigned cell, it looked like he had joined the getaway gang.

"Kimbro's one of them!! He escaped!" he heard a guard yell.

Warren, Devlin, and the others rushed out of their cells, which were unlocked that time of day, to look out a cell-block window. They could see a black escapee, shorter than Warren but with a similar complexion, hop the fence on County Street—and get shot by the police. The bullet hit his leg; he survived. He, like the other would-be escapees, were caught, returned to jail, and punished.

Panther George Edwards was held in the Whalley jail, too. He, too, determined to show the Man he was no patsy. He started hearing about the other detainees' long-held complaints about the conditions in their cells, the limitations on visits, the lack of access to outside phones. Edwards soon got in trouble with the prison brass for his mouth. He ended up in "the hole." Edwards had only the floor to sit on, only four blank walls to stare at, only an opening in the floor into which he could relieve himself.

The inmates declared a strike to protest the situation. They drew up a petition. The warden was a recent transplant from rural Connecticut; he wasn't ready for this. So he called in the state commissioner of corrections, Ellis MacDougall. Warren had met MacDougall once when the commissioner visited a Yale-run youth program where Warren worked.

Now MacDougall, a portly, neatly dressed white man of middle age, entered the mess hall, calm, composed. "I want to speak to the leaders," he said.

MacDougall looked at Warren. "Kimbro," he said, "I met you before. Let me tell you something. It looks like you're gonna be here a long time. First of all, you don't demand shit. You request. You're in no position to demand.

"Another thing. Never put your damn name on the top of a petition. 'Cause we'll know you instigated it!"

Warren didn't know what to say but "OK." He was getting another education.

Warren still hoped to salvage some results from the disruption; he requested state law books to research the corrections statutes. MacDougall, meanwhile, told the group he had learned to use incidents like this for a constructive purpose. He said he would look at their demands to see if any had merit, then raise them with the legislature. He could use the threat of inmate unrest to lobby lawmakers for money to support prison programs.

While Warren wondered when he would leave the Whalley Avenue jail, his nine-year-old son, Germano, wanted to get in. Germano's Uncle "Bubby," Ted Spurlock, took him one day. The guard let Bubby in while Germano was left to simmer unattended in the waiting room. Germano walked out to the County Street side of the jail. He called for his dad. Warren got the message, held his hand out of a window, and waved to his son. Germano could see the wedding band. He couldn't see his dad's face.

Germano missed his dad desperately. He started riding his red one-speed bicycle to the jail. He would circle the building and call out his father's name. Only once did he receive a response. "Who are you looking for?" an inmate asked from a window. Germano told him. "They moved him to the other side" came the response. So Germano raced to Hudson Street, shouted again. This time, no one answered.

After Little League games, Germano rode back to the jail. He wanted to tell his dad his batting average. He threw rocks at the walls to get someone's attention. He succeeded only in releasing steam. The postgame ritual wouldn't last long. The Whalley jail was a pretrial way station. Lesser criminals returned to the street. People facing charges like murder were transported to long-term confinement out of town. "I want to take these books," Warren said the night they retrieved him for the transfer to Montville Correctional Center, an hour east, near New London and the Rhode Island border. Warren still had the state statutes in his cell. "No," he was told. "These belong to the institution."

His new cell at Montville had something better than a law book: its own toilet. The cell was roomier than the one at Whalley Avenue. It had glazed brick walls. The only downside was his commissary—the candy, cigarettes, and other items he kept in his cell at the Whalley jail. He'd put them in a pillowcase for the ride to Montville. For weeks the guards wouldn't return it to him. An older guard of Irish ethnicity would leave cigarettes in Warren's cell.

CHAPTER 5

The Making of a Panther

DESPITE THE GRUMPY welcome wagon the night of Warren's transfer, the Montville guards turned out to be friendly. Then came Henry Karney. A short, tough ex-Marine, Karney took over the jail warden's office soon after Warren arrived. If he was going to have problems with anyone during his pretrial stay at this prison, Warren recognized, it would be with Karney.

Karney, too, had heard about Warren's rabble-rousing, about the petition he drew up over the George Edwards affair. So he made it a point of acquainting himself with the sort-of-celebrity inmate with the Afro, to make what turned out to be a generous offer.

"I hear," he said, "that you can write a little bit."

"Yeah," Warren responded, noncommittal. "I can write a little bit."

"Well," Karney said, "we want to start an inmate newspaper here."

Thus was born the *Montville Times*, with Warren Kimbro as editor. It was soon a hit with inmates and guards alike.

Prison life offered Warren a welcome respite after a half year of the madness of Pantherdom. At first, Warren maintained the Panther attitude. He insisted that he was innocent of killing Alex Rackley and that the cops had framed him.

Unfortunately, events in the world outside had a way of chipping at his self-confidence. The government's case was building. Lonnie McLucas appeared before a grand jury. Again, stories reached Warren about how Lonnie gave him up.

"I know you did it," Warren's mother, Maybelle, told him the first time she made the trip to Montville. Until then, only Warren's sister Betty and his wife, Sylvia, had been allowed to see him. Sylvia didn't come often. Betty made the drive up every Saturday; she wouldn't miss a Saturday visit for years, not even on holidays.

"I don't condone what you did," Maybelle told her son. "But you're still my baby, and I'll pray for you." Warren didn't want to hear about praying. The books in his cell revealed that he was, as always, busy reading—reading radical political tomes, not scripture. "Religion is the opiate of the masses," Warren had mimicked Marx in one of his street corner Panther speeches. He saw no reason to disavow it now.

The next morning, Warren was reading one of those books in his cell and smoking a cigarette. The cell block was quiet, deserted. Sergeant Eddie Burns, the Irish guard who gave him cigarettes, popped open the gate:

"Kimbro! Kimbro! Kimbro!"

"What?"

"Come on."

Warren slipped on his flip-flops and followed Burns's waves down the hall. They walked past one door. Burns pointed to another door. Warren walked in—just in time for Father O'Brien to start saying Mass in his Irish brogue.

A voice inside him, from his Catholic upbringing, answered, "Sit there; be respectful." The voice sounded suspiciously like Maybelle's.

Priests from New Haven had started paying visits to his cell. Father O'Brien visited him, too. He asked Warren, a former altar boy, to serve as one again. Warren declined. Then he asked Warren to take communion. How could he take communion without first going to confession? Warren wasn't ready to confess. Warren agreed to keep coming to Mass, though. And his determination to live the lie started weakening. Maybelle wouldn't confess to her son for years about her conversation with Burns that first day she visited Montville. But Warren could tell she had some hand in that first visit to Mass.

IN A WAY, Warren appeared to be returning to his roots. He grew up in a strict Christian household. As always, however, the truth was more complicated; from childhood Warren felt the competing lures of right and wrong. People in New Haven wondered what happened to Warren in 1969. They wondered how this promising and respected community leader could have become a member of the Black Panther Party.

Warren was born on April 29, 1934, two months early, barely three pounds. He was delivered at home. He grew up on Spruce Street, which ran for one block along the southern border of New Haven's downtown, at the edge of the Oak Street section of the Hill neighborhood. For generations the Hill had welcomed immigrants, including Southern blacks like the family of Warren's mother, Maybelle, who came by boat from North Carolina in the 1890s.

Warren's father, Henry, stood out on working-class Spruce Street. He carried himself as a model of refinement on his way to work as he greeted the Eastern European neighbors who affectionately called him "Hendry." He didn't look like someone who spent his days at a machine fashioning braided steel cables. Henry changed from a suit into overalls when he arrived across town at the American Steel and Wire plant. A firm believer in the virtue of hard work, Henry held his job with American Steel for thirty-two years; if family lore is to be credited, he never missed a single day. On the way home, he stopped for a beer or a game of bocce at the Idarolas' Fats Tavern or unwound at the public bath at the corner of Spruce and Oak.

An occasional lipstick smudge on a shirt collar betrayed Henry's imperfect grasp of the Sixth Commandment. To wife Maybelle's consternation, other women found Henry magnetic, with his good looks, sharply defined features, dignified manner, and quick-witted charm. But in her presence, Henry treated Maybelle with reverence. He never raised his voice to her, nor would he allow any of his children to show the slightest disrespect toward her.

Inside the Kimbro apartment Henry set a proper, stern tone. As Maybelle and their eight children gathered at the table, he chose one child to say grace, demanding reverent attention from the rest of the brood. He never raised his voice. The kids knew better than to ask for salt, lest they receive a scolding for "insulting *my wife's* cooking."

To Henry's immediate right sat Warren—within cheek-slapping range. Henry seemed to take advantage of that proximity as regularly as butter made its way around the Kimbro table. Warren was Henry and Maybelle's second-youngest, not to mention the freshest. Warren tested the rules, over and over and over.

"Pass the gravy," little Warren said, deliberately omitting the "please."

Slap!

"You're carrying it too far," Henry Kimbro admonished his son. "You're acting like a heathen."

Heathens had no place in the Kimbro home. Henry supported Maybelle's devout Catholicism. Though Henry himself seldom accompanied the family, he insisted the children attend Mass at St. John's.

Maybelle was a strong woman with both a fondness for corporal punishment and a weakness for her wise-alecky little boy. She was a loyal daughter of the Party of Lincoln, back when the Republicans were still known as the party that freed the slaves. She hated "socialism." She dismissed FDR as a "Bolshevik." Maybelle kept house in two adjoining flats at 37 Spruce Street, which held not just her and Henry and the eight kids, but Warren's godmother, Edie, as well. Henry's steady paychecks were supplemented by Edie's wages from cleaning homes. Somehow that was enough to feed an eleven-member household.

At St. John's school, Warren tested the rules. After one too many run-ins with the nuns, school officials told Warren to stay home for good. He spent a year and a half out of school before returning to St. John's. During that time he followed his godmother to house-cleaning jobs. He carried books with him; by watching his older siblings, he learned to read without much formal instruction.

Like most kids, Warren learned at least as many of his lessons about right and wrong, about survival, outside of the classroom as he did in it. Spruce Street stretched less than the length of a major league fly ball, but it contained a city's worth of stories, struggles, and dramas. Nearly a third of the neighborhood's families were first-generation immigrants: Italians, Russians, Irish, Poles, Greeks, a scattering of Asians, and blacks. One-block Spruce Street's pitted asphalt surface connected twenty-three properties, some of them tenements, some row houses, not one a single-family detached home. It was a street filled with businesses: a corner A & P grocery, the Joseph Horowitz junkyard, Afinitto's meat market, a pair of Italian clubs (one favored by Republicans, the other by Democrats), Jacob

Gutkin's tailor shop, Dorothy Cohen's Hebrew tutoring business, Bill Jones's trucking operation. It was a place crammed with hard-working people. The Tomback family of 8 Spruce Street, for instance, included Abraham the baker, Isidore the tailor, and Nathan the haberdasher. Number thirteen was home to Jim Apotrias the peddler, Philip Bonaguso the machine operator, Sam Cohen the peddler, Alex Kuczyski the grave digger, and Stanley Kuczyski the Taft Hotel houseman. Even in the depths of the Depression, the surrounding neighborhood had only fifty-five families on welfare, meaning that roughly 95 percent kept jobs of one sort or another.

Not all the jobs, not all the businesses, were models of civic enterprise. Charlie Brewster, for instance, ran a whorehouse at 40 Spruce Street. Over the objections of his father, Warren visited the whorehouse to take out Mr. Brewster's trash. Brewster paid 50 cents, twice the going rate.

"I want to be like Charlie Brewster," young Warren declared one day. "I want to be a pimp."

Henry Kimbro overheard. He called his son in for a sit-down talk. He had told Warren to stay away from 40 Spruce Street.

"Oh, you wanna be a pimp, do you?" Henry demanded. "Well, let me show you something." That "something" was a strap. Warren would still feel the sting of that strap almost six decades after the beating. Warren decided he didn't want to be a pimp after all. In fact, he decided that he hated pimps.

Spruce Street still offered plenty of other opportunities for easy money, especially for a kid like Warren. He was a hard worker and stood out to adults. He could relate to different kinds of people. And he had nerve. One neighbor paid Warren to go up to people and say, "Kiss my ass." Rhea Johnson paid young Warren to look out for the cops outside her illegal after-hours club at 39 Spruce Street, where visiting musicians like members of Duke Ellington's, Ella Fitzgerald's, and Count Basie's bands would end up after playing local gigs.

One night Warren rapped on the window at 39 Spruce.

"Miss Johnson! Miss Johnson! The cop is out there."

The cop heard. He chewed Warren out and shooed him off. Warren grew indignant. "You go down to Mississippi," he told the cop, "and stop what's happening to blacks down there!"

Warren didn't get in trouble this time. "This boy," Miss Johnson told his mother, "is gonna be great!"

Unfortunately, Warren's teachers felt differently. He dropped out of school at sixteen. Warren stumbled through a series of menial jobs—stock boy, furniture lifter, banana truck worker—and into reading, a habit that would later set him apart from his peers and allow him to grasp intoxicating ideas like those of Malcolm X and the Black Panthers. The small jobs frustrated him. At seventeen, he tested his way into the Air Force. He decided he'd make a good career officer.

WARREN SHIPPED OFF to basic training in Geneva, New York, at Sampson Air Force Base in 1951. Warren trained hard and mastered the care and use of firearms. But he lost interest in patrolling his fellow officers, which was the job he was assigned in Korea. It was tedious, and a pain, catching officers breaking rules. He'd entered the military a provincial teenager who believed in America, in the government, in its stated missions around the globe. Five years later he left the service with a more complex view of his country, of the world, after encounters with racism in the service and with Asians who weren't grateful for American protection.

By the time Warren returned to New Haven in 1957, home had changed. His father was dead. And Spruce Street was about to die, another victim of an effort under way in New Haven to create America's first slumless city. From 1954 through the end of the 1960s, the city, under the direction of an ambitious mayor named Richard C. Lee, embarked on the country's most intensive experiment in fighting poverty, earning New Haven the nickname "Model City." Over a half a billion federal and foundation dollars flowed through the city for "renewal." No other city in the country received even close to as many antipoverty dollars per capita. New Haven received $745.38 per citizen just from the federal urban renewal program; the next closest city, Newark, received $277.33. New York City received $36.77.

Urban renewal involved buying hundreds of low-end properties—virtually everything from Warren's childhood and adolescence—and bulldozing existing buildings. Then, the land cleared, small parcels were folded together to make big parcels, and these were used to build bigger buildings, serving larger owners, and displacing the people who'd lived there. This "renewal" was hard on many families, thousands of whom lost their homes.

Spruce Street was flattened, destroyed—every last stick of housing and commerce. The street itself disappeared, swallowed by a block filled with nothing but parking lots and, eventually, new stores. Warren had mixed emotions. He shared the dream of a better city, nicer homes, and helping people, but he didn't like seeing his whole neighborhood bulldozed. He would rather the city had selected rundown buildings to renovate, keeping the good, preserving community.

He was having trouble establishing a stable adult life both at work and at home. In 1959 he lived on and off with a divorcee. One day, when they were living apart but still going together, someone called Warren. "If you're looking for your woman and your money," the caller informed him, Warren could find them in a particular house on Shelton Avenue, where a well-known gambler named Earl Overby lived. Warren grabbed a knife his nephew had given him as a gift upon returning home from the military. He charged over to Shelton Avenue and broke down the door. He found his girlfriend in the bedroom with Overby. They were asleep.

Warren was beside himself. "Oh, bitch. *This* is how it is," he seethed.

His girlfriend moved to protect the gambler but was too late. Warren thrust the knife into Overby's chest. He could have killed him. In throwing herself on Overby, Warren's girlfriend got cut, too, badly enough to require stitches.

The man spent days in intensive care. He survived. Convicted of aggravated assault, Warren was given probation.

Almost immediately thereafter, Warren hooked up with Sylvia Banister. They married before the year was out. Sylvia was pretty and young, six years younger than Warren. Warren made her laugh. At twenty-five, after a series of bad relationships, Warren figured, she was as close to love as he would get. Plus, she was pregnant.

Warren finally put down roots, and blossomed.

Germano Kimbro was born in March, named after an old neighbor from the home on now-demolished Spruce Street. Warren was thrilled at his son's birth; he ran down the street handing out cigars. Veronica, conceived on Father's Day, arrived eleven months after Germano. Warren doted on both of them. He warmed their formula. As soon as they could walk, he drove them around town in his Mustang. They played Frisbee in the park. They ate kosher salami on rye and drank lemon-lime soda at Fox's Deli. Warren bundled them up for football games at Bowen Field. In summer the family would cook out at the beach.

The expanding Kimbro family moved to another apartment, on Orchard Street. Jazz and R & B music filled the house. Warren always seemed to be fussing with new toys. Veronica was the playful one, pushing limits. Germano, who idolized his dad, followed the rules. They spent hours in the backyard, Warren showing Germano the finer points of baseball and football. Early on Germano had a strong arm. At age three, Germano followed Warren to his football coaching duties at the Albie Booth League, carrying a water bucket that weighed nearly as much as he did. A year later Germano and his older cousin Boopie followed Warren on Sunday mornings to a side job cleaning up after shows at the Soundtrack Café; they took home the change they found on the floor or under the seats.

Warren supported the family through a series of jobs at several dry-cleaning establishments. He learned fast, rising to the position of manager. He was popular with customers. In discussions at work, in the community, he absorbed the political passions of the day. Black America's great ongoing debates of the twentieth century were heating up again: Should the race pursue integration with whites, or should it develop its own institutions and culture? Should resistance to racial oppression take nonviolent forms? Or is violence sometimes necessary in self-defense?

The differing camps were personified most of all by the Rev. Martin Luther King Jr. and Malcolm X. The Oasis, a black social club, sent Warren as a representative to the 1963 March on Washington. Warren heard King's famous speech that day, with its poetic repetition: "I have a dream that one day on the red hills of Georgia the sons of former slaves and the sons of former slave owners will be able to sit down together at the table of brotherhood. . . . I have a dream that one day, down in Alabama, little black boys and black girls will be able to join hands with little white boys and white girls as sisters and brothers." To Warren, the march felt like one big social event. Some of the celebrities seemed sincere. Others were preening, being seen. Even Warren was more interested in picking up pretty women than in picking up the vibes of the movement. He left with neither.

Warren believed in working within the system. He supported organizations that followed the vision of King, not Malcolm X. Still, he thrilled at Malcolm's fiery speeches, including one Malcolm delivered in New Haven. Malcolm gave voice to the frustrations gathering inside Warren. It prodded him to question and challenge liberal established power.

As a Christian, Warren had no interest in the Nation of Islam, the Muslim faction to which Malcolm X then belonged and which preached against "white devils." Nor did he buy the idea of black separatism. But Malcolm had a way of speaking truth about racism, of not using it as an excuse. He preached that black Americans had to take responsibility, not depend on white plantation owners who now dressed as enlightened politicians and government bureaucrats. They had to organize for themselves, develop their own businesses, not depend on the liberal dole. He cast black people as positive actors, not helpless victims.

Warren, like Malcolm, considered the March on Washington a sham.

"Most of the so-called Negroes that you listen to on the race problem usually don't represent any following of Black people," Malcolm would say. "Usually they are Negroes who have been put in that position by the white man himself. And when they speak they're not speaking for Black people, they're saying exactly what they know the white man who put them in that position wants to hear them say."

How those words intoxicated the pent-up Warren. He cheered Malcolm's break from the Nation of Islam in 1964 to pursue a truer (and colorblind) religious and political path. He agreed with Malcolm's broadening the American black struggle to an international human rights struggle, with a special attachment to African liberation movements. On the West Coast, Malcolm X was having a similar effect on an antipoverty worker named Bobby Seale and others who would soon found the Black Panther Party on Malcolm's principles of self-defense, on resistance "by any means necessary."

Those thoughts hovered in the background as Warren grew restless at the dry cleaners. He found he could rise only so high. He learned all he could about the dry-cleaning business: accounting, bookkeeping, advertising, and equipment. Whenever an opportunity arose to move up or become a partner, he was told, "You're too important to me in the job you're in right now, so I can't spare you." At one point his boss wanted to sell the business; the buyer insisted that Warren be part of the deal.

That's it, Warren decided. He wasn't going to be anyone's boy to buy and sell.

As he plotted his career shift in 1965, New Haven's economy had undergone a fundamental shift. Factories fled for the suburbs, the South, the Midwest, anywhere they could pay workers less and stretch out over cheaper, more plentiful land. That meant good jobs for unskilled people were disappearing, jobs like the one that enabled Warren's father to feed and house nearly a dozen people. Over Mayor Lee's tenure, a macroeconomic tidal wave would wash away more than half of the 33,000 factory jobs in town, more than half the local employers. In their wake, a new economy was spurred by all the federal War on Poverty money washing onto New Haven's shores. That's where hard-working high school dropouts like Warren Kimbro turned.

In conversations with friends and people around town, Warren had grown outspoken in his criticism of these government and foundation-funded programs. The top guns were well-paid whites with salaries as high as $30,000 ($173,000 in 2005 dollars). These technocrats conceived urban poverty as a clinical problem to be solved by expert use of taxpayer money. Some mistook the displacement of poor people from a neighborhood for the elimination of their poverty. Warren saw middle-class high-rise apartment buildings grow from the ashes of Spruce Street. They were geared to people from Yale, to professionals. No one from the old neighborhood could afford to live there. The high-rises and the wider roads obliterated any hint of the old street life.

"You're a bright guy," one of City Hall's black neighborhood power brokers, Eugene McCabe, told Warren. "We'll get you a job with the city."

Warren suspected that City Hall wanted to silence a critic, but he agreed to visit the Redevelopment Agency—the main City Hall department in charge of urban renewal—to apply for a position. "The job is yours," McCabe assured him.

One of the questions on the application asked about college education. Warren noted that he hadn't gone to college.

"So when do you start work?" McCabe asked Warren the next time they bumped into each other.

"I got a call. They said I wasn't qualified for the position."

"What do you mean you're not qualified for the position?"

McCabe called the office to find out why.

"You stupid sonofabitch!" McCabe told Warren. "Why didn't you say you went to a black college somewhere? They wouldn't have checked!"

Henry and Maybelle Kimbro's son said he didn't care. A lie, he said, catches up with you sooner or later.

"OK," McCabe said. He sent Warren to another agency, Community Progress Inc., or CPI, a City Hall–controlled, though nominally independent, umbrella for antipoverty programs. CPI hired Warren as a community organizer. This time he didn't need a college education. He had a degree from Spruce Street.

WARREN THREW HIMSELF into community organizing. He also remained buddies with black activists who criticized the programs from the outside, notably the leaders of the militant Hill Parents Association. The HPA saw liberal programs like those in Lee's Model City as a new form of white control, of white people making decisions for black people and keeping them dependent on government rather than helping neighborhoods obtain the tools to determine their own destinies. The HPA eschewed violence but warned of danger brewing in neglected neighborhoods like the Hill.

HPA's warning proved prescient on August 19, 1967, when New Haven had its riot—just like the other cities with less enlightened mayors and just a fraction of New Haven's antipoverty budget. The riot started in the Hill neighborhood after white restaurateur Ed Thomas shot a knife-wielding intruder of Puerto Rican descent; rumors about the incident swept the neighborhood, drawing crowds of people angered over a perceived racial attack. The police, disconnected from neighborhood groups like the HPA, found themselves unable to contain the subsequent outbreaks of violence. For four nights battalions of cops in the streets dodged bullets from and beat on rioters.

Buildings burned in the Hill, in Dixwell, in Fair Haven, almost all in black neighborhoods along the ravaged corridors of "renewal." State troopers and National Guardsmen poured in to claim control of New Haven's streets. The Hill neighborhood became occupied territory. The bonds were fraying between white New Haven and its quiescent black community. The old rules of manipulation and marginalization had grown as outdated as laws governing speakeasies and horse hitches.

A federal government commission on urban riots reported that the New Haven disturbances led "moderate Negro community" members to drift toward support of "at least two black militant organizations." Angry people who felt tugged in one direction by hopes for peaceful progress were increasingly propelled in the other direction by their frustrations with the limits of urban liberalism. They would find other—less pacific—leaders to turn to.

In the riot's wake, black community groups sought to take protection of their community into their own hands. Sixteen organizations, from the moderate NAACP and Urban League to the militant HPA, united under the banner of the Black Coalition. They took charge of keeping the black community calm when Martin Luther King was assassinated on April 4, 1968. They worked alongside cops, as partners, to give the community a chance to vent at a forum on the Green, without resorting to mass arrests or provoking confrontations. Unlike many other cities, New Haven did not erupt this time.

Warren was one of the community leaders called to help keep peace at the Green the day of King's assassination. He had moved to an exciting new job in the War on Poverty infrastructure. He was an "indigenous counselor" at an agency called the Residential Youth Center, or RYC. Warren loved working with kids. Warren developed relationships with, among others, the region's chief prosecutor, Arnold Markle, to help find ways to keep troubled kids out of the prison system.

Warren's exploits are trumpeted in the pages of *Build Me a Mountain*, a study of RYC written by Yale clinical psychologist I. Ira Goldenberg, RYC's founder. Goldenberg followed Warren around for a day, July 8, 1968, transcribing his colorful interactions with colleagues, kids, and muckety-muck around town. He devoted fifty-seven pages of his book to a riveting, rollicking chapter about his day with "Will K.," his pseudonym for Warren.

The picture is of a streetwise, golden-hearted superdude straight out of *The Mod Squad*. On the page he connects with everybody. He understands the bloods' anger at the Man. But he also knows the futility of trying to fight back with violence. Unlike the white do-gooders, he can reach the kids, show them a better way, help fight their battles. A lot is churning inside that passionate, charismatic thirty-four-year-old soul. "There is an almost indefinable 'presence' about him," Goldenberg writes, "a feeling of strength and tenderness, passion and loneliness—all these things together, sometimes muted and mingled, often stark and alone."

Will K.'s day is a roller-coaster ride of disappointments and small miracles. He is all energy. At a morning staff meeting, Will K. squirms in his chair, doodles, lights cigarettes, cracks jokes, jumps out of his seat, and bows to punctuate a point. He convinces a coworker not to party with his charges. He offers another coworker tips on finding a home for a needy family. He solves a conundrum over how to discipline kids involved in a fight over a fire extinguisher. Then Will K. turns the meeting into a draining encounter session; he draws out the boss about the pressure and inner turmoil he's feeling on the job. "You got to understand," Will K. then tells the others, "that this is especially hard for Scotty. Scotty never had nobody to turn to and to open up to. I know. Believe me—I know." The staff rallies around Scotty.

All by 12 o'clock.

Then Will K. zips around town in his powder-blue 1966 Mustang with the "black American Flag" on the bumper. ("The black stands for black consciousness and the red is for the blood spilled by black people in this country ever since we were brought here. The sword stands for strength and perseverance, and the leaves for peace and prosperity.") He visits the mom of a former RYC charge who is doing well in a new job but, to his mom's consternation, has come out of the closet as a homosexual. Warren promises to keep tabs on the alleged problem. He wrestles with bureaucrats to deliver a check to a young inmate at the Whalley Avenue jail. He talks political strategy with the head of the city's Black Coalition. Over the phone, he convinces a benefactor to pony up $450 ($2,600 today) for a prep school scholarship for an RYC kid. After hanging up the phone, he "does a jig" in the office. He slaps colleagues five, then declares, laughing, "Now all I got to do is make that big-assed fool put his mind to school. And he'll do it, too, or you'll all see one skinny-assed nigger smack one big fat-assed nigger kid all over New Haven."

In a swing by the Yale Bowl, Will K. makes sure Ron, an RYC teen, works hard at a summer "Neighborhood Youth Corps" job preparing the stadium for football season. He also wants to follow up on something.

"I hear you had a little problem last night," Will tells Ron.

"No problem," Ron responds.

"Shoot," Will says, "no problem. When you're making like to kill people, that's a problem. What happened?"

Ron spills the story. He admits to trying to pick up a gun on the streets after someone stole (then anonymously returned) his ten-dollar ring:

WILL: "Good thing our friends on Legion [Avenue] didn't give you a gun."

RON: "I tell ya, Will, I'd a shot all them guys."

WILL: "Well, they can only fry you once."

RON "Hell, I know that. But it wasn't the money, it was the principle."

WILL: "Would it be worth getting fried for ten dollars?"

RON: "Hell, no, but God love me I was hot, Will. Really hot."

WILL: "I know you was hot. You think I don't know that? But you'd be a helluva lot hotter if they fried you."

RON: "I tell you honest, Will. I don't really think I'd a shot anyone. That's not my style. You know."

WILL: "I don't know shit. All I know is that I don't care how hot you get. That gun shit out. Dig? Out!"

As at the dry-cleaning business, Warren worked his way up at RYC. A sense of mission unified the racially diverse staff. They overcame their differences to work together. Everyone, including the director, maintained a caseload, worked weekend shifts, took turns cooking. They saw each other's success or failure as their own. They were reaching kids. These were heady days for Warren. Each day he saw real-life evidence that the system could work, a counterpoint to Malcolm X's belittling of integration and the Great Society.

But outside the RYC offices, in New Haven, in cities across the country, people like Warren who helped to wage the War on Poverty struggled with how their work fit into the long-term effort to improve the plight of black America. In his famous 1903 book *The Souls of Black Folk*, W.E.B. DuBois argued that the "Talented Tenth" of black Americans should lead the race's emergence from the crushing weight of white oppression. Will K. was a Talented Tenth guy, and was acting out the role prescribed by DuBois as he worked in the War on Poverty.

Later in his life, DuBois came to acknowledge that members of the Talented Tenth might abandon the interests of less talented blacks, leading to "a sort of interracial free-for-all, with the devil taking the hindmost and the foremost taking anything they could lay hands on." Radical blacks like the Panthers, who were establishing themselves in Oakland and several other cities (though not yet New Haven), criticized "bourgeois blacks" for grabbing the good jobs and fleeing the ghetto, returning only to pray in church on Sundays. The Panthers provided a radical reinterpretation of the mission of the Talented Tenth. According to the Panther vision, the educated vanguard elite would team up with the least fortunate blacks in creating a revolution that would spring the entire race from the grip of white exploitation.

The Black Panther Party emerged at a time when the image of the plantation still served as a vivid symbol for blacks' place in the U.S. economy, albeit in a form updated from the pre–Civil War era. The antebellum South had built its racial ideology, and its core economy, on the plantation system—a system that could not turn a profit absent unpaid slave labor. The sharecropping system that followed emancipation of the slaves in 1865 relied upon the extraction of profits from the backbreaking effort of tenant farmers, often black ones. As the mechanization of Southern farming undermined this system, blacks moved to Northern cities in increasing numbers, especially after World War II. Many of the Panthers belonged to families with exactly this history. Here, again, "black" rhymed with "bottom": The white-led unions as well as the white factory managers consigned black workers to dead-end, low-end, high-sweat jobs.

As in the South, the system enabled white bosses and workers alike to prosper economically. The black migration north peaked at the worst time, just as factory jobs began moving south and abroad, trapping Northern urban blacks in poverty. So for most urban blacks, opportunities for advancement were vanishing; meanwhile, the most talented urban blacks, like Warren, found new opportunities in the subsequent 1960s War on Poverty.

The '60s-era social programs were designed to help the poor. However, in the eyes of black critics like the Panthers, the War on Poverty created a new variation on the plantation system: The economic interests of white-led government and social-service agencies (like housing authorities) depended on keeping down poor blacks. If blacks rose from poverty, those bureaucracies would lose their customers. Here, in stark contrast to the whole history of American racism, whites seemed to derive their economic status from unproductive blacks, not from productive ones. The economic marginality of blacks in Northern cities seemed to some a nearly perfect inversion of the old plantation economy—an arrangement by which "poverty pimps" and social-service providers enriched themselves by serving blacks who failed even to be exploited in the old-fashioned ways of farm and factory.

JUST MONTHS AFTER Warren's day as "Will K.," downtown decision makers decided they wanted Warren to run a different agency, CPI's outpost in Dwight, a working-class section just west of Yale and downtown. Warren went to work in a one-story storefront office at the corner of Platt Street and Edgewood Avenue. He had a $10,000 salary. This income—nearly $58,000 in 2005 dollars—placed Warren solidly in the ranks of a growing black middle class. His family moved into a nice home in a townhouse at nearby Ethan Gardens, a government-built complex designed for a racial and economic mix of people.

As Warren and his family joined the ranks of the burgeoning American middle class, a black cultural explosion was underway. Warren's eight-year-old daughter Veronica had long, straightened hair; now she wanted an Afro. New sounds, new styles, new smells swirled everywhere.

One day Warren and Sylvia were home, smoking cigarettes, when Veronica rushed in. She'd been hanging outside a hippie leather goods shop around the corner.

"Oh mommy, daddy, I need some cigarettes for my friends," she reported.

"What friends?"

"My friends on Chapel Street."

"What friends on Chapel Street do you need cigarettes for?"

"Well, they're so poor, daddy, that they have to have one cigarette, and they have to pass it around to everybody." They'd been sitting on the floor in bare feet. Veronica felt so sorry for them.

Warren walked around the corner. He confronted the group of tokers with an unrealistic demand. "Don't you ever smoke that shit around my kids again!" he ordered.

For all the excitement within the Kimbro family about their new apartment, Warren noticed corners being cut as builders completed work on Ethan Gardens. (Warren informally christened the complex with a different name: Malcolm X Village.) Warren's neighbors noticed the problems, too. They turned to him to make their case. He was elected the cooperative's board president.

Warren had been following the debates, in New Haven and nationally, over President Lyndon Johnson's directive to give poor people more control over decision making in antipoverty and urban renewal programs. The catchphrase was "maximum feasible participation." Warren figured that meant government beneficiaries like the families at Ethan Gardens had some power. They could hold up issuance of the final government checks promised to builders if the builders tried to cheat them; in Warren's view, the builders were cheating the residents of Ethan Gardens. He looked at the project's architectural plans. They called for circuit breakers in all apartments. Warren didn't see circuit breakers in the apartments. Instead, the apartments had been outfitted with cheaper fuses. If the lights went out you would have to fiddle with screwing in a fuse instead of being able just to push a button. That didn't seem right to Warren.

Warren helped turn out a room full of families for a meeting with the developer.

"OK," Warren told him, "where are the circuit breakers?"

"Well, these are better for you."

"Don't bullshit me. A woman who's a single head of household, who isn't mechanically inclined, it's easier for her to push a button, to turn the power back on if she pops it off, than to find a fuse-stat that's fifteen amps, thirty amps, twenty amps."

The developer promised to knock money off the rent.

"And you didn't do three coats of paint, like you were supposed to do, three coats of non-lead-based paint."

The developer didn't believe him. So Warren pointed to a spot on the wall. It was bare drywall. How often, he asked, does a painter manage to miss the same spot three times?

The developer reported back to the city. Someone called Ernie Osborne, Warren's brother-in-law who worked with the city. Ernie told his wife, Betty, Warren's close sister. Betty told their mother.

Maybelle phoned Warren.

"Don't embarrass your brother-in-law and your sister," she pleaded.

"OK, Ma, but this stuff isn't right."

Then, one Sunday, the developer visited Warren's apartment unannounced. Warren was watching television. A black-and-white television.

"You know," Warren would remember him saying, "we could finish your basement. We could panel it. Put a nice color TV in there."

"I don't have money for that crap," Warren snapped.

"You could get it. You could get it."

"You know what?" Warren said. "This sounds like a bribe. Get the hell on out of here."

Promises to Mom aside, Warren refused to sign off on the project's completion on behalf of the coop board until the developer addressed the problems.

IN HIS NEW job running CPI's Dwight office in the fall of 1968, Warren saw another chance to put ideas into action. "We're going to make this a self-sufficient neighborhood!" Warren declared. He thought back to what one of his old dry-cleaning customers, a steel company president, used to tell him about the difference it would make if inner-city neighborhoods could become self-sufficient rather than relying on government help.

Warren had his eye on a factory at the corner of Orchard Street and Legion Avenue. In World War II it made rubber rafts; now it was empty. Maybe the neighborhood could buy that factory, figure out a product to manufacture, and plow the profits back into the community.

He decided to run the idea by Joe Downey, his supervisor at CPI. He got the chance not long after he took his job, when Downey visited him on his rounds of neighborhood offices.

"Why would you want to do that?" Downey responded. "Because if you do that, they won't need *us*."

"Bullshit," Warren thought to himself. "They tell me to come in here and say, 'We're going to get people off welfare, we're going to make people self-sufficient, we're going to empower people.' When we have a real opportunity to empower people, we don't want to."

Warren's impatience increased when he learned of the Redevelopment Agency's plans to tear down buildings in Dwight and build new ones. Warren heard about them not from Redevelopment officials, not from the politicians or the bosses at CPI, but from a friend who happened to notice blueprints in a downtown Agency office on Chapel Street by the corner of Park Street.

As at Ethan Gardens, Warren knew officials would need some form of neighborhood approval to draw on federal dollars. He had attended enough meetings at which officials would spring detailed proposals on residents for quick ratification; people had little chance to scrutinize plans, mull them over, offer suggestions. He was determined that wouldn't happen in Dwight. Warren figured no one in Redevelopment would share the plans. So he and a friend snuck into the building. It had no alarm. They grabbed a copy of the plans.

Warren justified the caper to himself. While it was illegal to break in, they weren't trying to steal anything. They just wanted to know, needed to know, had a right to know, what the planners had in mind for their neighborhood.

In the plans, Warren noticed that an auto body shop would be replaced with senior housing. Warren and his fellow neighborhood organizers wanted the city to give them the site, or some site in the neighborhood, for a youth center. The plans didn't have one.

So when officials convened a Dwight meeting to discuss the plans, Warren had a crowd ready to oppose them. Warren wondered, if they couldn't have the body shop property, then how about a vacant church at Chapel and Sherman? The planners didn't budge. Neither did the neighbors—led by Warren, who still held a city job designed to promote, not oppose, City Hall's ideas.

Just as Warren's neighborhood organizing was gaining in momentum, the Panthers came to town. Through 1968 New Haven had never had an official chapter. Although Warren had heard of the Panthers, he didn't set eyes on them until January 24, 1969, when he went to a funeral at St. Luke's Church for a twenty-three-year-old named John Jerome Huggins. Huggins was the son of a middle-class family much admired in New Haven's black community. Mr. Huggins, John's father, managed an exclusive society, the Fence Club, on Yale's campus. Mrs. Huggins worked in Yale's Sterling Memorial Library. John, a smart kid on whose shoulders rested the promise of continued progress from the civil rights era, attended the elite Hopkins Grammar School in New Haven. But by the mid-'60s he, like many young blacks, had grown impatient with the prospects of peaceful, gradual social change. After a tour in Vietnam, he went to a teachers' college, where he met another idealistic, aspiring teacher, Ericka Jenkins.

The two drove to California to join the Black Panther revolution. John was a campus leader at UCLA, where he was gunned down in an ambush by members of a rival black militant group called United Slaves, or US. It would later be revealed that the gunmen were FBI informers; they produced the desired results of J. Edgar Hoover's directive to sow suspicion among black radical organizations. The murder emboldened the FBI to continue using informers and planting incendiary rumors among US and Panther members to trigger an "internecine struggle" that could, as a Bureau memo put it, "grant nature the opportunity to take her due course."

Warren didn't know John Huggins, but he knew several Hugginses. His sister-in-law married a Huggins. He showed up at the funeral to pay his respects to the family. From his seat in St. Luke's, Kimbro looked at the parade of Black Panthers, guys ten, fifteen years his junior. He stared at their berets and turtlenecks and black leather jackets. Some looked sincere, upset, dedicated, defiant. Others looked as if they were putting on a show. He'd heard they ran free breakfast programs for children in the ghetto. He'd heard they preached black self-determination. He'd heard their members went to jail for their beliefs. He could support all that. But John Huggins's death, shoot-outs with other black activists, wildly exaggerated claims to fight cops—these things didn't make sense.

Warren noticed one Panther above all: twenty-one-year-old widow Ericka Huggins. Everyone noticed her. She had brought her husband's body home along with their three-week-old baby girl. She was grieving, but she never looked the meek widow. She stood straight and tall, just under six feet, her slender body some 130 pounds. Her hair was cut short. Composed, she had the steely self-confidence of a warrior. The first glimpse of her electrified Warren.

Soon after that day, Warren was visited in his office by José Gonzalvez, a Black Panther trying to organize a chapter in the Connecticut city of Bridgeport. Gonzalvez wasn't making much progress. He was looking for a local recruit to jump-start a New Haven chapter. "Are you with us, Brother Warren?" he asked.

Any other year, it's hard to imagine Warren saying yes. Even if he were inclined to challenge the system from the outside, he would not have seen self-proclaimed revolutionaries like the Black Panthers as viable. But this was 1969, a time when anything seemed possible—except change from within the confines of American democracy. Fidel Castro and Che Guevara had taken Cuba with a few hundred guerillas. More than fifty anticolonial uprisings had succeeded around the globe since the early part of the century. Many young people truly believed that revolution was on its way in America, or at least didn't immediately discount the notion. The Vietnam War sent home America's young men either in body bags or doped up and disillusioned with their country. The civil rights movement hit a wall; the country's "silent majority" elected a new president, Richard Nixon, with a barely unspoken mandate to put the hippies, the coloreds, and the Vietcong back in their places. A decade born of idealism came to be defined by the initials of heroes gunned down at the threshold of dreams: JFK, Malcolm X, MLK, RFK.

Whether it is was due to the times or because of Ericka, Warren started showing up at Black Panther meetings. Ericka led political education classes. The national office in California had suggested she stay in town and help organize the chapter. Warren hadn't stopped thinking about her since the funeral. She was so pretty. That sad face—she looked, in Warren's imagination, like someone who needed to be held. He started making inquiries: How old is John Huggins's widow? Is she staying in town?

One evening, as a small Panther meeting broke up, Warren seized the chance to offer Ericka a ride home, get to know her.

On the ride home, Ericka asked Warren's advice. Her mother-in-law was upset; the city's urban renewal bureaucracy had informed her that it was taking the family's home. The plan was to knock it down and replace it with senior housing. Did Warren know of any way to help the Hugginses save their house?

Warren would have liked to have played Superman, but he had to be honest. He had seen urban renewal in action. Usually, once the downtown bureaucrats decided on a new destination in the march toward "progress," no human story, no extenuating circumstances, no reasoned critique could stand in the way of the bulldozer. Warren told Ericka how he had seen entire streets, including the one where he grew up, disappear. The Hugginses may have just buried their son weeks before; that they now stood to lose their home, too, would not sway government decision makers on their behalf.

Soon the two were going everywhere together: speaking before audiences at Yale or in churches; trying, unsuccessfully, to convince black community leaders to support the Panther breakfast program for kids; traveling to New York to retrieve Panther newspapers or Little Red Books to resell at a profit on New Haven streets.

Many of the Panthers, including Ericka, believed deeply that a revolution was brewing in America. They were in the middle of it, leading it, with only two likely endings: victory or death. They believed that black people had a chance to take control of their own destiny. Warren recited the same sentiments with conviction. He followed the line, played the Panther he imagined Ericka believed in, down to his beloved wardrobe. He put away his dashiki in favor of a Panther-issue safari jacket to go along with his black jeans and dark shoes; the Panthers rejected "back-to-Africa" style as an outdated relic associated with "cultural nationalism." "Off the pigs!" Warren called out from platforms he shared with Ericka and José Gonzalvez.

Ericka came across as tough in public, hard-edged. She ran party classes like a martinet. Yet to Warren, Ericka moved to the strains of "The Age of Aquarius." Ericka was pretty, strong, passionate, tough; yet there could be a disarming sweetness about her. When the cameras were off, when the "cadres" weren't in the room, when political education class was over, when she was alone in the front seat of the Mustang with Warren, the elder member of the New Haven contingent, or at least the grown-up, the father with a job and a wife and a nice home, Ericka let down her guard. She offered glimpses of vulnerability beneath the revolutionary armor. Warren came to know the hippie who spoke of dropping acid in college, the astrology buff, the woman who wrote poetry. He loved her long fingers, her slender hands, her caramel skin. With her erect posture, Warren thought that Ericka looked like a model in her jeans and leather boots. She was growing her hair out frizzy and free. In the presence of worldly, dreamy Ericka, so deep beyond her twenty-one years yet youthful and sexy, Warren was putty. He had enough stars in his eyes to light up all the marquees on College Street.

Warren cherished their longer trips, the errands to New York. On one such journey, he and Ericka drove down the Merritt Parkway, through tony Fairfield County, Connecticut's "Gold Coast." Ericka continually pointed to the side of the road.

"Look at those nice houses," she said. "Isn't it a shame that after the revolution, we're going to have to take those away from people?"

With frequent trips like these it didn't take long for people to start whispering about Warren and this attractive young woman constantly at his side. Not surprisingly, Warren's wife, Sylvia, resented Ericka. When the Panthers moved into Warren's home at Ethan Gardens, after being evicted from their previous headquarters, it became an all-hours crash pad. To Sylvia, these strangers were the houseguests from hell. They might as well have put their names on the mailbox. They slept on the floor, on the couch. They held their meetings in her home. They helped themselves to cigarettes lying around the kitchen; these were now "the people's cigarettes." They helped themselves to the food in the fridge. "The people's food," they called it.

It was Ericka's presence that rattled Sylvia most of all. Everyone was talking about Warren and Ericka. Now Ericka felt free to roam right through Sylvia's house. Sylvia got an up-close view of the pretty young girl who attracted so much attention. To Sylvia, Ericka didn't look like a "sister." *Sylvia* had been the pretty young girl when she had married Warren nine years ago.

One night Sylvia exploded. That damn record was on again—Eldridge Cleaver making speeches. Jazz and soul used to fill the house, before the revolution. Not any longer. Sylvia was trying to get to sleep. She had to wake up early the next morning for her job at a drug treatment center. It seemed as if that record kept playing over and over again. Sylvia stormed down the stairs. Visions of Annie Oakley swept through her mind: she imagined grabbing that rifle the Panthers kept in the house, grabbing the other guns, and shooting all those Panthers down. I'm going to throw that stereo out the window, she thought to herself.

Her face must have told the story. All those brave revolutionary Panthers flew out the door, as though Sylvia had pumped bullets into the air.

This wasn't a place to raise her kids, not anymore. This wasn't her home anymore. That week, Sylvia moved out with the kids and stayed with a relative in town.

Soon after Sylvia's departure, Warren's long-awaited moment arrived.

It was at night, a lull in the meetings, the classes, the shuttling around town. Ericka felt down. Warren could see it.

They sat in the living room. As usual, Warren was focused on Ericka. He told her she could use his bedroom for some time alone. Then he followed her upstairs and closed the door. One of the girls in the downstairs living room watched Ericka's baby; everyone had known for a while what was bound to happen.

Perched on the bed, Warren and Ericka talked. Then Ericka started crying. Warren held her. She spoke of how she hadn't been with a man since John's death. "This is someone who needs caring for," Warren said to himself. He also told himself, "Warren, this is another notch in your belt."

Call it comfort, or call it inevitable. The Panthers believed in free love—as long as it was consensual. (That proviso proved a challenge to enforce.) When the talk about Ericka's relationship with Warren became truth, she didn't resist.

Love making provided momentary escapes from the conflicts Warren and Ericka encountered every day with the local police, with other Panthers, with people in New Haven. Paranoia hit a boiling point, stoked from all sides.

Warren didn't need to file a Freedom of Information request to know his phones were bugged; it was a widespread assumption in New Haven by then that police were tapping all the radicals' phones. When he left the house, he'd wave to the undercover officers sitting in their parked cars. In the middle of phone conversations, he'd remark, "Pigs, we know you're listening." In the privacy of Warren's Mustang, the Panthers wouldn't turn on the radio; they were convinced that it would activate a police bug.

To his old friends throughout town, Warren had gone off on his own inexplicable trip. Buddies like Wes Forbes from the RYC shared Warren's and the Panthers' idealism but disagreed with the violent rhetoric.

Forbes still considered their friendship intact enough to express his concerns. One afternoon he encountered Warren and Ericka and asked to speak with Warren alone. Warren said that wasn't necessary. Forbes said he was worried about Warren, that he had a bad feeling about where the Panther trip was taking him. Forbes had had a nightmare: he saw a skull and bones in Warren's face. He urged Warren to take an RYC director's job that was open in Cleveland. Warren said he'd get back to him.

Warren did call Forbes and told him not to worry. He was fine. Later that week, Alex Rackley's corpse was discovered along the muddy banks of the Coginchaug.

CHAPTER 6

Five Hail Marys

MAYBELLE COACHED HER son Warren on how to pray. Rather than asking God to spring him from jail, Warren should ask God to guide him, to help him figure out a way to get himself out of jail. A new Warren—or, as Maybelle saw it, the old Warren—emerged at Montville. This Warren was the model prisoner. He was the enthusiastic student in the "Guides for Better Living: Success through a Positive Mental Attitude" class and respected by guards and inmates alike; he put out the newspaper and attended Mass. He was reexamining his life, including his role in taking the life of another black man who did nothing wrong besides show up at the wrong revolutionary crash pad at the wrong time.

His children missed him terribly. Veronica had nightmares about her father. In one dream, her dad was under the ice of a frozen lake. Veronica saw his face. She couldn't break through the ice to get to him. Warren wrote letters home to his children, who were rarely brought up to visit him. Veronica cherished the letters. Warren sealed the letters with melted wax, with an imprint of his ring. Veronica saved all the seals.

Outside jail, an hour away from Montville, the city Warren left behind entered into a new era. On July 7, 1969, New Haven's Mayor Lee called it quits, announcing he wouldn't run for a ninth two-year term. His official explanation: time for new challenges.

"Sixteen years is a long time," Lee reflected in his official two-page announcement. "There always arrives a time in a man's political career when he should do other things, pursue other challenges, and mine is now."

In truth, Lee had no bigger challenges planned. He had passed up the chance to run for the U.S. Senate. He would continue, through a series of soft-landing private-sector posts, to see the mayoralty as his one true professional challenge, his life's work. As he also noted in his announcement, "I am sure that never again will I do anything so important as running a city, for this is where all the problems of my generation are focused—the problems of inequality, of crime, of equal employment opportunities, of poor housing—the problems of the inner city in America." Dick Lee tried as mightily as any mayor in America to tackle those problems. Lee made no mention of the Alex Rackley murder, no mention of the 1967 riot, no mention of the new brand of militancy behind the increasingly strident community attacks on government. They clearly opened the exit door that he now had no choice but to pass through.

The liberal Democratic civil rights era was over, in New Haven and across America. Government would no longer dance with the radicals or even the liberals; battle lines were hardening. The country signaled as much in electing Richard Nixon president months before the Rackley murder. Nixon ran on a law-and-order platform against the hippies and the protesters. He won office on an antiblack, anti–civil rights "Southern strategy" that would realign American politics for decades to come, under which even Democrats who got elected had to convince Southern whites they would limit government activism and send blacks to the electric chair.

As attitudes across the country hardened against dissenters and convicts, Warren may have had less than sincere motives when he first signed up for the jailhouse "Guides for Better Living," a Norman Vincent Peale–style inspiration class. The state's corrections commissioner was promoting the class. He dispatched two teachers, an ex-inmate con man named Jim Wilcox and a corrections employee, to bring the class to Montville. Karney, Montville's new warden, was suspicious of the class. So Karney asked his pal Warren to "cover" the class for the prison newspaper—and serve as Karney's eyes and ears, like a Cold War–era journalist doing double duty for the CIA.

Warren encountered lectures about mental attitudes, about "thinking for a change." The words sounded trite to him. He also knew that participants received a certificate upon completing the class; the certificate could help build a record for a prisoner hoping to get out of jail early. So Warren asked not just to cover the course but to enroll. Unfortunately, the instructors informed him, the course was open only to sentenced inmates, not to people awaiting trial.

Warren visited Warden Karney. "I'm gonna be in there every week, writing about it. Why can't I take the course?" he asked him.

"You're damned right!" Karney responded. He got Warren enrolled.

Warren didn't start out a model student. "This is corny bullshit," he told instructor Wilcox. "It won't work."

"Warren," replied the ex-con turned ideological con man, "if you believe it won't work, it won't work. If you believe it will work, it will work."

Soon enough, Warren realized, it made sense to keep his doubts to himself so as not to get on Warden Karney's wrong side. However, he took more interest in the readings as weeks progressed. He agreed with the idea of looking for opportunities to achieve goals. One week the instructors assigned students to write their personal goals in their workbooks. "I want to do the shortest life sentence in the history of the state of Connecticut," Warren wrote. As far as he knew, the record was six and a half years.

His goal didn't impress the teacher. "Warren, put down something realistic," Wilcox told him.

"You said this stuff works," Warren responded. "Why can't I try to make this happen?"

WHILE WARREN TRIED to think of matters other than the murder, the government got a big break in the Rackley investigation on August 7, when police in Toronto caught up with George Sams. He had slipped across the border dressed as a priest.

Sams was ready to cut a deal. The state seemed exceedingly eager to believe anything this man—with a long trail of bizarre stories, lying, psychotic episodes, and a recorded IQ of 75—was willing to tell them. Sams delivered a grand eleven-page tale with the desired punch line: He said that none other than national party chairman Bobby Seale had personally ordered the Rackley murder.

Within days, the Nixon Justice Department formed a special unit for the "purpose of instituting federal prosecution against the BPP [Black

Panther Party] and associated groups throughout the United States and any areas where sufficient evidence is available to support federal prosecution." Ironically, the unit included attorneys assigned to the department's civil rights division. In the wake of Sams's delectable "confession," J. Edgar Hoover informed the New Haven FBI office that two attorneys from the special new unit were arriving in New Haven. Nixon's assistant attorney general also directed the FBI to reinterview "individuals who were connected with the murder of Alex Rackley . . . in an effort to develop information which would indicate that Bobby Seale played a role in Rackley's murder."

Hoover had his troops scrambling to confirm Sams's story. Agents conducted the reinterviews—and reported back that they had no evidence to tie Seale to the murder. The New Haven police, upon whose information the FBI so heavily depended, believed Seale was mixed up in the affair and had probably given the order to kill. They, too, failed to produce information to back up Sams's account. "We had no solid evidence to link him to Rackley's death or torture," Chief Ahern would write. "Despite my personal feelings about the case, it was a fact that there was not sufficient hard evidence against Seale, and the New Haven Police Department never requested an indictment against him, nor did we expect that [prosecutor Arnie] Markle would ask for one."

Markle shocked Ahern by doing just that. In August, Bobby Seale was arrested in California on a warrant in connection with the Rackley murder, based on Sams's story. On the heels of the New York bombing-conspiracy case and the coast-to-coast raids, the government had fourteen Panthers imprisoned for the Rackley case alone. All the Panther leaders were in jail, out on bail preparing to face trial, or in exile.

For antigovernment protesters, a new cause was born. From New Haven to California, struggling chapters were energized. It was time to print up new posters—the Panthers had a new martyr. The government was framing the party's chairman. It was setting up Bobby Seale for the electric chair.

"I never saw Rackley in my life," Seale told a United Press International reporter in a jailhouse interview; he reported that George Sams had been kicked out of the party for stabbing a fellow Panther, then reinstated at the urging of black leader Stokely Carmichael, whom Sams once served as a bodyguard. Seale called his arrest in the Rackley case a "frame-up operation connected with the fascist tactics used by the black racists and the racist police."

Three hundred Panther supporters crowded a San Francisco courtroom where Seale's attorney unsuccessfully argued for bail in the case. Two of the supporters raised their clenched fists. "Power to the people!" they shouted. The judge sentenced them to five days behind bars for contempt of court.

Similarly, it seemed that police also had a renewed sense of purpose. They desperately needed to find someone to second George Sams's "facts" about Bobby Seale. Someone who, according to Sams, also heard Seale give the order to kill. Someone like the Panther gunman sitting in Montville, attending Mass.

WARREN WAS INDEED sitting in Montville, and he was moving toward changing the story he had told the police. He thought he might be ready to shed the Panther armor and come clean. He thought he was ready to change his not-guilty plea to guilty. Maybelle had a hunch a confession might be forthcoming. Word of a potential confession rippled to prosecutor Markle, who decided to bring a visitor from down South up to Montville. The visitor, who wasn't on Warren's list of desired guests, showed up in January. It was Warren's fifty-year-old brother, William—Sergeant William Kimbro of the Dade County, Florida, police department.

Warren wasn't happy to see him. He had always resented his brother ever since William, fifteen years his elder, beat him up as a kid to try to get him to go to school. Detective DeRosa of the New Haven force, as well as a state police corporal and an FBI agent, accompanied William to the Montville jail. William came to try to convince Warren to corroborate Sams's story about Seale.

Warren was called, unchained, unescorted, to meet his visitor. He noticed an open gate along the way between the men's wing and the women's section. The path led straight out of the prison. There were no barbed wires or guards in sight. An irrational thought flashed through Warren's mind. Upon arriving and seeing his brother, Warren told the guards, with whom he was on a first-name basis, about the unprotected exit.

"And if you would have ran," William cut in, "*I'd* have been the first one to shoot you."

So that was how it still was—William playing the hard ass, the tough guy. Well, screw him, Warren decided. *He's still someone I won't tell anything to.*

They talked for an hour or so in a room in the women's section of the jail. William urged Warren to say that Seale had been inside the Ethan Gardens apartment and issued the execution order.

"Papa would want you to do the right thing," William pressed. "You've got to be honest."

That's right—honest. Warren swore he never saw Bobby Seale come into his house. He sure didn't ever hear Bobby Seale give any orders about Alex Rackley, let alone any orders to kill. Warren was determined to go straight. He wasn't willing to lie, even if that helped him. (Years later William would tell Warren that the FBI had been ready to put him in a witness protection program, change his name, move his family, if he had given up Seale.)

Even though he wasn't about to corroborate Sams's implication of Seale, Warren could no longer deny that he had pulled the trigger. He'd run out of excuses, no matter how culpable he still believed the government may have been in the case. One January day, Warren sat in the New Haven courthouse in the second-floor office of prosecutor Arnold Markle. Markle called Warren's attorney, George Johnson, to the room. He said it was important.

Johnson didn't know about Warren's change of heart. He arrived in Markle's office to find Warren sitting without handcuffs next to his wife, Sylvia. Warren, feeling the effects of prison isolation, was groping at Sylvia, trying to kiss her; Sylvia squirmed, resisting. Johnson also saw Warren's brother William there. William had the air of a man in charge. Markle sat to the side with a triumphant grin.

Warren informed Johnson he wanted to plead guilty. Determined to admit his mistake and straighten out his life, Warren had already worked out a deal to plead to the lesser charge of second-degree murder. The lawyer was stunned. Even if Warren would ultimately cooperate with the state, Johnson didn't think he should rush into any deal. He felt he would be letting Warren down if he jumped ahead and signed on.

Markle gestured grandly to a small anteroom. "Why don't you go in there?" he suggested. Johnson huddled with his client. He'd known Warren before the arrest. Johnson helped found a white activist group in

New Haven called AIM, which supported Panther programs. In the early '60s Johnson had been a Peace Corps volunteer. After his first year at Yale Law School, he joined with SNCC (Student Non-Violent Coordinating Committee) to register black voters in Mississippi as part of 1964's Freedom Summer.

Johnson liked Warren and Ericka. He liked the Panthers, even if he thought some of their rhetoric was over the top. He didn't believe they could win a fight with the police, and he didn't think that more violence was the answer. He certainly didn't appreciate getting urgent calls from Panthers demanding to borrow his car to drive to Bridgeport "to stop a race war." Too many Yale students who said yes to such requests had a banged-up car returned, or no car returned at all.

Still, Johnson had been happy to help with the case when he got the call the day of the arrests. Months later, the case consumed the bulk of his days. And it wasn't paying the bills for his solo law practice.

"Tell me what the hell is going on," Johnson pressed Warren in the anteroom. Warren told him he sincerely wanted to plead guilty. Johnson could see Warren had thought about it and made up his mind. Warren was tired of pretending he hadn't done wrong. He was tired of the Panthers. At the time, the Panther newspaper included anti-Semitic screeds featuring drawings of Jews with big noses and big lips. That bothered Warren. He told Johnson about Christmas cards he'd received in jail from strangers; all but one came from Jews.

"Warren," Johnson said after hearing him out, "if this is what you want to do, by all means do it. But remember, this is forever, and you haven't given me a chance to do any negotiating. You could probably get a lot better." Second-degree murder brought with it a mandatory sentence of life in prison, with no parole for at least twenty years. Sure, that beat the electric chair. But, Johnson reasoned, given how badly the state wanted to convict Bobby Seale and Ericka Huggins, Warren could demand a lesser charge.

"No, I just want to do it," Warren said. "It's the right thing to do."

They rejoined Markle and the rest. Markle pressed to grab the next available court date, January 15, 1970. That happened to be Martin Luther King's birthday.

"That's wonderful," William Kimbro said. "It will be a fitting memorial."

"No," Johnson insisted. On this much, at least, he could take a stand. "We're not doing it on Martin Luther King's birthday."

They did it on January 16 instead. Warren showed up in court wearing a gold tie. A loose-fitting brown suit covered his skinny frame. The suit used to fit snugly, an Ivy League cut, when Warren first bought it at the Herman Pickus haberdashery on Church Street.

Johnson still didn't know what to do. He believed Markle had put unfair pressure on Warren through his brother. In 1964, the Supreme Court, in *Massiah v. United States*, forbade the state from eliciting statements from a defendant without his or her lawyer present, once the defendant has hired a lawyer. Markle had violated that ruling, using William Kimbro as a go-between. Johnson expressed qualms when he told the judge, a strait-laced, no-nonsense Irish-American, Roman Catholic Democratic pol named Harold Mulvey, that Warren wanted to plead guilty. He said Warren had been pressured.

The judge surveyed their faces. He called Warren forward.

Are you making this plea of your own accord, free of intimidation? Mulvey asked him.

"That is correct," Warren responded.

Mulvey couldn't be sure, but he accepted the plea. He also accepted Johnson's request to be dropped as Warren's lawyer. Mulvey informed Warren that he could have a court-appointed lawyer. Then he sent Warren back to Montville. Warren could take time with a new attorney of his liking to hash the issue out. This was too important to rush. In deliberate consultation with his new lawyer, Warren could choose to continue with the guilty plea or to ask the judge to withdraw it.

The news of Warren's plea made the front page of the *New York Times*, which noted that Warren "joked briefly" with prosecutor Markle and "smiled broadly" at Sgt. Nick Pastore, "who headed the investigation of Rackley's murder." The news stunned the Panthers and their growing legions of supporters, especially when word seeped out about Sergeant William Kimbro's jailhouse visit. The fact of the visit seeped out, but not the facts of what actually happened. No matter; the Panthers felt they knew those facts anyway.

The local Panthers held a press conference at their new Sylvan Avenue headquarters, a storefront office in the Hill, to accuse the cops and the state's attorney's office of "illegal activities" in using Sergeant Kimbro to "intimidate" his brother to plead guilty to "something he knew he didn't commit" in order to avoid life in jail or the death penalty. Warren—not Alex Rackley—became the torture victim whose travails the Panthers trumpeted. The Panther newspaper and the party's supporters continued to portray Warren as a reluctant participant in the state's case. In a book published three years later, a Yale professor would continue to suggest, inaccurately, that Warren pleaded guilty because "he may have been convinced that a fair trial was impossible."

Back at Montville, Warren had another confession to make. He made it the next Saturday.

"Bless me, Father," he told Father O'Brien. "I confess that I have sinned. I accuse myself of the following sins."

When he said, "Father, I have to confess, I shot and killed a man," Father O'Brien broke in.

"Oh no, Warren," Father O'Brien exclaimed, "don't tell me it was you!" He had recognized Warren's voice.

"Yes, Father, it was me."

"Are you truly sorry for what you have done?" the priest asked.

"Yes, Father, I am truly sorry for what I've done."

They discussed penance. Warren figured he'd have a barnload of prayers to recite.

"For your penance," the priest instructed, "say five Our Fathers and five Hail Marys."

What?

"Five Our Fathers and five Hail Marys," repeated the priest. "It's not the amount of prayers you say. It's for how truly sorry you are for what you have done that God forgives you."

Warren returned to his cell to say his five Our Fathers and five Hail Marys. Yes, he was truly sorry for killing Alex Rackley and for what he now considered his even bigger sin—denying the existence of God. He took communion that Sunday. And, responding to an earlier request by Father O'Brien, he became an altar boy once more.

BETTY AND ERNIE Osborne, Warren's sister and brother-in-law, knew that Warren meant it when he said he wanted to plead guilty, and they wanted to help in any way they could. They made an appointment to see Milt DeVane, a friend at one of New Haven's white-shoe law firms, Tyler, Cooper.

During their conversation, the visitors mentioned the name of Larry Iannotti, a forty-year-old attorney at the firm. They'd heard he was a sharp trial lawyer. DeVane called Iannotti into the room. He asked him if he wanted to take on Warren's case.

Iannotti wasn't sure. He didn't do criminal work; he specialized in corporate law. The lawyers willing to help the Panthers, often at no cost, tended to be movement people. Radicals. Activists. Larry Iannotti was nothing of the sort. A product of New Haven's conservative, working-class Italian-American Wooster Square neighborhood, Iannotti made it to Yale Law School via the Naval Academy. He clerked for a federal judge. He was a full-fledged member of the establishment.

And yet a few encounters in uniform with Southern racism had given him a sense that there was something amiss with the way blacks were treated in this country. By the time he met Ernie and Betty Osborne, he had concluded the country needed a change when it came to race relations, and he was open to playing some modest part in that effort. He disliked the tactics of the Black Panthers; he preferred less confrontational efforts to improve life in the city. He helped organize a group called School Volunteers for New Haven. Through his involvement with Our Lady of Mt. Carmel Roman Catholic Church in the suburban middle-class suburb of Hamden, Iannotti was an incorporator of Christian Community Action, which ran soup kitchens and family homeless shelters in New Haven's Hill neighborhood.

Ernie and Betty pressed Iannotti to help Warren. They impressed him, too; these were solid, sincere people. He agreed to consider representing Warren. First, though, he wanted to meet him. Stare him in the eyes. See how serious he really was.

Iannotti phoned Arnie Markle, the pugnacious prosecutor making the case against the Panthers. Iannotti told Markle he might represent Warren. He asked how to find Warren, how to obtain permission to visit him. "I have to tell you," Markle told him. "When the detectives told me they had the guy who had done the job, and that guy was Warren Kimbro, I said, 'You've gotta be kidding. He's not that kinda guy.'"

The drive to Montville took longer that Saturday than Larry expected. He'd never heard of the town before Markle told him about the jail.

When he met Warren, Iannotti was on alert. He served on a state panel for posttrial appeals and had already heard all the sob stories.

Warren looked at this man with neatly trimmed hair and beard and thought: If this doesn't look just like that guy in the Schweppes commercial, Commander Whitehead!

Don't tell me whether or not you're guilty, Iannotti began. Tell me about you.

They spoke for hours. To Warren, the conversation felt more like one he would have with a therapist rather than with his legal counsel. He described his life, his philosophy, his dreams and frustrations. He told Iannotti how he'd spent hours and hours at night awake wrestling with his predicament. He felt that he had to act for himself now, and not try to fulfill someone else's idea of how he should behave. His role in life, he said, was to be a decent citizen, a productive citizen.

Iannotti kept waiting for the tip, for the signal that Warren was blowing smoke. Warren seemed genuinely torn. He seemed genuinely remorseful about killing Alex Rackley.

"Well, what do you think?" Iannotti finally asked him. "Do you want to go for a jury trial?"

"I don't wanna go for no jury trial," Warren responded. "I want to get this off my back." Warren told him how he did pull the trigger in the swamp. He knew, deeply, that he was wrong. He offered no excuses.

You realize, Iannotti noted, that you'll have to testify for the state against other Panthers. That wouldn't lower Warren's sentence, but it could be crucial to winning a later appeal to suspend the sentence. Warren had mixed feelings about this. He knew testifying was in his own interest. He was still loyal to many of his old comrades. Not to Lonnie McLucas, maybe, who gave him up. Not to George Sams, or Landon Williams either. But to some of the others, especially Ericka.

Yes, Warren said, he knew he had to testify.

Iannotti was won over. He respected the man he heard baring his soul. And he already liked him. A lifelong friendship was born that day in the Montville jailhouse. Iannotti would represent Warren on one condition. First, Iannotti had to research the issue more before making a recommendation about whether Warren should maintain his guilty plea or bring the case to a jury. As long as Warren listened to that recommendation, he could make his own decision about whether to proceed, and Iannotti would be his attorney.

Warren agreed.

After weeks of investigation, Iannotti concluded that Warren was making the right decision. Warren reappeared before Judge Mulvey to confirm that he meant his guilty plea, that no one had coerced him. "I'm sick and tired of being used," Warren said. "The only pressure that was on me was the pressure of my conscience."

CHAPTER 7

Leading Lady

For all his activity behind bars, Warren slipped away from the barricades of the revolution. At first the Panthers rationalized his guilty plea. They portrayed him as a victim. As he prepared to testify for the state, it became clear that Warren had changed sides. He morphed into a symbol of turncoat piggery for Panther supporters.

Ericka Huggins, on the other hand, was fighting. Unlike Warren, she didn't make friends with the warden or the guards. She made trouble. Ericka and the other Panther women arrested in the Rackley sweep were housed in a prison known as the "State Farm for Women" in the town of Niantic, some forty miles east from New Haven on Long Island Sound. Officials there housed Ericka and the other Panthers in their own tier. "Administrative separation," it was called. The rationale: given their views, these women could start a riot among the other prisoners. The other Niantic women, many of them imprisoned for drug or prostitution offenses, tended to be apolitical.

Although the Panthers were pretrial detainees, not convicted offenders, they lived by the same restrictive rules the convicted women did, and then some. Niantic officials opened their mail, refusing to deliver some of it. They denied Ericka many visitors, including newspaper reporters. The Panthers' phone and recreation privileges were restricted; they were forbidden from having doctors of their choice visit them. The warden banned Ericka from receiving books sent over by lawyers or friends. Chinua Achebe's influential novel about the Ibo in Nigeria,

Things Fall Apart, was considered too dangerous. So were Lenin's *State and Revolution*, Joyce Carey's *Mr. Johnson*, Ho Chi Minh's essays, Eldridge Cleaver's *Post-Prison Speeches and Writings* (even though the jail's own library stocked it), *Ramparts* magazine, and the Black Panther Party newspaper.

Philosophy and spirituality texts passed through the filter; Ericka dove into them. Her old Panther comrade Elaine Brown found Ericka to be "very brave" during a visit to the jail. Ericka cried about being separated from her daughter, whom her mother-in-law would bring up to visit.

As on the outside, Ericka the inmate flitted between two personalities: the hard-edged, resolute revolutionary and the flower child writing prison verses like these:

> the oldness of new things
> fascinate me like a new
> feeling about love about people
> snow, highways that
> sparkle at night, talk,
> laughter. . .
> that old longing for freedom
> that this place constantly
> renews—it all makes
> me know that humankind
> has longed to be free ever forever
> since its break from the
> whole
> maybe the longing for
> freedom will soon make
> others homesick for our
> natural state in/ with
> earth, air, fire, water
> earth, air fire, water
> not dead
> but living
> not asking for freedom—
> but free

Ericka and the other Panther women ate meals separately from the other women in the jail. Other inmates who managed to communicate with them were punished for doing so. Ericka and the Panthers' lawyers helped other inmates get lawyers. The prostitutes had been abandoned by their pimps, their only previous support; Ericka looked out for them. Behind bars, as in Panther houses, she was a natural leader.

Three of the Panthers were pregnant. When Panther defendant Frances Carter's water broke, jail officials insisted, incredibly, that she remain shackled to her bed in the hospital while she delivered the baby. Ericka led a protest over the pregnant women's lack of medical treatment. Ericka went on a hunger strike until the jail agreed to bring them green vegetables and prenatal vitamins with iron. The protest succeeded.

Ericka watched Niantic inmates wrestling with drug withdrawal—without much help from the prison administration. The corrections system, like society at large, was still in the early stages of understanding how to deal with people's drug addictions. Ericka and the other Panthers smuggled in cigarettes and candy for women undergoing detox.

One night screams from another part of the prison reached the Panthers' segregated tier. The screams came from a lower floor housing women suffering through drug withdrawal. Ericka was used to hearing screams from detox cells, from heroin addicts suffering cravings, muscle spasms, nausea. These screams sounded more desperate than usual. Ericka and the other Panthers started banging on a door that led to their tier. They yelled through the bars of the windows onto a quadrangle of buildings: Help! A woman is dying! No response.

The woman's screams melted into moans. Then the prison turned silent. Ericka stayed up all night hoping to learn more. The next morning an ambulance crew arrived to take the body away. Ericka asked the matrons, as the female guards were known, what had happened to the shrieking inmate. She went to the hospital, a matron said.

"We know that," Ericka responded. "We think she's dead. What do you think?"

Ericka got word to a newspaper reporter, who found out the woman died of colonitis, related to heroin addiction. Niantic officials denied any responsibility.

Though locked up, Ericka communicated such drama and her passion to supporters in the world outside. She stepped into the role of new Pan-

ther hero—the first hero*ine*, actually, in a role central to the Panthers' survival, that of victim of the "Amerikkkan" police state. The Rackley case
had quickly become a boon to the party. Whenever the party seemed in
danger of collapsing, the death or imprisonment of its leaders paradoxi-
cally resuscitated its fortunes. From their inception, the Panthers won the
most notoriety, public sympathy, recruits, and rallies when Huey Newton
sat behind bars, when Li'l Bobby Hutton perished in a hail of police bullets, when a judge had Bobby Seale literally gagged in a Chicago courtroom. Each arrest, each trial offered fresh variations on the script,
presented a new cause with literal black-and-white demarcations of heroes
and villains. The details—like the questions of whether Huey Newton
really did kill a white cop or pistol-whip a tailor or whether the Panthers
themselves bore even some of the responsibility for Alex Rackley's
death—were beyond the point. The facts weren't even afterthoughts.

Ericka's face popped up all over Yale's campus on "Free the New Haven
Nine!" posters. Her raised-fist picture appeared in Panther newspapers.
Women's groups from New York traveled to Connecticut to demonstrate
on her behalf and on the behalf of the other female Panthers. The "New
Haven Women's Liberation Rock Band" entertained 150 women inside
Niantic's prison gymnasium; forbidden to get up and dance, the inmates
swayed in their folding chairs.

Ericka brought attention to the plight of women in ways that both
mainstream America and radical America had largely ignored, in this case
the plight of nonviolent women inmates. Even Panther leader Eldridge
Cleaver, a convicted rapist, joined the effort to cast Ericka as a symbol of
women's advancement in the revolution. In an open letter, written from
exile abroad, Cleaver cast Ericka's jailing "and suffering" as "a stinging re-
buke to all manifestations of male chauvinism within our ranks. That we
must purge our ranks and our hearts, and our minds, and our understanding
of any chauvinism, chauvinistic behavior, of disrespectful behavior toward
women. That we must recognize that a woman can be just as revolutionary
as a man, and that she has equal stature along with men, and that we cannot prejudice her in any manner, that we cannot relegate her to an inferior
position. That we have to recognize our women as our equals."

ERICKA HAD PRESSED the feminist fight from the moment she joined the
party. All the traits she demonstrated in prison—leadership, compassion

for the downtrodden, a fierce resolve sometimes masked by a flowery ex-
terior—were visible from childhood. Growing up in the segregated
southeast section of Washington, D.C., Ericka was active in the Girl
Scouts and in her church. Adults recognized her intelligence and her
fire. She was steered to college-track McKinley Senior High School in
northwest D.C. Ericka was suddenly face-to-face with white people all
day. Meanwhile, through her church, she volunteered to escort poorer
kids on shopping trips. She also volunteered at a community center summer program, where she noticed that the kids came from inadequate
schools and homes where parents were rarely around. The experience
convinced her to "do something for children." At fifteen she witnessed
an event that cemented that conviction: alone, defying her parents' orders, she went to the 1963 March on Washington at which Martin
Luther King Jr. gave his famous "I Have a Dream" speech. Inspired,
Ericka resolved to ditch the middle-class, nuclear-family dream. She
would join the crusade to better the world. After all, her parents, even if
they'd wanted her to stay away from the Mall that day, had always talked
about the need to "step forward for our people and to make a difference."

At first she thought she'd do that by becoming a special education
teacher. She dreamed of opening a school for children with birth defects.
That was her goal, anyway, when she enrolled in Cheyney State College
in Cheyney, Pennsylvania.

A year later, she transferred to Lincoln University and immersed herself in the student radical movement. Like so many women active in
protest politics from the mid-'60s through the early '70s, Ericka found
herself fighting two simultaneous battles. One involved challenging society at large. The other pitted women against the macho culture within
movement groups. She went to a meeting of the militant Black Student
Congress. A male organizer, an intellectual, a powerful speaker, barred
her entry. You wear your hair too straight, he told her. She appealed, but
the male majority stuck by the leader.

She and her new beau, John Huggins, found what they read about another group, the Black Panthers, a lot more logical, more relevant to the
fight at hand. The Panthers were taking on racist police brutality in
deed, not just rhetoric. They appealed to black pride while also working
alongside sympathetic whites. They challenged capitalism instead of

preaching "cultural nationalism." John and Ericka drove west to find the party and join the revolution.

In the L.A. Panther office, Ericka resumed the two-front battle. "Sister, can you type?" the men in charge asked when she signed up. "Can you cook? Can you clean?" The Panthers were like the rest of society in that respect: women played subservient roles to the male heroes. Plus, the Panthers attracted tough guys from the street, who expected women to submit to them; at some other chapters, gang rapes were reported.

Thanks to the intellectual pretensions of their militant rhetoric, the Panthers also attracted strong women. Ericka found other women in the L.A. chapter to join her in demanding respect. Indeed, Panther women were doing much of the work behind the scenes. They helped shape policy and make plans and did the day-to-day chores of organizing events. Kathleen Neal Cleaver emerged as a key intellectual force in the party, one of three central committee members.

The men's attitude irritated Ericka, especially when white female groupies followed the men back to headquarters after speaking engagements in West Hollywood and Beverly Hills, all made up, flicking their hair. Ericka and the other Panther women would be exhausted and disheveled from round-the-clock work, subsisting on the meager communal fund and, in some cases, welfare checks. They were also dodging bullets only to be treated like furniture by the men returning with their harems.

So Ericka and fellow Panther Elaine Brown wrote a tract on the subject. They called it "Position Paper on the Influx of the White Pig Bitches." They complained to party leaders like David Hilliard. They and some other feminist Panthers became known as "the clique." Some men referred to them as "smart bitches" who merited silencing. But they got some results, including party rules, in some cases enforced, protecting women from unwanted sexual advances. The Panthers believed in free sex—that is, consensual free sex. Officially, at least, "no" meant no. Ericka got people reading Friedrich Engels's *Origins of the Family, Private Property and the State*. Through group discussions on sexism in the party—sometimes bitterly unproductive, sometimes effective—she and others tied the oppression of post-slavery American blacks to the "ownership" of women and children in traditional families. If we're going to move history forward, Ericka argued to the men, you can't "own" us. We have to march together.

Ericka was in the communal Panther pad on Century Boulevard, taking care of her three-week-old daughter, when she learned that two unnamed black men had been shot at UCLA. Ericka—who had turned twenty-one just twelve days earlier—just knew her husband was dead. A report on the radio confirmed Ericka's premonition. When Elaine Brown arrived later with the news, Ericka made coffee. She began packing a bag so someone could take her daughter from the apartment. Some twenty minutes later, seventy-five or more police officers burst through the apartment door to drag Ericka and everyone else to the station. They confiscated all of the guns on the premises. They also grabbed the baby and ripped off her diaper for a body search. Everyone in the apartment—including Ericka—was charged with "conspiracy to commit murder." After being grilled for hours and locked up, Ericka was finally released, the charges dropped. As she prepared to leave for Connecticut, this young widow had fresh evidence for her view of law enforcement as enemy number one of the black community.

ERICKA DECIDED TO stick around New Haven after her husband's funeral. The Hugginses offered to let her and the baby move in with them and lead a quiet life. She lived with them for a while before taking her own apartment in the Hill neighborhood. Even though her in-laws didn't support the Panthers, Ericka certainly could use help with the baby.

At first Ericka was mired in grief, if not full-on depression. Her mother in D.C. noticed it. Her mother-in-law in New Haven saw how the outgoing, friendly, open girl she'd met years earlier had grown shy, withdrawn, quiet. Ericka and Elaine Brown kept in touch on the phone; their conversations inevitably turned to how much Ericka missed John.

As February 1969 progressed, Ericka heard from the Panthers' national headquarters. She learned that two Panthers, José Gonzalvez and Lonnie McLucas, had come east to start chapters in Connecticut. She agreed to visit the Bridgeport office. That got her out of the house. Once a week she taught "political education" classes there.

The group soon shifted to the more fertile ground of New Haven. Gonzalvez, Ericka, and Warren emerged as the three visible local chapter leaders. They each played different roles. Gonzalvez, the "state captain," was the menacing swaggerer. He threatened the life of a top FBI agent in New Haven, Ted Gunderson. In a speech in the Fair Haven neighborhood, Gonzalvez vowed to hang the heads of drug dealers from telephone poles. He wrote leaflets with incendiary language:

> We Black People, Brown People and Yellow People are an organization to organize our people and an Army. We fight this battle with political means. Then if this has failed we will carry on to the future with the only symbol of justice the pigs know: Pistols, rifles, shotguns, machine guns, and grenades. . . . We're going to walk all over this nation and say: "Put 'em up MOTHERFUCKER, this is a holdup, we're coming for what's OURS." . . . We can do this by going to the low down rotten politician and saying: "Look Bastard, we're the people; you're not out to help the people, you're not out to help anyone but yourself, you're not out for the community, we voted you in now we're voting you 'OUT,' if not we'll shoot you out."

The FBI couldn't have scared New Haven further away from the Panthers if they had written the flyer themselves. In fact, when agents did forge documents designed to do just that, in one case they lifted the flyer by Gonzalvez and changed only a few words. Warren and Ericka, who did most of the real day-to-day work, eventually grew suspicious of Gonzalvez.

Warren played the role of resolute but reasonable grown-up. He was, after all, a good decade or more older than the rest of the Panthers. When rhetoric like Gonzalvez's provoked protests from a public-school parents' group and a Republican mayoral candidate, the *New Haven Journal-Courier* quoted Warren responding to such "misinformation": "We are not terrorists, we do not hate white people. The thing we're trying to fight is oppression. . . . The Panther doesn't believe in violence, it believes in self-defense. . . . It is not a gang; we do not identify with riots or disturbances."

Meanwhile, Ericka was the keeper of the flame. She taught classes in ideology to the couple of dozen volunteers who sought party membership. She spoke around town about her vision of health clinics and free breakfast centers that avoided relying on government money. She was also the master of intimidating rhetoric when people dared to question the Panthers' militaristic approach to social change.

Ericka's intimidation talents were on display the last Sunday of March, 1969. Some seventy-five Panther supporters, mostly white, attended a talk by Ericka, Gonzalvez, and Warren at Bethesda Lutheran Church on Whitney Avenue, the main thoroughfare in the Yale/liberal northern stretch of New Haven. A group called the Coalition of Concerned Citizens called the meeting to allow the Panthers to set the record straight about their mission.

The Panthers had a script; they made clear who was there to talk, who was there to listen. Male Panthers stood guard, stone-faced, throughout the event at various entry points to the hall. One stood sentry behind Ericka, Warren, and Gonzalvez.

One attendee had the nerve to deviate from the script.

"Do you honestly feel it does any good to call the police pigs?" this gray-haired woman asked from the back left corner of the room. "Some policemen are members of your own race."

According to an account in the *Hartford Courant* account, Ericka "got a little angry" in response. "She is young and tall and she did not like the woman in the back of the room very much."

But Ericka did respond.

"I lived in Los Angeles. Have you ever seen the L.A. pigs when they oink? They walk around in their uniforms and boots and helmets and never talk. They just walk around. If the chief says, kill, they just kill. If the chief says use a shotgun, they use a shotgun. They don't think twice. They have no individual minds. They're robotic."

So much for that question. The woman with the gray hair did pipe up again later in the evening. She suggested the Panthers were "asking for" a "socialism" that seemed "very close to Communism." That led to groans in the audience, and to another woman in the audience asking the woman with gray hair if she were a teacher. The answer was no. "Thank God," the questioner responded. Another audience member accused the woman of being a "plant" to make the Panthers look bad. She denied the accusation. Then she stopped talking.

In the end, "everybody clapped" for the speakers, who "applauded the audience" in return.

In later years Ericka would revisit the gray-haired woman's initial question. She would wonder whether the use of violent rhetoric attracted people who destabilized the party. In 1969, the wounds still raw from her husband's murder, more violence and signs of betrayal surrounding her every day, Ericka was preoccupied with survival. She wasn't ready to let down her guard and entertain such questions.

She and Warren did keep an eye on José Gonzalvez. He acted more erratically than ever, and they wondered if he were a plant. He returned from trips out of town making wild boasts. The national office reprimanded him for trying to organize a chapter in North Carolina without permission. Gonzalvez left the Oakland apartment of a Panther leader, who discovered a sweater, a watch, and $20 were missing.

Ericka called national headquarters. She took up the matter at a "central staff" meeting at the New Haven headquarters. Following the meeting she sent a letter to national headquarters. "This letter is to inform you," it read, "that the state captain of Connecticut, José Gonzalvez, Jr., has been stripped of his rank as captain because he has consistently broken numerous party rules. He has misrepresented the party to the people and to the party members. We have through investigation found out that he has made exaggerations of our efforts in New Haven to Bobby Seale, Masai and some of the Chicago Panthers and to us. He has rejected the party's discipline while really not serving the people. He has failed to provide adequate leadership."

Plus, the letter noted, he "does not study."

Gonzalvez disappeared. No one ever saw him again.

Ericka was the one Panther who remained above suspicion when the national team of Panther leaders arrived on the East Coast to weed out informers. Her loyalty to the party was indisputable. In jail, she remained a loyal Panther. Her work—and her turn as leading lady—had just begun.

CHAPTER 8

Welcome to New Haven

T HE RACKLEY MURDER and bust had destroyed the New Haven Black Panther Party chapter. So national dispatched a crew from Boston to New Haven to pick up the pieces. The party assigned Boston's Doug Miranda, a twenty-one-year-old short, mustachioed martinet who earned his Panther stripes at San Francisco State University, to take charge. Miranda's new assignment displeased Nick Pastore of the New Haven police—for two reasons.

Reason one: Nick had maneuvered his own informants into taking charge of the Panther chapter after the Rackley bust. He felt he now ran the party. He liked it that way. The cops and the FBI were convinced they had the Panthers on the run for good, if they just kept up the heat. William Sullivan, J. Edgar Hoover's assistant director, placed a call to Ted Gunderson, coordinator of the bureau's counterintelligence programs in Connecticut. "I attribute the downfall of the Black Panther Party to you, your squad, and the New Haven police department," Sullivan congratulated Gunderson.

Reason two for Nick's displeasure: Miranda had included his name on a list of FBI and local police "pigs" needing to be "dealt with."

Knowing in advance of the plan to send Panthers from Boston, Nick had the bus bringing them to New Haven surveilled. As soon as Miranda settled into an apartment near the corner of Orchard and Henry Streets at the northern edge of the Dixwell neighborhood, Nick paid the new leader a visit. He kicked in Miranda's door.

"Here I am," Nick declared to the surprised Panther. "You're looking for me?"

Nick told Miranda he better not hear any more threats to the lives of law enforcement agents, or there would be repercussions.

Then Nick left Miranda with a simple message: "We mean business."

So did Miranda. Buoyed by the attention drawn to the upcoming trial of Ericka Huggins and Bobby Seale, the chapter got busier than ever. A "hard core," as the local FBI office put it, of thirty active members coordinated the work. They set up office again in the Hill district, on Sylvan Avenue. They got into occasional scuffles with the local cops, at one point igniting a mini-riot. They also conducted a purge of local Panthers. Among the expelled was Ted Spurlock, Warren's brother-in-law and Germano's "Uncle Bubby." Spurlock's manifold alleged offenses included "individualism," "subjectivism," "disregard for organizational discipline," "spreading erroneous information [lying to people]," "liberalism," "consciously cashing false checks in the Party's name," and "he did not adhere to the policy and ideology laid down by the Central Committee and selfish departmentalism."

Ideology classes resumed Wednesday nights on Columbus Avenue. The Panthers got the free breakfast program up and running for real at the Newhallville Teen Lounge on Shelton Avenue. They named it after John Huggins and fed seventy to eighty kids each morning. They opened an outpost of the program at the Legion Center in the Hill. They launched a free clothing program. This is the kind of work Warren and Ericka tried to get started but never saw take form. And they summoned supporters for rallies outside the courthouse on days of pretrial proceedings in the Rackley murder case.

At the center of this round-the-clock bustle was Doug Miranda. Like José Gonzalvez and George Sams before him, Miranda talked tough, barked orders, relied on intimidation to keep New Haven conscripts in line. But unlike his predecessors, Miranda was a keen strategist, an intellectual. There was method to his menace.

One day in Boston, for instance, Miranda decided to deal with the chapter's habitual latecomers. He ordered them to stand with arms in the air.

"Repeat after me," he demanded. "'Tardiness is a hardy corrosive that would destroy the party. I would rather destroy my arms than destroy the party!'"

They repeated the chant, arms raised. They came to Panther meetings on time from then on.

In New Haven, Miranda kept the chapter afloat through a talent for dealing with widely divergent constituencies, from students to Panther "cadres" to trust-fund babies—the "Muffys" of the world. Depending on the audience, he could move from academic discourse—as in a Yale debate over Marxism with an undergraduate member of Students for a Democratic Society—to cajoling, from chutzpah to sudden sangfroid.

The local FBI office sent J. Edgar Hoover an account of Miranda at work in a memo dated February 19, 1970, about a wiretapped phone conversation with a backer named Kitty, concerning a bunch of "LNUs" ("last names unknown"):

MIRANDA asked when the money from MUFFY (ph) (identity unknown) was going to arrive. KITTY said she didn't know, but she would let him know when it arrived. They talked about RITA (RITA ZEICHNER). DOUG said he was trying to get some money from her. It was mentioned that MARSHA (LNU), DIANE (LNU), and PAM (LNU) might be joining the party soon. . . .

DOUG told KITTY she would have to meet PONCHO (LNU) who he described as a crazy white nigger. . . .

With regard to money, KITTY said she would have five for DOUG by this Friday (2/20/70). She followed by saying that would be all for quite a while until she got things straightened out with her brother. She mentioned that PHYLLIS BLAN (ph) was trying to raise money for New Haven. MIRANDA said he needed more than five, that he needed twenty to implement all his proposed programs. DOUG told KITTY that she would have to go back to Milwaukee and get things straightened out with her brother.

During the conversation, KITTY's parents' last name was mentioned, HARDING (ph). KITTY said she had no source of wealth from home other than her stocks. MIRANDA asked her how much money MUFFY would probably send. KITTY said she had no idea but that it might not be more than a two zero figure. She said she expected it tomorrow. MIRANDA said that they could make some money off

MUFFY if they tried. KITTY said . . . that MUFFY mostly got money by begging for it from her parents.

The memo was forwarded to the Milwaukee FBI office.

PERHAPS THE MOST energy went into producing the chapter's own newspaper. That job fell to Charles "Cappy" Pinderhughes, a journalist who'd dropped out of Beloit College to return home to Boston and join the revolution that he, like other idealistic, educated Panther recruits, saw just over the horizon. Pinderhughes had put out the Boston edition of the Panther paper, so he was sent to New Haven to do the job there. Working day and night, he wrote and edited stories, laid out pages, drove to the printer, put papers on the street. Sometimes a Panther would be assigned to ride in a car with Pinderhughes just to keep him awake.

Pinderhughes was prolific, his *People's News Service* paper a blend of Panther propaganda, verbal and cartoon attacks on "pigs," and critiques of power in New Haven. The paper reported on neighborhood efforts to hold the antipoverty agency CPI to its rhetoric on decentralizing power. Stories ignored by the mainstream media—the complaints of public-housing tenants beset by brutal cops or of activists frustrated by accommodationist black leaders—found their way into the Panther paper.

In the January 25, 1970, issue, activist Maurice Sykes wrote an article about "holier than thou" black clergy ducking problems of injustice to maintain their relationships with City Hall. Addressing himself to the clergy, Sykes wrote, "Did it ever occur to you that when the Mayor is gone you still have to face the black community? And that the Mayor will no longer get jobs for your relatives, and keep you in a political position? Well, if you're that type of clergyman, then wake up! It will be quite embarrassing if your church was picketed by people who know that you are a part of the Mayor's game." (Years later Sykes would become a minister and take a city government job.)

The same issue featured an article entitled "King Yale: Enemy of the People." It criticized Yale's role in helping to design urban renewal programs that the university's planners allegedly "conceived as a means of dividing the black community, while giving to it merely token benefits. . . . Not only were black people moved from their houses by Yale's urban renewal program, but were also forced to compete against Yale's students for renting houses in our community. . . . Yale University has not only deprived black communities of its housing and jobs, but it has also used black people as experimental patients for their untrained doctors."

The paper weighed in on local controversies with truly alternative spin. It blamed the police force when a black officer was shot in the Hill. In an article entitled "Pig Offed in Self-Defense," Pinderhughes called the cop an "undercover pig" who "instigated crime" by "willfully involv[ing] Black people in the Hill section in numbers games, and the receiving and selling of stolen goods, and [buying and selling] dope, on the assumption that a dope addict can't be a revolutionary." So, the article argued, it was the "Racist Pig Cops of New Haven" who had blood on their hands when a man shot back during a confrontation with the officer.

Like any good community newspaper, the People's News Service offered practical advice for readers—full-page lists about how to deal with police, including a "pocket lawyer" outlining detainees' rights. And like any good community newspaper, the paper made room for school kids' writing. Nine-year-old Michael Gallyot, whose mom worked for the party, contributed an article entitled "Revolution in Our Lifetime." Gallyot resented the amount of time his single mom devoted to the party. But he found it exciting to hang out with older guys. He shared the excitement about participating in a revolution. He also saw cops beat people up in his neighborhood and get away with it. All of that proved a combustible brew for an impressionable preteen, enabling him to write words like these:

> All of you people out there with houses and color T.V., if you voted for that muddle-headed pig Nixon, I think I know why. . . . He probably told you that he would do all this good stuff for the people. Now that he has been elected by you, you should be able to tell that he was a liar, just by looking at his warlock face and all you people lying to your children about that motherf—er pig Santa Claus; why don't you tell your children the truth—tell them that Santa Claus is a big fat capitalist pig. I'm telling you this so that on next Christmas Eve when he comes down your chimney—blow his mother–ing head off.

Tell that bald-headed punk pig policeman he better . . . stay out of our community or we'll snatch his head off in the name of revolution and liberation. You should realize by now that this fascist government is robbing you and using the money to send people to the moon and kill people in Viet Nam. But you must remember!! If there is going to be revolution and liberation, we're going to have to fight for it.

ALL POWER TO THE PEOPLE

Michael Gallyot

Age nine

New Haven, Conn.

Most of all, each issue kept the wider circle of Panther sympathizers in touch with the latest heroines and martyrs behind bars, pumping a steady flow of adrenaline and outrage. When permitted by prison authorities, imprisoned Panthers occasionally spoke to the paper or got letters printed in the paper about mistreatment behind bars. On February 16, 1970, Ericka wrote the following account of events in jail; her story appeared in the Panther paper:

This whole week has been hell! After the Chicago 7 and the sentencing of Kuntsler and Weinglass, we were about ready for anything. Well, this morning we found out Frances was in the dungeon for not going in her room on some b.s. Anyway we went down stairs for recreation and we hollered to her and Rose told her not to worry and stuff. A 'guard' (I'm trying not to call him a pig) told Rose if she did that again she'd be locked in her room and she said she didn't care, she'd shout the truth, because what could they do that they haven't done already. So the guard said O.K. Come on!

So we turned around and marched back upstairs knowing that the guard was going through all these changes to inflate his ego. We got upstairs, right? The guard said, 'All right Rose you going in you [*sic*] room or do I have to get help.' Rose said yea, I'm not going in my room, she hadn't done anything but talk to her comrade. So the guard got help—the biggest fattest, most egotistical guard on the farm. Moriarity. He said Rose, I want you to go in your room, Now!!! She said no—all of us talked for a while and he said O.K. He went and called reinforcements—he said if we were going to fight it may as well be even (?) Then, he closed Ida's door (with her in there). We all waited. Another security officer came (oh, by the way, the reason Rose was to be locked was due to insubordination to an officer!) by this time. Moriarity had started moving chairs out of the way in the kitchen area and putting his hooves on Rose. He asked her again if she would go in her room, all the while intimidating her. Of course she couldn't answer. I told him to let her answer the question and like a pig he said 'you got 30 seconds.' She said well get to counting because I'm not going anywhere until you get out of my way. . . .

Two other guards came smiling, ready for a battle. They all lifted Rose up, twisted her arms, one had her by the neck, one had her arms one had her feet. Meanwhile I was screaming let her go and holding onto her head so they couldn't hit her there. One of them twisted my arm pulled away and grabbed Rose again. Moriarity hollered 'get that one' and somebody (don't worry I know his name) twisted my arms behind my back. I kicked him and he threw me down. I hit my head. I be cool though, cause my foot got a couple of em!! Then I heard scuffling in Peggy's room. They had her between her locker and the door trying to restrain her. They had dragged her down the hall to her room, one of them punched her in the breasts and then ran out and locked the door. Mine was already locked by then. (Ida's was reopened).

Then one began choking Peggy and Rose. Peggy was o.k. but I got no answer from Rose, she was knocked out. They had slammed her on the bed and she grabbed one of them. As he turned around to leave she hit him. He knocked her onto the floor, her arm twisted in a chair with the chair on top of her. Her room must look like Chicago after the 1968 convention. She was out for 5 minutes. We were ready to burst then. I called her and called her. Finally after the matron went to get the nurse, she woke up, or regained consciousness. As the nurse came to the door, the guards (2 of them) followed. Rose told them to get away. He locked (slammed the door) them both up together and the nurse left and almost cussed the guard out. The nurse found out that she had a pulled muscle in her arm and the other arm is scraped. Her neck is extremely sore, her head is aching, her back hurts and her arm is in a sling. ALL SELF-DEFENSE. (Hey they probably enjoyed it). . . .

Amerikkka is disruptive, fascism is disruptive, it disrupts your life! . . .

Down with imperialism abroad and fascism at home

Free all political prisoners

Love and Power

Ericka

THE PAPER'S DRAMATIC accounts made a particularly strong impression on one long-distance subscriber in Washington, D.C.: J. Edgar Hoover.

In a March 8 memo to New Haven, the FBI chief ordered the local office to "furnish six copies of this bulletin on a regular basis. . . . You should insure that it is being analyzed on a continuing basis for lead material and for other data of possible interest." If the Panthers had a copy of the memo, they could have excerpted blurbs for a promotional campaign. "Paper is chock full of reports—from jail, from New Haven black neighborhoods, about police confrontations, conditions at Elm Haven, diatribes against the system, news on national Panther cases," Hoover wrote. He added that the paper retained "real local flavor, and hateful 'pig' rhetoric."

Hoover's men kept on top of the Panther press all over the country. The FBI considered the party's national newspaper "one of the [party's] most effective propaganda operations." Its circulation peaked in 1969 at an estimated 139,000. A 1970 memo directed FBI field offices in Chicago, Newark, Miami, Los Angeles, San Diego, San Francisco, New York, and New Haven to devise plans to disrupt the paper's operations. Subsequent plans ranged from smearing a powdered form of a chemical agent called "Skatol" on the papers to convincing United Airlines to charge higher rates to transport bundles of them.

Hoover's men indeed remained loyal readers. They kept on top of speeches the local Panthers were giving, too, about the upcoming trial of Bobby Seale and Ericka Huggins. With each report, the bureau grew increasingly convinced of a possible explosion on the streets of New Haven. In all capital letters, one FBI memo began: "Extreme caution must be exercised during all encounters with members and associates of the Black Panther Party as they are attempting to prearrange the location of interviews in order to kill FBI agents. Due to their proven record of attempts to kill police officers, all Black Panther Party members and associates are considered armed and completely dangerous."

"The BPP in New Haven and Hartford is continuing to obtain weapons for the 'revolution that is coming,'" read another memo. "Specifically, they have ordered all members to obtain personal weapons and to maintain weapons at all times in their homes." When Cappy Pinderhughes exhorted an audience at the University of Hartford's Gengrass Campus Center, "Kill ten pigs and die yourselves," the quotation shot around the FBI wires.

Panther homes were raided; other raids, or potential raids, were exposed in advance in "Pigs Set to Vamp" flyers the party distributed in public. Fears on both sides fed each other. Meanwhile, the temperature was fast rising. The leading man to Ericka Huggins's leading woman was about to enter, stage left: Bobby Seale was coming to town.

CHAPTER 9

Plane Ride from California

Nick Pastore was in California, on the phone to New Haven. "Arnie," Nick told Markle, the prosecutor in the Rackley case, "I'm not going back on that plane."

Nick was still recovering from the flight to California. He and some of Markle's people had flown west in a puddle jumper. The weather was stormy, the ride bumpy. Several times they had to stop.

Now they had a celebrity Black Panther to transport to New Haven: the national chairman. Just ten months earlier, last May, Bobby Seale left New Haven a hero. He had the Yale students who crammed Battell Chapel for his speech hooting and hollering at the notion of killing cops and informers. They whooped and applauded as Seale thundered: "Today's pig is tomorrow's bacon!" At that climactic moment, Alex Rackley lay bound and imprisoned nine-tenths of a mile away at Panther headquarters.

Seale was a prisoner contesting two cases in two cities. He faced murder, kidnapping, and conspiracy charges in the Rackley case in New Haven. Under Connecticut law, those charges could land him in the electric chair. He was also appealing a four-year contempt-of-court sentence handed down during a trial on incitement-to-riot charges in Chicago for his role, along with Jerry Rubin's and that of Abbie Hoffman's Yippies, in disrupting the 1968 Democratic National Convention. A mistrial was declared in that case. But Seale drew the contempt sentence after a test of wills with the iron-fisted judge, Julius Hoffman. After surgery prevented Seale's attorney, Charles Garry, from representing him, Hoffman denied Seale's request to represent himself. Seale shouted at the judge, expletives pouring over the courtroom in torrents, and claimed his constitutional right to choose his lawyer. Hoffman ordered Seale silenced and bound. Chains fastened him to his courtroom chair; adhesive tape gagged his mouth. It made quite a picture for radicals and Nixon's silent majoritarians alike.

Without doubt, Seale had developed a menacing reputation, what with his incendiary speeches, his role as national chairman of the Black Panthers, as right-hand man of Huey Newton from the early gun-drawn confrontations with the Oakland cops. And, perhaps understandably, Seale didn't want to come to Connecticut. Unfortunately for him, the Panthers' nemesis, California governor Ronald Reagan, ordered his extradition.

Meanwhile, Nick was worried more about another ride on that plane than about Bobby Seale. He didn't bother bringing a gun; he didn't expect Seale to cause trouble. In a routine prearranged with the local cops, with no advance word to the press, Nick and crew went to the lockup holding Seale. They formally arrested him. Seale was congenial. He caused no problems as Nick explained the itinerary for the trip back.

Markle came through with a better plane, a Lear jet formerly owned by golfer Arnold Palmer. Nick sat next to Seale. Between them they dispatched a fifth of Cutty Sark and a whole lot of conversation. Both men liked to talk. Seale spoke expansively about why the Panthers confronted the cops, how their goal was self-defense, not attacking people. His words impressed Nick. The guy seemed sincere, thoughtful. But Nick couldn't forget Alex Rackley. "By the best I can determine, Bobby," Nick said, "this guy was innocent." Seale didn't argue. "I don't know anything about it," he said. He claimed to have nothing at all to do with Alex Rackley.

To himself, Seale thought: Why's this guy playing with me? Does he think I'm stupid? The Black Panther Party was founded to tell people their rights, to tell black people what to do and what *not* to do around cops. Seale taught black people not to answer when a cop asks you about a case for which you're under arrest.

Seale did have something to say about the Rackley case. He said it before the flight, in a pre-extradition interview to be published in the Panthers' New Haven paper the week after his arrival. In the article, head-lined "Bobby Seale Raps on the New Haven Panther Trial," Seale iden-tified Rackley as "a brother in good standing."

Unlike Nick, of course, Seale saw the police as the guilty party. He identified George Sams as a police agent who set up Rackley, oversaw his torture and murder. "The federal government and the establishment press has used all this to try to animalize the Black Panther Party, to try to smash the Black Panther Party and blame it on Party members," Seale said. ". . . It's another murderous operation that went down."

As for the upcoming trial, Seale said, "we have a lot of things we have to bring out."

One of many things that would not be brought out until many years af-ter the conclusion of the trial was a memo to J. Edgar Hoover the day of Nick's flight home with Seale. On March 13, the San Francisco FBI office offered details on future Panther plans: "Reliable source this date reported not aware of any planned violence contemplated by BPP leadership. Source states that BPP intends to 'educate the people' concerning New Haven court charges against Bobby Seale. This 'education' will be ac-complished by a massive propaganda campaign through BPP newspaper, other printed matters and public appearances of leadership. . . . Source states BPP leadership decided to refrain from violent confrontations inas-much as it would cause them further legal difficulties and other organiza-tions now appear to be doing a satisfactory job in the field of violence."

To Nick, the goals of Bobby Seale and the Panthers sounded good enough. Even without knowing that Panther leadership was about to start taking it easy, as others were "doing a satisfactory job in the field of violence," Nick would have been likely to view Bobby Seale with more sympathy if the plane ride from California had occurred a few years ear-lier. The line between good guys and bad guys, cops and criminals, law enforcement and law breaking, between people who stood to make his-tory and people who stood to make trouble, had bent and curved and moved back and forth before Nick's eyes his entire life.

Nick grew up a few short blocks from the Kimbros in the polyglot Oak Street section of the Hill neighborhood. Nick's parents were factory workers. Mom put a net over Nick's bed so rats wouldn't bite him in his sleep; Nick put paper in his shoes to block the holes. Like other Italian immigrants, Nick's grandfather made his own wine, four barrels at a time, in the basement. Once a year, when he'd come upstairs with the barrels, it was cause for celebration, singing, and feasting. He'd crack open the best barrel for the family to drink. He'd sell off the others for $2 a gallon. The worst batch went to wine vinegar—or to the vice cops who snooped on Italian immigrants' homes. Technically, they were looking to raid home-brewers. In reality they came to shake the families down. They loved the elder Pastore's wine, even the fourth-best barrel.

As Nick got old enough to leave the house on his own, he got to know all the characters on the street. He loved people; he loved bustle. The neighborhood's thoroughfares, like Legion Avenue, teemed day and night with hustlers, bakers, jewelers, laborers, entertainers—black, Jewish, Italian, Irish. They didn't meet inside each other's homes; many black families were confined to the shabbiest row of fire traps in the neighborhood. Everyone came together on the sidewalks. They fought, bartered, and joked. Nick played basketball and softball with Warren Kimbro's brother Martin in the Scranton Street schoolyard and in the park at Davenport Avenue and Asylum Street. He earned coins as a *shabbes goy*, turning on lights for religious Jewish neighbors on the Sabbath.

At age ten Nick set up a shoeshine stand. He did more than buff footwear. He helped Nutter Koletsky, New Haven's very own Meyer Lansky, look out for the vice cops. When word came of an imminent raid, Pastore hid Koletsky's bookie slips in the shoeshine box. In high school, Nick got a job in the store that served as a front for Nutter Koletsky's profitable black-market operations.

In January 1957, months short of graduation, Nick dropped out of high school to enlist in the armed forces. Later that year, orders from President Dwight D. Eisenhower sent Pastore's unit to Little Rock, Arkansas, to confront an opposing army: Governor Orval Faubus's National Guard. Faubus took a stand against the school desegregation ordered by the Supreme Court in *Brown v. Board of Education*; he defied an order to allow black children into an all-white high school. With some half-dozen fellow soldiers, Nick was assigned to escort one of the black girls to school amid death threats from crowds of angry whites. Each morning Nick went to the girl's home. The girl was scared to go to school. "This is important," her mother told her. Nick rode on the back of the truck taking the girl to school. "Go home, you nigger-lovers!" white women yelled at the soldiers.

The harsh realities of Little Rock all seemed memories from another world when Nick returned to New Haven upon finishing his two-year stint. In 1962 he joined his friend Mike Sullivan in taking the test to become a police officer. He got hired and quickly earned a reputation for knowing the street. Since Nick had always felt deprived by the limited education he had received growing up in the Hill, he devoured courses on policing. He would also pursue a college degree on the side. His street contacts, his reservoir of information on safe-crackers and numbers runners, helped the department arrest crooks like Eddie Devlin, Warren Kimbro's pal from St. John's who landed on the FBI's Ten Most Wanted List. By 1967, a year shy of his thirtieth birthday, Nick made detective.

Shadows of his Little Rock encounter came back to him in August that year, when riots broke out in New Haven. Nick found himself marching down the street en masse with fellow police officers like army troops. They put out fires, confronted groups of black citizens, searched for snipers. They herded people like cattle. People punched Nick. Nick punched back. He looked in the rioters' eyes. He saw that fervor he'd noticed in the eyes of the demonstrators in Little Rock. Now it burned in black—not white—faces.

Nick was in his hometown. He was in the neighborhood he grew up in. Only now people were burning it. And he saw strangers: They didn't know him even if they knew who he was. He didn't know them even when he knew who they were. New Haven in August 1967 felt more like Little Rock than his hometown. Nick felt that by turning to violence, agitators were using the rhetoric of a just cause as an excuse for criminal behavior. He came to feel that way even about law-abiding civilians who had begun using civil rights rhetoric to justify law breaking or to advance their careers. In Nick's eyes, they used militant rhetoric to shake down the government for money.

The next year Nick took charge of the police intelligence division. He had no qualms about monitoring militants, the way he did the bookies and protection rackets that remained the division's top priority. In his view, the militants endangered his city. So Nick was ready when the Black Panthers came to town in January 1969 for John Huggins's funeral. He had an extensive network of informants in place—people like Kelly Moye, whom Nick originally met on March 3, 1964, while on traffic duty. He stopped Moye for failure to obey an overhead signal. They struck up a conversation. He learned that Moye was a liquor delivery man. Could you get me discount liquor? Nick asked. Sure, Moye said. Soon Moye was making regular deliveries to the home of his new friend, Officer Pastore. As time went on, Nick encouraged Moye to apply to the police department. Moye did. His application languished for years. In the meantime, Nick enlisted him to spy for pocket change. He started Moye on neighborhood drug dealers. Now, with the Panthers coming to town, he had a new assignment for him.

If the Panthers planned to shoot a cop or cause trouble or raise money, Nick determined that he would know who, how, and when. If the Panthers were recruiting new members, he would be glad to supply them with convincing supporters who earned side money as police informants.

Nick knew the owner of the storefront next door to St. Luke's Church the day of John Huggins's funeral. He rented the second-floor apartment in order to secure a prime balcony spot for the Panther procession. Watching through a telephoto lens, Nick recognized many faces among the mixed multitude streaming into St. Luke's Church. To Nick, who made his reputation working organized crime, the St. Luke's gathering felt like a mafia funeral: You watched who showed up. You noticed who gathered alongside whom. You decided which ones merited further monitoring.

THE FBI WAS ready for the Panthers, too. Nick invited agents from the Connecticut office to the second-floor balcony. Like other police "red squads" across the country, Nick's intelligence division worked closely with the FBI as part of COINTELPRO ("counterintelligence program"). The program was FBI Director J. Edgar Hoover's pet project aimed at destroying dissident groups in the United States. Hoover directed agents nationwide to "expose, disrupt, misdirect, discredit, or otherwise neutralize" black militant groups. Hoover launched COINTELPRO in 1956 out of frustration over Supreme Court rulings that limited intelligence gathering on citizens who disagreed with the government. The program lasted fifteen years.

"In essence, the Bureau took the law into its own hands, conducting a sophisticated vigilante operation against domestic enemies," an investigation by a U.S. Senate Select Committee on Intelligence would later state. The committee concluded that COINTELPRO "aimed squarely at preventing the exercise of First Amendment rights of speech and association, on the theory that preventing the growth of dangerous groups and the propagation of dangerous ideas would protect the national security and deter violence. Many of the techniques used would be intolerable in a democratic society even if all the targets had been involved in violent activity, but COINTELPRO went far beyond that. The unexpressed major premise of the programs was that a law enforcement agency has the duty to do whatever is necessary to combat perceived threats to the existing social and political order."

Even before COINTELPRO, Hoover considered integrationists and black civil rights leaders as threats to the social order. His agents' duties under COINTELPRO included illegally breaking into the homes of members of dissident groups to seek evidence of law breaking or to compile names and addresses of other dissidents (one agent would later write that five hundred such "black bag jobs" occurred against targets in Chicago alone in the 1950s); planting informants in organizations to obtain information and spread false accusations; forging letters and making anonymous phone calls to stoke rivalry within groups and between groups; writing flyers and letters in the name of dissident groups to scare away members of the public; and preventing dissidents from obtaining jobs or public speaking engagements. COINTELPRO's first target was the Communist Party USA. The campaign's targets expanded to include the Socialist Workers Party, white hate groups, the white New Left, and "black nationalist-hate groups."

The latter category of groups became an official target in August 1967, following riots in cities across the country. Hoover included a wide range of organizations under the black "hate" umbrella, from the nonviolent Southern Christian Leadership Conference to the Deacons of Defense and the Nation of Islam. Leaders from Martin Luther King Jr. to H. Rap Brown were targeted. Hoover expanded the black "hate group" section of COINTELPRO from twenty-three to forty-one field offices on March 4, 1968. The reasons included preventing a "coalition of militant black nationalist groups" that could lead to a "Mau Mau" in the United States and thwarting the ascension of a black "messiah" like King, Carmichael, or Elijah Muhammad, who had the potential to "unify and electrify" black protest groups.

The Panthers didn't become an official COINTELPRO target until the fall of 1968, when Hoover dubbed them "the greatest threat to the internal security of the country." By the following January, when the FBI played at least an indirect role in John Huggins's murder, the party was already becoming an obsession for Hoover and the primary focus of COINTELPRO's campaign against black dissident groups. Of 295 officially authorized COINTELPRO actions against "black nationalist" groups, 233 were taken against the Panthers. The pattern of using informers and anonymous messages to provoke discord, which led to murder in L.A., would repeat itself in cities like San Diego, Chicago—where the FBI sought to drive a wedge between the Blackstone Rangers youth gang and the local Panthers—and, ultimately, New Haven.

Hoover personally directed the New Haven office to focus on the Panthers after Panther José Gonzalvez publicly called for the elimination of COINTELPRO chief Ted Gunderson. Hoover ordered the office to launch an "intensive probe" of the local party aimed at "establishing information indicating a possible violation of the assault on a federal officer statute." The "plot against the life of ASAC [Assistant Special Agent in Charge] THEODORE GUNDERSON" showed up in memos sent to FBI offices across the country. FBI offices regularly appended the background briefing to memos about the Panthers. It emphasized a 1968 quote from the national Panther newspaper: "Black men . . . Arm Yourselves. . . . Use the gun. . . . Kill the pigs everywhere."

Gunderson responded by dispatching agents to keep the Panthers under surveillance, to stop them on pretenses of committing crimes, and to haul them in for interrogations. That didn't satisfy J. Edgar Hoover. "To date," an impatient Hoover wrote, "you have submitted no concrete recommendations under this program concerning the Black Panther Party, despite the fact that this extremely dangerous organization is active in four cities in your Division." That was an exaggeration. Hoover referenced a January 30 letter that instructed "all BPP offices to submit biweekly letters to the Bureau containing proposed counterintelligence maneuvers aimed against the BPP and accomplishments obtained during the previous two-week period." "By 4/14/69, and every two weeks thereafter," Hoover demanded, "submit to the Bureau your proposals to disrupt the BPP and fully comply with the instructions."

Despite Hoover's fears, the Panthers organizationally were never a match for the FBI. They couldn't control the entry of risky converts.

Hundreds of active members were street criminals. In seeking to unite black intellectuals with the angry proletariat, the party welcomed hustlers with lengthy criminal resumes. While some organizers exhibited great intelligence and dedication, most were barely old enough to vote; virtually none had experience managing a complex organization, much less one that proposed to take on the law enforcement community at large.

Resources for training leaders, staffing command groups, coordinating local chapters to meet national goals, creating and distributing media releases, controlling misconduct by members and officers—none of these essential ingredients of organization were at any time available to the Black Panther Party. Real surveillance of rival organizations, or of law enforcement, was beyond reach. The Panthers built popularity among urban blacks and white intellectuals bitter about the system's brutality and corruption. But unlike the anticolonial revolutionary movements on which they patterned themselves, and despite their analysis of America's "revolutionary" conditions, the Panthers had no nationwide large constituency of oppressed people ready to take to the streets to dismantle the government in favor of militant black followers of Chairman Mao.

The U.S. employed well over 400,000 full-time law enforcement officers in 1969, backed up by more than 100,000 jailers and prison officers (numbers that would rise sharply in coming years). As part of that army, Nick Pastore may have understood people on the other side like Bobby Seale, but he also knew he was in a war. He had no doubt which side he was on.

CHAPTER 10

Super Chimp

A CHOICE ROOM awaited Bobby Seale in Connecticut. Upon his arrival, he eclipsed Warren as the leading man in the Connecticut Panther drama. So he received the celebrity suite, or at least the state corrections system equivalent—the Montville prison, with its large commode-equipped cells, glazed-tile back walls, and outdoor views.

On the theory that two leading Panthers shouldn't be kept at the same institution, authorities moved Warren to a jail in rural Brooklyn, Connecticut, a half hour further from New Haven in the eastern part of the state. Built in 1896, the red-brick jail, across from a strawberry field, looked like an old schoolhouse.

George Sams was also at the Brooklyn jail. Warren was assigned to a different cell block.

Warren's cell contained a concrete commode. Warren had the only single cell, locked unto itself. The other cells were arranged in groups of six; they opened out to a common area with a shared toilet.

The first day in Brooklyn, Warren was called to the warden's office. "Oh shit," he thought. The salad days he knew in Montville were over.

Warden Richard Hills offered Warren a handshake hello. Warren noticed that Hills had beefy farmer's palms. Hills looked like a big old swamp Yankee.

"Sit down, Kimbro," he said. "Somebody wants to talk to you."

Hills dialed the phone. "Commissioner MacDougall, please," he said.

Warren relaxed. His friendly relationship with the man at the top of the state corrections hierarchy could only help his prospects here.

Hills handed Warren the phone.

"Warren," came the voice on the other end of the line, "I hated to move you. But see what kind of programs you can start here."

"Sure, *Ellis*," Warren said. He enunciated to ensure that Warden Hills noticed Warren was on a first-name basis with his boss.

After the call, Hills asked Warren about the Guides for Better Living program. Should it come to Brooklyn? Hills expressed his dissatisfaction with the current state of the *Tier Tribune*, the prison paper. An inmate who served as the jailhouse barber edited it.

Warren sensed an opportunity as well as a danger. The guards arranged a meeting with the barber/editor. How would the editor take the suggestion that this new guy was going to waltz onto his turf and make the newspaper better?

The two inmates met in the prison library. The barber/editor offered Warren a coil stinger to heat his coffee. Warren demurred. He feared a set-up. The two checked each other out like boxers entering a ring. Warren discussed his ideas for the paper. They met again. Eventually the guards convinced the barber to turn the paper's reins over to Warren. It turned out not to be a problem. As jailhouse barber, the man had an identity, a position of respect, to fall back on.

The newspaper office moved from the library to a room out front, right by the warden's office, a perch from which Warren could view goings-on at the jail. Warren even convinced the warden to have Warren's khakis pressed. If I'm going to sit where visitors will see me, Warren reasoned, shouldn't I look sharp?

Every Friday in the mess hall, guards as well as inmates eagerly awaited the arrival of the latest four-page *Tier Tribune*. The paper started winning statewide awards for prison journalism. Warren added a front-page motto accompanied by a drawing of an hourglass: "Don't count time—make time count." Under the pseudonym "Mark Fox"— the "M" and "F" enlarged to suggest a popular Panther epithet—Warren produced a gossip column teasing inmates and guards alike, even the warden. "Mark Fox" would hear that "Mr. Regis," one of the guards, was bragging again about catching a big fish on his time off. Maybe the inmates could expect fish chowder, "Mark Fox" wrote—but don't count on it.

Pecking out the pages on an Olivetti typewriter, Warren made the columns of type right-justified to give them a more professional look. He also incorporated journalistic practices gleaned from a journalism textbook brought to him by an old friend, Jim Tipton, who taught sociology at the nearby campus of Eastern Connecticut State University. Tipton and two colleagues agreed to teach Warren college-level courses behind bars; the courses would earn credits from ECSU.

Warden Hills came to trust Warren enough to assign him an inventory of equipment at the jail. Inside a room behind an iron door, Warren came across shotguns. No one else was there. "I'm not touching them," Warren told himself. No matter how trusted he was, he couldn't shake the paranoia.

Navigating prison culture required more than finessing the warden and the guards. Warren had to maintain credibility with a tougher audience: the other inmates. While in Montville, he had honed the split personality needed to survive, the ability to switch from altar boy to tough guy when the occasion warranted. He began with the perfect credential for prison culture, murdering an informant. He kept to himself his certainty that Alex Rackley wasn't an agent. Occasionally, Warren learned, you had to smack people—when a group discovered an inmate stealing somebody's stuff or provoking a fight, for instance. If you didn't join in, you'd be marked as a future target. Also, you needed a weapon. On the brick in his cell, Warren fashioned a sharp point on a loose piece of metal that he'd bent off a mop. He never used it. He just made sure someone heard the grinding and spread the word.

In the Brooklyn jail, as in Montville, because of his favored treatment, Warren needed to avoid resentment from his fellow inmates. He needed to earn stripes as a leader rather than a rat. A hardened street criminal from Hartford, a former boxer named Asa Boyd, helped him out. Boyd concluded that Warren was useful. Warren could show inmates how to work the system. Boyd agreed when Warren told him and the other inmates, "You have to learn to play the game to get out of here. You're not going to beat the system."

Somewhere a Panther was turning in his grave. Warren's new message had come far from his recent rhetoric about tearing down the system.

Warren was a warden's dream. "The only way the system will change," Warren told the inmates, "is if someone gets out of here and gets in a position to influence policy. You have to be like a chimpanzee. You have to be trained to respond to the system."

Usually, "chimpanzee" was a racial taunt, not a model for a black man. The image could sear any prisoner. Pharmaceutical companies were using inmates to test products during Warren's incarceration; one company executive was quoted in the press saying that inmates were cheaper than chimpanzees or monkeys. Warren knew inmates agreed to participate in product testing for the money; he nevertheless editorialized against the practice in the *Tier Tribune*. Yet he felt comfortable invoking the chimpanzee in urging his fellow inmates to work the system. There was no denying it, Warren reasoned; like chimps, they lived in cages. They needed to do their best to get out.

Other inmates calculated that Warren would help them earn chits to shorten their time in jail and make the time behind bars better. Guides for Better Living did come in. Warren took a position as a counselor for other inmates. He arranged with guards to take four or five inmates at a time to job interviews beyond the walls.

One day, Asa Boyd and some of the other guys got their hands on a toy chimp. They made a button and put it on the chimp. They presented it to Warren. "Super Chimp," the button said. Warren took it as a compliment.

Part II

CHAPTER 11

Disorder in the Court

THE COURTHOUSE WAS under round-the-clock guard when Bobby Seale made his first pretrial appearance in New Haven's state superior court on Wednesday, May 18, 1970. A new sign relegated demonstrations to at least five hundred feet beyond the building. Seale, in an olive windbreaker and blue shirt, appeared in court for ten minutes. He uttered five words to Judge Harold M. Mulvey: "Yes, I'm here. I'm present." Defusing one potential controversy before the case started, Mulvey ruled that the flamboyant California-based attorney Charles Garry, who had represented members of the Black Panther Party thirty-eight times in courts across the country since 1967, could serve as Seale's lawyer in the case even though he wasn't a member of the Connecticut bar. A recent Yale Law School graduate, David Rosen, would assist Garry during the case and do the real work of preparing arguments and motions.

"Right on, brothers!" Seale, clenched fist in the air, told a half-dozen Panthers in the spectators' section as guards led him out of the courtroom and back to the armored van that returned him to Montville.

Of the fourteen Panthers arrested in connection with the Rackley murder, three, including Warren, had pleaded guilty. The state dropped charges against three others. Of the remaining eight, the state planned to proceed first with prosecuting Ericka, Bobby Seale, and Lonnie McLucas, the other man besides Warren to shoot Rackley. In a tactical mistake, the prosecutor moved to have McLucas tried separately, first, seemingly as a warm-up to the main Ericka-Bobby event. Already, in pretrial hearings, the state had to reveal key points of its strategy to the defense.

Meanwhile, New Haven's FBI busied itself preparing background memos smearing the Panthers' civil rights–oriented attorneys as menaces to the American way. Theodore Koskoff, Lonnie McLucas's lawyer, chaired the local chapter of Henry Wallace's People's Party in 1948, one memo reported, noting that the Communist Party "dominated" the People's Party. "Koskoff was noted to confer regularly" with the Communists' state party chairman back then, the memo added.

Ericka's lawyer, Catherine Roraback, was depicted as a former "associate" of local Communists back in 1950, when she represented them on Smith Act charges. The state's leading Communists contacted her "on several occasions" in the 1950s, the FBI reported. The next sentence of the memo noted, "Roraback traveled to Mississippi in 1964 in order to assist the handling of legal problems that arose from Negro voter registration." In the FBI's worldview, Communists jailed for conspiring to one day advocate the overthrow of the government were little different from people beaten or jailed for trying to register Southern blacks to vote; anyone who helped protect their rights was suspect.

Little had changed since the dawn of the modern FBI political surveillance apparatus, when opposition to lynching or efforts to build black economic power automatically branded people, white and black alike, enemies of America, branded them Reds and made them targets. The same man who directed the FBI's anti-radical campaign after World War I, J. Edgar Hoover, was still obsessed with "racial militants" like Katie Roraback and Ericka Huggins who, in his view, pursued the "Communist" goal of dismantling the all-American barrier separating black from white.

The goal of keeping up this barrier was always tied to Hoover's fascination with black language, culture, and sexuality. There was a constant emphasis on those within the Bureau learning to talk black. Under pressure from Hoover, the office churned out ideas for disrupting the Panthers through forged letters and anonymous messages. The idea was to seed paranoia, even when it was clear that such a tactic would increase the likelihood of violence.

More than eight months after Alex Rackley's murder on suspicions of informing, the New Haven office prepared a glossary on how to sound "black" when preparing new forgeries. The glossary appeared in a February 27, 1970, memo about an anonymous letter being prepared to convince national Panthers headquarters that a New Haven Panther "is skimming money from BPP contributions and hav[ing] sex with white girls." The memo counseled including "grammatical errors to indicate the person writing has no formal education." Then it gave definitions for suggested "terminology":

- Dig the threads: look at the clothing
- On your main man: [name deleted] is wearing
- When you blows in: on coming to town
- Vamping ain't my bag: an informant I am not
- But [name deleted] is raking the scratch: he is taking BPP money
- And play stud with the gray girls: having sexual relations with white girls
- Dig it: listen
- We all is for one: BPP members are for BPP members, a.k.a. united
- But our man is an oreo: black on the outside, white inside
- He getting to be like a house nigger: becoming [a] black that is allowed to live-in as a white servant
- cuase [*sic*]: because
- All he hits on is: has intercourse
- gray leg: white girls
- an who paying: BPP is paying for activities HUH?
- He think we don't know what going down: we are aware of his activities HE THINKS WE ARE UNAWARE?
- But we think he is in some deep shit: his action will be dealt with

The New Haven FBI office also prepared a point-by-point anonymous flyer rebutting the Panthers' ten-point program. Supposedly written by black dissenters, the flyer was intended for distribution in the black community. The FBI distributed an attack on the Panthers by "A Concerned Merchant" in a black neighborhood where the party wanted to buy a house. It wrote anonymous leaflets supposedly published by the Panthers to confuse people who received similar flyers on the street about the trial in the New Haven courthouse. Another letter, supposedly from a Yale "alumnus," sought to pressure the university to bar Panthers from the campus. Anonymous letters went to columnists like William F. Buckley with information that ended up in their syndicated pieces. A Hoover-approved anonymous letter to national Panther headquarters reported transgressions by a New Haven Panther leader (probably Miranda; the FBI blackened the name before declassifying the approval memo) whose standing needed to be "undermine[d]" because of his success in strengthening the local chapter. The alleged transgressions included misuse of funds, which Hoover's approval memo acknowledged "has not been verified," and "promiscuous activities," which, the memo claimed, were "true."

THE NIGHT AFTER Seale's brief March 18 court appearance, national Panther Chief of Staff David Hilliard set the tone for the coming weeks at a speech to two thousand students at the main campus of the University of Connecticut, outside of Hartford in the rural eastern Connecticut town of Storrs. Hilliard's theme: the role of young white people in stopping Bobby Seale's "criminal execution."

"Not only will we burn buildings," Hilliard vowed, "we will take lives. We will blow up buildings. We will kill judges, and we will do whatever is necessary to make white people understand that we're not going to be passive to a genocidal plot that's been perpetrated against black people." Hilliard implored the white students to join the effort. "If you want to break windows, if you want to kill a pig, if you want to burn the courthouse, you would be moving against the symbols of oppression." Hilliard noted that massive demonstrations would soon take place in New Haven. Afterward, if the "pigs" continued to insist on imprisoning and trying Seale, "we're going to unleash a race war on the pigs of America, and it's up to you, as white revolutionists, to support the struggle of black people."

The FBI forwarded an account of Hilliard's remarks to, among others, presidential adviser John Ehrlichman; memos traveled from office to office within the FBI warning of violence-bent crazies descending on New Haven. Every rumor, no matter how specious or unconfirmed, shot adrenaline into the law enforcement bloodstream.

"A rumor is spreading in the ghetto area of New Haven," reported a March 31 memo, that if Seale was convicted, Arnie Markle "will be murdered." From Washington came a summary of a phone call between the New Haven and Berkeley Panther offices: "Conversation suggests the possible transportation of implements of violence by David last name unknown to New Haven and their intended use to stop the murder trial concerning Panther Chairman Bobby Seale."

As part of a $75,000 security upgrade, workers installed bulletproof glass in the Elm Street courthouse's first-floor windows; new drapes hid the rooms from public view. Twelve to fourteen extra police officers were put on standby during working hours.

Some 1,700 people, mostly white Yale students, filled Woolsey Hall to hear national Panther Elbert "Big Man" Howard, an incendiary speaker and Central Committee member who edited the Panthers' national paper and represented the party in speeches abroad. He predicted that if the state succeeded in convicting Seale and Ericka, New Haven would see a flood of "crazy niggers in your streets. . . . There's going to be freedom for everybody or freedom for nobody. We're going to advocate killing those motherfuckers who kidnap us. We're going to advocate killing pigs who kick our doors in."

"Either you're with us or against us," Artie Seale, Bobby's wife, told the crowd.

The sidelines were vanishing outside of the courthouse, and the point of no return for those people still wondering where they stood finally came the next day, April 14. The big news of the day concerned the crippling of the Apollo 13 spacecraft. "Hey, we've got a problem here!" came the words from the Space Center in Houston. Meanwhile, in New Haven, the state courthouse—the local command center—had difficulties of its own maintaining order.

The problems in New Haven began before the start of the court session at a pretrial hearing in the cases against Ericka, George Edwards, Lonnie McLucas, Rose Marie Smith, and Margaret Hudgins. Hoping to see Bobby Seale, 150 students left nearby Wilbur Cross High School to attend the session. A group of the students, along with some adult Panther supporters, entered the courthouse lobby chanting slogans. State police arrested two of them; Judge Mulvey promptly gave the pair, a seventeen-year-old boy and an adult woman, twenty- and twenty-five-day sentences, respectively. The police removed the rest of the group from the building.

The crowd reconvened across the street on the Green for an im-promptu rally. The students heard Artie Seale and Doug Miranda un-leash a new volley of outrage. The rally broke up around noon. Some of the students left the rally and started looting the area of the Chapel Square Mall, the block-long symbol of Dick Lee's efforts to keep subur-banites shopping in downtown New Haven. The students broke win-dows, scuffled with cops, snatched purses, and knocked a woman to the sidewalk at Temple and Chapel streets. Police made five arrests, includ-ing a Yale graduate student who was placed in custody for the crime of photographing the police. He was doing that on the steps of the court-house. An emergency directive banned cameras or tape recorders from the premises, even the outdoor perimeter.

That afternoon, David Hilliard—the highest-ranking national Pan-ther *not* behind bars or in exile—attended the pretrial hearing. He sat in the spectator section next to beret-clad French author Jean Genet and Black Panther Minister of Culture Emory Douglas, an artist responsible for the look of the national Panther paper, most notably the porcine drawings of police. Someone, perhaps Ericka, handed a note to Hilliard through Charles Garry. According to one account, Bobby Seale wrote the note in advance. As Hilliard looked at the note wrapped in yellow paper, he said something to Douglas, and the cops rushed at him. They grabbed at Hilliard and at the papers. Douglas tried to pry them off Hilliard. A scuffle ensued as Jean Genet stood by, berating the police in French.

The officers hauled Hilliard and Douglas, handcuffed to each other, before Judge Mulvey. Each was immediately given six months in jail, the maximum sentence for contempt of court. No bail was granted, and no further questions were asked. Mulvey even had the note impounded. Frenchman Genet, who was white, received no punishment. In the black community and on the Yale campus, Hilliard and Douglas's sen-tence made some skeptics and fence-straddlers more inclined to believe the Panther refrain, or at least seriously consider it.

A wave of urgency transformed Yale's campus. Weeks of meetings, protests, and threats would follow, leading up to the big event. The Pan-thers were calling radicals from all over the country to descend on New Haven for a rally at the Green on May 1.

Usually, protest organizers highballed estimates of protesters, while authorities would downplay the numbers. This time, the Panthers and the FBI competed for who could invoke a scarier number of expected ruffians. Agents passed along Panther estimates as gospel. "As many as half a million persons," an FBI teletype predicted the same day as the Hilliard jailing.

Anticipation spread up the New England coast. On April 15, in Cambridge, Massachusetts, an offshoot of the white radical group Students for a Democratic Society (SDS) organized a march at Harvard to protest the New Haven Panther trial. Fifteen hundred demonstrators showed up at 7 P.M.—only to find the Harvard gates along their parade route locked shut. Incensed demonstrators rampaged through the streets. They smashed windows, threw rocks, lit fires in and around Harvard. The crowd of protesters swelled to as many as three thousand. Two thousand police officers were called in from surrounding towns. Demonstrators threw bricks at the cops, and the bricks were thrown right back. It took hours to disperse the crowd. Tear gas filled the air as police clubbed marchers, including women from Radcliffe College. Some 214 people were hospitalized; an estimated $100,000 of property was destroyed. At the rally, Yippie leader Abbie Hoffman vowed that the marchers would burn down Yale on May 1.

The patricians entrusted with Yale University's future knew it was time to swing into action. First order of business: they arranged a picnic.

CHAPTER 12

The Magic Bus

Mary Brewster filled the wicker basket with a meal fit for a king—or, more to the point, for "King," Kingman Brewster, eleven generations off the Mayflower, president of Yale University. Mary was devoted to her husband, King. She prepared Cornish hen. She packed a bottle of white wine and glasses of martinis for King and his friends.

Brewster and his young assistant, Henry "Sam" Chauncey Jr., traveled to the appointed meeting place beside a brook in a field in Sturbridge, the western Massachusetts town that sang the virtues of the New England era in which Kingman Brewster's patrician roots claimed the soil. There they met up with a colleague from King's days on the Harvard Law faculty, Archibald Cox.

Despite the bucolic setting, the world didn't feel peaceful that afternoon. King and Chauncey needed to rendezvous with Cox somewhere removed from the turmoil tearing at their campuses. Cox was the top Harvard official dealing with campus unrest. He was investigating how such a smart institution could have handled a protest so unintelligently. Fresh from combing through the ashes, broken glass, and dried blood on Cambridge's streets, Cox might help King figure out how to avoid an even messier implosion in New Haven.

The group originally considered eating at the Sturbridge Publick House. Upon reflection, they decided to seek privacy. Like the radicals at their wrought-iron gates, Brewster and Chauncey watched over their shoulders as they traversed the daily battlefield of 1970 campus life. They also imagined spies on their trail. They had good reason for their imaginings. They knew that New Haven police listened in on private phone calls, and not only the phone calls of bookies or other outlaws. They eavesdropped on Yalies, too. Brewster and Chauncey began each day with a 6 A.M. phone call. Starting in 1969, they noticed that information they had discussed in those phone calls would show up in other people's conversations. Eventually, they tested the tappers. They would pretend that a noted visitor was coming to campus; hours later, a reporter would call to ask for details on the visit. Like the Panthers, Yale's vanguard caught on to the government spies and adjusted their movements accordingly.

Also, like the Panthers, Kingman Brewster drew the ire of the government. New Haven politicians resented Yale's power, its privilege, its history of high-handed dealings with the townies. The Nixon administration resented Yale, too. The Ivy League represented the old East Coast establishment, which never viewed Main Street Republicans like Richard Nixon and Vice President Spiro Agnew as equals, as products of the right breeding, the right intellectual training, even the right kind of money. The Brewsters hailed from the old Republican Party. With a mix of motives—noblesse oblige, class prerogative, financial self-interest— their families had opposed slavery, formed the American Civil Liberties Union, donated fortunes to the preservation of fine arts and the pursuit of intellectual inquiry. Socially, they were liberals. Nixon, who came to public prominence hunting Communists, represented an ascending white middle-class and, eventually, working-class Republicanism. Spiro Agnew represented the self-seeking—eventually criminal—side of this invasion. They both played on hostility to elites. They echoed the idea that the Ivy League snobs, the liberal judges, egghead intellectuals, and scruffy upper-class rabble-rousers threatened America by weakening the nation's military resolve in Vietnam or by supporting upstart blacks who could steal white jobs, move into white neighborhoods and schools. To Brewster, Nixon and his ilk were dangerous. He saw the true threat to American values in 1970 as their anti-intellectualism, their contempt for civil liberties and for civil rights activists, and the escalating bombing in southeast Asia.

Brewster was pushing the limits of Republican ideology. Years before it became more acceptable for establishment figures, Brewster joined his friend Dick Lee at a press conference to denounce the Vietnam War. Although he feared the intolerance for dissent he saw among too many campus radicals, Brewster had grown even more disgusted with many of his peers' antagonism to those demanding change. Harvard President Nathan Pusey, for instance, feared the protesters and avoided them. This mind-set led to the riot in Cambridge. Instead of hiding from student protesters, Brewster listened to them. He loved talking with students, mixing with them on campus. Like FDR during the Great Depression, Brewster saw protests not as a threat, but as an opportunity to strengthen the system.

In that sense, Brewster's agenda diverged from that of the Black Panthers and the student radicals who were now trashing him in public. Both sides feared Nixon, opposed Vietnam, and spoke out against racism. But Brewster sought to save the system. He and liberals of his generation saw the rise of the CIA as an idealistic enterprise, an intelligence-gathering mission in the fight against the international evil unmasked in World War II. Brewster wasn't troubled by the existence of cloak-and-dagger government agencies. He opposed the misuse of those operations by less-than-noble power seekers.

Meanwhile, the Panthers, SDS, and the Yippies saw the system as the problem. They wanted to replace it. They looked not to the New Deal or the ACLU for models, but to the Vietcong and Mao's Cultural Revolution. Kingman Brewster's Yale trained the capitalists, the war planners, the liberal defenders of the status quo whom the radicals hoped ultimately to overthrow.

Archibald Cox (who would later stand up to Nixon as Watergate special prosecutor) and Sam Chauncey were Brewster's kindred souls. Like Brewster, they wore their class privilege as comfortably as their silk smoking jackets. But, also like Brewster, they viewed "nobility" as a character trait to develop, a challenge passed down to better society, rather than a crown inherited as a license for complacency. Like Brewster, Chauncey descended from a line of elite New England WASPs, including a Yale founder and a Harvard president. Chauncey's father founded the Educational Testing Service in 1947 in a quest to transform private colleges from bastions of inherited wealth into a meritocracy.

A generation later, Brewster brought that battle to Yale. He opened Yale's gates to black students; before Brewster, Yale classes had only a handful of African-American students. Yale also went coed in 1969 and welcomed more students of modest means, making Brewster a target of the defenders of the old order among Yale's alumni. Conservative Old Blue William F. Buckley, incensed at the welcoming of women and blacks to the portal of power, led an effort to dethrone King from the presidency. To Buckley, Brewster and the Black Panthers belonged on the same side of the gates he wanted to slam shut.

At the picnic in Sturbridge, the gate metaphor became a literal imperative for Kingman Brewster. Archibald Cox relayed the Big Lesson of the Cambridge disaster: Harvard should never have shut the campus gates and blocked the path of the protest march. That frustrated the marchers. It focused their rage, originally targeted at the New Haven Panther trial in specific and the system in general, on the physical landscape of Harvard University. It produced a combustible brew, merging mob rage with provocation and a handy target.

When the tens of thousands of radicals descend on New Haven for the pro-Panther May Day protests on the New Haven Green, Cox advised, Yale should learn from Harvard's mistake. Yale should keep the gates open. After an earlier rampage at Columbia, Cox had performed an investigation there, too. He concluded that Columbia's authoritarian attitude toward students and protesters exacerbated the problem and contributed to violence. Cox conveyed to Brewster and Chauncey information he'd picked up from intelligence sources. A contingent from a violent underground group planned to travel from Boston to New Haven for May Day. This worried Brewster and Chauncey. They felt confident about Yale protesters' peaceful intentions. They had faith in Yale's black student groups. Through Tracy Barnes (a former CIA agent, who helped plan the ill-fated Bay of Pigs operation) and Warren Kimbro's brother-in-law Ernie Osborne, Yale worked with the students and New Haven black community groups to keep the peace.

On the other hand, Yale had less confidence in the outside groups coming to town. Outsiders were unpredictable, capable of provoking violence for their own ends. There were white motorcycle gangs threatening to cause trouble, too. The Nixon administration could be counted on to heighten the tension. Some of the white radical groups clearly were seeing New Haven and Yale as the next stop on the California-Chicago-Cambridge overground railroad of mayhem. On New York's radical radio station WBAI, Abbie Hoffman predicted the biggest riot in history in New Haven.

Cox had surveillance photos of provocateurs from the Cambridge rampage. Chauncey took the photos back to New Haven. He and Brewster could use them as they continued cobbling together a strategy for saving their university. Chauncey took the photos to Jim Ahern, the police chief whose brother's crew was illegally wiretapping Chauncey and Brewster. Ahern's intelligence network extended beyond New Haven, and Yale was going to need it. Chauncey and Ahern would soon discover—when Brewster met with New Haven's mayor, Bart Guida, to discuss May Day—that they were also going to need each other.

Guida, a product of New Haven's working-class Italian-American Democratic machine, resented Yale. His party's boss, who had battled with Dick Lee over patronage and control of the city, handpicked Guida to succeed Lee in order to send a message to New Haven and to Yale: the liberals, reformers, racial integrationists, and Yalies were out. Unlike Lee, Guida didn't lunch with Yale presidents at the on-campus club, Mory's. He didn't hammer out plans for new Yale buildings; he saw Yale as an encroachment on his city, gobbling up taxable land. More importantly, he didn't trust Yalies. Nor did he appreciate this crisis. He worried about riots and had no interest in the whinings of privileged student radicals. He put the blame for all this *agita* on one culprit: the Ivy League behemoth across the Green and its fashionably liberal president.

Of course, Brewster never wanted to have to deal with this May Day protest. It began over a murder and a trial quite separate from Yale, and it had overtaken his life and complicated it as much as it had Guida's. Now he discovered he would have to confront the crisis without an ally in the city government.

Chauncey and Ahern were present at the City Hall meeting of Guida and Brewster. Ahern would compare the sight of Brewster entering Guida's office to that of "a medieval patrician confronting a frightened peasant." Guida let Brewster know that he wanted any problems with May Day to occur within Yale's gates, because, in his view, this trouble was at least in part Yale's doing. The meeting produced no concrete plans and no hope of official cooperation. Afterward, Ahern called Chauncey. They needed to work together, he said, because their bosses couldn't.

Chauncey agreed. Ahern revealed that Guida had instructed him to leave Brewster out of the loop on plans for policing the protest, which included driving protesters onto Yale's campus at any sign of trouble.

"I want you to know," the Irish cop told Brewster's WASP assistant, "I'm not going to do that." Ahern made it clear that he, not Guida, would make the decisions on May Day. And he wanted Chauncey and Brewster in the loop.

The first matter of business for these newfound allies was thwarting the violent contingent from Boston. Through intelligence reports supplied by the Massachusetts police force, Ahern learned that the group had rented two buses to take its members to New Haven. He hatched a plan with Chauncey: They'd arrange for state troopers to masquerade as the bus drivers, who would then prevent the radicals from coming anywhere near the rally. Chauncey said Yale would cover the costs if the radicals trashed the buses as a result. He never had to put the guarantee in writing; Yale's oral promise satisfied the bus company's insurer.

An ideal spot to pull over was in the town of Hopkinton, a rural stop along the Massachusetts Turnpike. The troopers would have no trouble pulling over, popping the hood, disabling the engines. As darkness covered the hills of western Massachusetts, another trooper would "happen" to drive by right then and whisk the drivers away. The troopers would leave behind two stranded busloads of cranky, mayhem-bent radicals.

CHAPTER 13

Panther, Panther . . . Bow, Wow, Wow!

Bulldog! Bulldog!
Bow, wow, wow
Eli Yale
Bulldog! Bulldog!
Bow, wow, wow
Our team can never fail
When the sons of Eli
Break through the line
That is the sign we hail
Bulldog! Bulldog!
Bow, wow, wow
Eli Yale!

—YALE FOOTBALL FIGHT SONG

WHILE BREWSTER, CHAUNCEY, and Ahern could keep some of the more incendiary activists from coming to New Haven on May Day, Yale and the city still had to contend with those who were already in town and on campus. Inside Yale's buildings, Doug Miranda, the young Panther leader sent from Boston to revive the New Haven chapter, urged students to burn the campus as May Day neared.

"Man, if you really want to do something," Miranda exhorted one gathering, "you ought to get some guns, and go and get Chairman Bobby out of jail!"

Incredulous students shouted back objections. One of Miranda's fellow organizers retorted that the students should "at least" burn down Yale's rare-book library. Miranda stepped back as a heated argument ensued; he smiled as the shouting continued. Then, feigning disgust, he reclaimed the floor to herald a dramatic exit from the room. "We'll be back!" he vowed. "You all better get your shit together."

William Farley, a Yale sophomore from Pennsylvania, and some of his fellow black students caught up with Miranda outside the room. "You ain't serious about that shit you were running," one of them asked, "are you?"

"This same shit worked at San Francisco State," he answered.

"But this ain't San Francisco State! You can't expect these Yalies to get guns and go marching down the New Haven Green to the courthouse!"

"Hell no, I don't expect those whites to do that," Miranda agreed. "But they ain't done shit yet except talk. We're trying to get a strike going here, man! Now, you can't just tell them, 'Strike!' You've got to give them something more extreme, and then you let them fall back on a strike."

If you want a fair trial for Bobby Seale, you don't demand a fair trial for Bobby Seale, Miranda told Farley. You demand that people risk their lives to bust him out of jail.

"You may get some of these people hurt," Farley objected.

"Man, I don't care about these whites. I'm just using them to get Chairman Bobby out of jail. And I'll use them any way I have to," Miranda responded. "We're in a fight for survival, brother!"

Miranda needed Yalies, black and white alike, to stir up the city, because the Panthers had drawn little active support from black New Haveners beyond a core of several dozen hard workers. To lure the Yalies, Miranda bobbed and weaved, sometimes jabbing, sometimes reaching out: one day, debating with would-be proletarian Yalies on the finer points of Marxist theory; another day, a call, before a rally at Woolsey Hall, for white students to shoot police "pigs."

Farley felt caught between self-serving "pseudo-revolutionaries" and an unjust system. It was a position in which black students like Farley increasingly found themselves in 1970. Miranda simultaneously irritated and intrigued Farley. The young student had enrolled in Doug Miranda 101, studying the Panther's every move. Immersed in argument, Miranda would catch sight of Farley on the sidelines and wink. On one occasion Farley sat in Dwight Chapel as Miranda debated socialism with leading campus SDSer Mark Zanger. (Zanger would become the prototype for the character Megaphone Mark Slackmeyer in fellow Yale alum Garry Trudeau's *Doonesbury* strip.) Farley didn't find the substance of the debate interesting; it seemed more like a macho who's-more-radical competition. But Farley did take notice of how Miranda, representative of a party that claimed to speak for the brothers on the street, paced the room. As he ambled, Miranda dribbled a basketball—or tried to.

Farley was one of ninety-six black students in the class of 1972, the largest contingent in Yale history. (By contrast, Yale had admitted just six blacks in 1963.) They were drawn to New Haven as part of Kingman Brewster's vision of a vanguard of leaders who would diversify America's ruling class. Farley was on that road. Son of an agronomist and a social worker—one of only three black students at his high school in Mennonite-dominated Lewistown, Pennsylvania—Farley came to Yale determined to save the world. In addition to his studies, he ran Yale's Ulysses S. Grant Foundation, which tutored black children from New Haven. He was already an emerging campus leader when events catapulted him to a central role in the oncoming May Day tempest.

Mixed emotions tore at Farley, just as they tore at the other black students who struggled with their roles at a changing Yale and in a changing America. The students contended daily with Yale's culture, the product of centuries of almost exclusively white students. They felt the pressure of being the first generation with the chance to claim a black spot on white America's highest rungs of power. They assumed the burden of opening doors of opportunity for "the race." From radical groups like the Black Panthers, however, they felt the sting of being branded Uncle Toms, of abandoning their people to pursue material success.

In spite of Miranda's glaring lack of hand-eye coordination, Farley and his black classmates couldn't ignore Miranda. They couldn't ignore the Panthers. They couldn't abandon them. Nor could these students fully embrace the Panthers. The students had a stake in Yale. They wanted to improve it; they didn't want to burn it down. Plus, they had committed themselves to causes important to New Haven's black community, like pushing Yale to open a day care center for its employees' children. The students feared that the frenzy over May Day would sap momentum from those efforts. They'd have to revive the campaigns once the May Day swarm left town for the next glitzy protest. Whatever their views of the Panthers (generally sympathetic to their agenda, but opposed to violence), the black students cared deeply about injustices faced by black Americans in the criminal justice system. That was the central issue of the protests over the upcoming murder trials. It drowned out everything else. The students focused on the two celebrity defendants: Bobby Seale and Ericka Huggins.

Another promising member of Farley's class, Henry Louis Gates Jr., today head of Harvard's Afro-American Studies Department, would later write of his peers' soul wrestling: "What would becoming a true black leader entail—for ourselves, in the classroom, and for people outside those hallowed Ivy Walls? What sort of sacrifices and obligations did this special ticket to success bring along with it? We worried about this, and we worried out loud, often, and noisily."

Gates had met John Huggins's mother at her job at Sterling Library; now he started seeing Ericka Huggins's picture on posters around campus. Her determined face "became the revolution's logo." Idealistic black students' role models were changing form, fast. Before Yale, Gates had believed that "the blackest thing you could grow up to be was [Supreme Court Justice] Thurgood Marshall, or Martin Luther King." Groups like the Black Panthers buried those role models in landfills reserved for "bourgeois" middle-class blacks. Replacing those allegedly accommodationist rejects were symbols of truly "black" people who knew that being "real" equaled being "down with the people," who wore Afros and spoke ghetto argot.

DOUG MIRANDA COULD use these emerging archetypes on the black students. A different form of guilt marked idealistic white students as Panther prey in Northern city campuses across the country, where Panther chapters tended to take root.

The political debates of the late 1960s focused white students' attention on the contrast between their elite life at Yale and the poverty in neighborhoods surrounding campus. The author John Hersey watched the gap widen as he dealt daily with students as "master," or resident faculty member in charge, of Yale's Pierson College. (Most Yale undergraduates live in one of twelve residential colleges.) Hersey interacted with all sides of the May Day tempest. His own outlook mirrored that of concerned but nonviolent critics of the system, like the black students, like Warren Kimbro's brother-in-law Ernest Osborne, who was working as a key aide to Kingman Brewster; he was assigned to building bridges between Yale and the black community. On principle, Hersey raised money for the Panthers' legal defense. "The demoralizing fact of life for most white radicals was their possessing too many, not too few, of society's goodies, and having come to loathe them," Hersey wrote shortly after May Day.

The journalist Jeff Greenfield, a Yale Law School alum, commented, too, on the role of student guilt. "Yale, after all, sits in the middle of a not-very-rich community, a constant symbol of power and wealth," he wrote in a contemporary account of May Day. "A half-billion dollar endowment, a student body from some of the richest families in America, on a large plot of land which pays no property taxes to New Haven. It employs hundreds of members of New Haven's communities—black and Italian—at wages of less than a hundred dollars a week. What had begun to happen in the late 1960s was an understanding among a part of the Yale community that they were part of a privileged class" served by poor and working-class New Haveners.

It only exacerbated matters that white radicals had a wicked crush on the Black Panthers. The Panthers—posing as heroes with their guns and defiant glares—may have fulfilled perverse white fantasies of the noble savage who, in his "genuinity," cannot restrain his violent nature. The Panthers offered adventure, an invitation to revolution—and a chance to shock the parents. Like any crush, the Panther infatuation—"Panthermania," Warren Kimbro's sister Betty dubbed it—crossed the wires of normally lucid young people's brains. It led them to embarrassing leaps of illogic. Such excesses are the birthright of the young, of course, especially college students who have the luxury of testing a universe of ideas while figuring out their identities. Indulging such excesses can carry with it a blindness to individual suffering. Amid all the agitation over the case, Yalies wrote or chanted precious few words about the victim, Alex Rackley, except to add him to a list of casualties of the system's war on the Panthers.

The infatuation extended to some of the students' elders. It captured playwright Donald Freed, a humanities professor teaching at Yale at the time. He threw himself into Panther support. He also detailed his observations in a book about the experience, *Agony in New Haven: The Trial of Bobby Seale, Ericka Huggins and the Black Panther Party.* A photo on the back jacket shows the author, a white man in shirt and tie, holding a pipe, lecturing a college class. Inside, the author, an avowed opponent of racism, in language that could practically come from the mouths of anti–civil rights racists, patronizes black leaders who paid for their activism with their lives.

Martin Luther King was a "*Negro,*" Freed wrote; King represented the "infantile" nonviolent civil rights movement. "It was a Southern, agrarian, Christian, matriarchical movement. . . . It put itself at the mercy of those who hold power. . . . It was metaphysical, and political only in its implications." According to Freed, Malcolm X had a legitimate voice; he represented "the first generation of black men" stepping "out of the ruins of the Negro," Freed writes. But ultimately Malcolm X, too, offered a "swindle" to the ghetto.

The "mature," "political," "revolutionary" black leader, according to Professor Freed, was none other than an advocate of violence who (with the support of white people like Freed) got away with murdering, raping, and extorting protection money from more African-Americans than 99 percent of the white men in America—and bragged about it until his death.

"Suddenly the heir of Malcolm X appears in the streets," a breathless Freed writes. "Huey P. Newton—the armed intellectual who could, as Eldridge Cleaver was later to say, 'bring out the niggers who were under the mud'—stands there with his gun and his love.

"The third phase of the American human-rights revolution has now gotten into clear view. The birth pangs are over."

Practically any intellectual or student engaged in controversial issues, swept up in passions of the day, will produce words that haunt or embarrass years later in the clarity of historical distance. However, some white intellectuals who were caught up in May Day took a left-leaning stand without abandoning their brains or their compassion. It required an ability to hold one's compatriots to the same standards as they held their opponents.

Michael Lerner did that during the height of Panthermania. A Yale graduate student, Lerner helped organize May Day protests focused on keeping peace in the streets and advocating racial fairness in the court-room. At the same time, he put together an essay, called "Respectable Bigotry," about the double standard he saw in fellow white Yale lefties, students and professors who denounced bigotry.

Lerner observed that violence by working-class whites provoked out-rage while violence by poor blacks summoned sympathy. Likewise, Chicago Mayor Richard Daley's malapropisms revealed him as an ignorant thug, whereas the Panthers' profanity and butchered syntax revealed them as "authentic." Ghetto violence is "'understood' and forgiven; the violence of a Cicero [Illinois] racist convinced that Martin Luther King threatens his lawn and house and powerboat is detested without being understood." "Lower-middle-class" Poles and Italians and cops made for "safe objects" for jokes or "pig" taunts.

Lerner proceeded to note that a *New York Times* columnist, speaking for many white liberals legitimately shocked by Mayor Daley's police assault on protesters outside the 1968 Democratic convention, wrote that "those were our children on the streets of Chicago." Lerner analyzed the unspoken assumption behind that liberal outlook: "[The] *Times* columnists and the hip radicals did not understand a nation that approved of the police action in Chicago because its children were in the streets of Chicago too. Its children were the police."

ELITE WHITE STUDENTS in New Haven were only too ready to romanticize and be swayed by figures at home looking to imitate their anticolonialist Third World brethren. Doug Miranda was one such figure. He played his trump card in a speech on Sunday night, April 19. Some 1,500 Yalies jammed Battell Chapel for a "teach-in" on the Panther trial. Miranda had good news for the students discomfited by his dares. "I'm not going to tell white students to go out and kill pigs at this time, because that would be idealism," he said.

Shoulders relaxed as Miranda proceeded to the Big Ask. "The most minimal level you can participate on is a call for a student strike," he declared. "We're saying, take your power and use it to save the institution. Take it away from people who are using it in a way it shouldn't be used. You can close Yale down and make Yale demand release. You have the power to prevent a bloodbath in New Haven."

Miranda's argument was that Yale, aka The Man, The System, controlled the courts. By shutting down Yale, by shutting down the classes that educate future corporate and government leaders, students could force Yale to have Bobby Seale freed, or at least fairly tried. The logic mattered less than the opportunity Miranda's plan offered to students. They could do something to "free Bobby." And that something required no bloodshed. It required no taking up of arms. Miranda cast the action as a way to *prevent* violence. The plan required little risk beyond missing a few days of classes. They could stand side by side with the Black Panthers at the moment of their chairman's pending crucifixion.

Miranda—realizing that he had the crowd with him—pressed on, invoking the spirit of Dapper Dan, the bulldog mascot of Yale's football team.

"There's no reason," Miranda declared, "why the Panther and the Bulldog can't get together! . . . That Panther and that Bulldog gonna move together!"

The assembled Yalies leapt to their feet, applauding. The artists in Yale's Jonathan Edwards residential college got to work running off T-shirts with the Panther-Bulldog logo. Activists pressed fellow students to support a strike. "Shut it down!" they chanted, fists raised.

The entire campus was now consumed with the Panther trial. In the law school, for instance, students voted not to strike. The law students formed a committee—cochaired by future First Lady and U.S. Senator Hillary Rodham (Clinton)—to monitor the trial, offer legal advice to demonstrators who got arrested, and help prevent violence at the May Day rally. Rodham's cochair was a close friend named Jerry de Jaager. (Bill Clinton wouldn't arrive on campus until the following fall.) De Jaager would remember Rodham as a voice of reason whenever anyone grew too emotional about the course of events. Rodham's calming influence become indispensable when, in the days leading up to the big protest, someone started a fire in the law school basement. Rodham was known on campus from the moment she arrived because of coverage of her anti–Vietnam War commencement address at Wellesley the previous year. She quickly made an impression as a careful, moderate voice of dissent. Even then, she came across as someone who knew better than to jeopardize her career with rash actions or comments.

Decades later, in an attempt to derail her political career, right-wingers would twist Rodham Clinton's role to make it appear she supported the murder of Alex Rackley and sided with radicals advocating violence. Hillary Rodham Clinton never chose to shed any light on her role on campus during that time. In writing and speaking about the period, she never mentions cochairing the committee. She has also limited her public recollections to helping clean up after the law school fire and responding, along with other students, to the dean's plea "to organize round-the-clock security patrols for the remainder of the school year."

Black undergraduates, many still wary of Miranda, joined the front lines of his march toward a strike. Propelled to leadership roles, students like William Farley and Kurt Schmoke, the future mayor of Baltimore, learned the kind of negotiating lessons that customarily come years after college. Farley was selected as the head of a steering committee to plan for the strike. Secretly, he met with Kingman Brewster and Sam Chauncey. They discussed details, not theory. Both sides wanted to prevent violence. "If anyone comes to us" with questions about how to get involved in planning for May Day events, Brewster told Farley, "we'll send them to you."

Farley found himself frustrated by Yale officials (he said as much in a speech outside Woodbridge Hall, the administration building), but he liked Brewster. The university president seemed committed to preserving lives. He wanted to allow the pressing issues raised by the Panther trial, the issues convulsing the campus, to receive a full, open hearing. That impressed Farley.

"You know," Farley told Brewster at the conclusion of a planning meeting, "we're going to close the university down."

"We're going to try to stop you," Brewster responded.

"OK," Farley said. Like two Yale gentlemen, they shook hands.

Everyone—from J. Edgar Hoover to frightened New Haveners making plans to leave town—believed the city was about to explode. Paranoia and overheated rhetoric from all sides contributed to that sense.

The Panthers continued ratcheting up the threats despite Miranda's sort-of-soothing words at Battell Chapel. At a rally in New Haven's Beaver Pond Park attended largely by black high school kids, the party distributed a picture of Chief Ahern labeled "Wanted Dead." Elbert "Big Man" Howard repeated threats of "physical attacks" in the event of Seale's conviction. On April 20, at the University of Connecticut, pro-

Panther students beat another student, the dormitory "president," with a tire iron, badly enough to hospitalize him, when he objected to the announcement over an intercom of a pro-Seale rally. Order was rapidly breaking down. It seemed that Yale, of all institutions, was joining arms with, of all people, the Black Panther Party for Self-Defense, or at least with a small group of scruffy, spoiled students.

On the evening of April 21 a mass pre–May Day meeting convened in Yale's whale-shaped hockey arena, Ingalls Rink. The rally followed on triumphant news for Panther supporters, as well as for advocates of a fair trial. That day Judge Mulvey reversed his decision to keep Panther court observers David Hilliard and Emory Douglas locked up on contempt charges. After a private conference, the Panthers agreed to apologize to Mulvey in open court. More important, Bobby Seale told the judge, "I respect your honor very much for allowing me to have a fair trial." New Haven wasn't—and, by implication, wouldn't become—Chicago, Seale declared. In Chicago he'd been denied the right to counsel of his choice. He told the judge. "I understand that you are trying to see that we defendants have a fair trial. . . . We also understand the necessity for peaceful decorum in the courtroom." In other words, Seale signaled his supporters to stay cool. Panther supporters could claim victory in the release of Hilliard. Mulvey had control of his courtroom. It was a turning point in the case. The judge then suspended pretrial proceedings until after the May Day rally.

In front of the 4,500 to 5,000 people spilling from the stands onto the floor of Ingalls Rink that evening, though, David Hilliard changed the script. Introduced and hailed like a conquering hero, he took the podium surrounded by Panther bodyguards, who seemed to have discovered a way to glare out from behind dark glasses.

After the requisite call and response of "Power to the people!" and "Right on!" Hilliard revealed he had lied when he apologized to Judge Mulvey.

"That statement was necessary to allow us another day of freedom," Hilliard said. "But just because we were crafty enough to outwit the stupid, demonic persecutors of black people in this country, we're going to take the opportunity to say, 'Fuck the judicial system!' Next time we're going to rot in jail rather than compromise! And that's my confession to Yale."

Hilliard proceeded to advocate murdering cops: "Everybody knows that pigs are depraved traducers that violate the lives of human beings, and that there ain't nothing wrong with taking the life of a motherfucking pig."

To his surprise, the audience—exactly the type of college audience that was normally putty in the paws of a Panther—started booing. Hilliard snapped into his well-rehearsed intimidation, guilt-trip mode. A product of tough Oakland streets, Hilliard, the party's national chairman, took the Panthers' ideas seriously but rose to his position because of his street smarts and organizational abilities. He lacked the rhetorical discipline of the party's intellectual leaders. He had a habit of losing control, of slipping into careless threats when he felt attacked, as on one occasion when he publicly threatened the life of President Richard Nixon. Spurned, Hilliard now shot back at the Yalies: "Boo me right out of this motherfucker! Boo me right back to Litchfield jail! Go boo me again, racists!

"Boo Ho Chi Minh. Boo the people that you pacifists are guilty of continuous bombardment. Boo all of your enemies. Boo the Latin Americans. Boo the Koreans. Boo the Africans. Boo the suffering blacks in this country." Hilliard followed with a threat: No way would he "stand up here and let a bunch of so-called pacifists, you violent motherfuckers, boo me without me getting violent with you." He dared someone to finish the job, as he portrayed the booing—to come up front, stab or shoot him. Bring it on! "I say, fuck you!"

That stunned the audacious crowd into silence. Hilliard huddled with his entourage, then returned with a peace offering.

"Now you got me talking like a crazy nigger. You got me talking like your mothers and fathers talk to you. I've called you everything but long-haired hippies." For the second time that evening, he offered to take back his words, this time to the students rather than to Judge Mulvey. In return, he asked the crowd to "repudiate your boos." They complied with cheers.

A light-skinned man stumbled toward the stage. Hilliard's Panther bodyguards pounced on the man. They tore into him with kicks and punches. Then they flung him back into the crowd, stunned and staggering.

The crowd, still stunned, started booing again. Hilliard tried to defend the beating as a "humane" response to a dangerous "reactionary." This time the crowd remained against him. So Hilliard left the stage with two parting messages. To the Yalies, he called out, "Fuck you! All power to all those except those who want to act like a bunch of goddamn racists." To his toughs: "Kick all these motherfuckers' asses."

The victim was later revealed to be a harmless Lebanese architecture student with mental problems, including a habit of disoriented wanderings.

Even after the contentious appearance by Hilliard, students returning to their residential colleges held meetings that, in most cases, led to endorsements of Doug Miranda's call for a campuswide strike.

Kingman Brewster tried to stay ahead of such events. To some extent, he played William Farley's compatriots, played the other students, even his faculty, as deftly as Doug Miranda played them.

Brewster and Chauncey—heeding Archie Cox's advice—decided to leave gates open during May Day. Most important, they would make sure to keep open Phelps Gate, the main portal to Yale's Old Campus. Filling a city block, the Old Campus consists of the original stone dormitories and classrooms of pre-twentieth-century Yale surrounding a large courtyard. Across the street from the western flank of the New Haven Green, site of the May Day protests, Old Campus could offer a refuge from trouble. Yale would welcome most of the out-of-town protesters (minus two derailed busloads of Boston radicals). The protesters were coming whether or not Yale liked it, and the university could either be prepared for the inevitable or try to lock its gates in a vain attempt to guard against the worst.

Yale would coordinate sleeping arrangements and mass granola feedings in residential college courtyards with the students and college masters. Still, Brewster and Chauncey waited to reveal the full extent of their plans. They said no at first to opening up the campus. They wanted the protesters to feel they'd won a victory when Yale "relented." Dealing with Miranda's requested strike was a trickier issue. How could a university agree to suspend teaching? Brewster needed to safeguard Yale's mission— to educate. Free intellectual inquiry formed the basis of a free society; the idea of forcing classes closed reeked of anti-intellectualism, even fascism.

Brewster wanted to allow students space to focus on the burning social questions that were rendering them oblivious to regular academic concerns, but he also needed to protect the considerable portion of his faculty and student body immune to Panthermania, whose voices were being shouted down in the pre–May Day hysteria.

Predictably, a tempestuous debate erupted among the faculty about the best way to handle the coming storm. Some professors reacted in horror to the strike proposal, while other factions battled over the details of how Yale should best respond. Brewster faced a new threat of fragmentation to his besieged campus seemingly every hour. He presided over a mass faculty meeting on April 23 that approved a plan to suspend academic "expectations" for the rest of the semester. This was not a genuine strike, since faculty members could still hold normal classes if they wished, free of harassment. Others could spend the final days of the semester, either in class or outside class, focused on addressing the issues raised by the Panther trial instead. No students would be punished; they would be given the option of writing papers over the summer to meet course requirements.

Activists could crow about pulling off a "strike," yet Brewster hadn't actually endorsed staying away from classes. He permitted it, as part of a short-term response to a crisis that had students thinking hard about the future of their country. Nevertheless, moderates, both in Yale's faculty and outside Connecticut, saw it differently. To them the "strike" defied comprehension.

The headline of an editorial run by the liberal but establishment *New York Times* read "Murdering Justice." The *Times* opined that "those students and faculty members at Yale who are trying to stop a murder trial by calling a strike against the university have plunged campus activism into new depths of irrationality." "Those at Yale who are engaged in trying to shut down the university in order to coerce it to use its power to stop a trial which it has no power to stop are only jeopardizing the future of the university as they attempt to thwart the course of justice. This is the road toward legal, moral and intellectual chaos."

To conservative professors and students, Brewster sold Yale out to a band of thugs. Indeed, viewed one way, a profanity-prone twenty-one-year-old college dropout, Miranda, had almost single-handedly brought a world-class university to a halt. Still, the reaction to the strike compromise was mild compared to the outpouring of vitriol that greeted a one-sentence comment Brewster made at a faculty meeting. That's when, in some quarters of the establishment, it appeared that Yale's blue-blooded president had truly lost his mind.

CHAPTER 14

Calling the Question

THE FACULTY MEETING took place inside Yale's resonant Sprague Hall, normally the site of classical music concerts. More than four hundred professors showed up; one thousand students demonstrated outside. The meeting lasted several hours as different factions of professors debated proposals. In a break from Yale tradition barring student speakers at faculty meetings, black student leader Kurt Schmoke was allowed in to deliver remarks. Schmoke stunned the faculty (or at least those who didn't know him) by seeking their counsel instead of berating them or making outlandish demands. Many of the students protesting outside the meeting "are committed to a cause, but there are a great number of students who are confused, and many who are frightened," Schmoke said. "They don't know what to think. You are our teachers. You are the people we respect. We look to you for guidance and moral leadership." His thoughtful words eased the tension inside Sprague Hall.

Brewster spoke next, from a prepared text. He began by explaining why Yale, as a not-for-profit institution, could not meet demands to contribute money to the Panthers' defense. As an institution, Yale must remain neutral, Brewster said. He encouraged people, in their "individual" capacities, to get involved in the case if they felt strongly. He encouraged people to speak out—which he proceeded to do. He delivered the sentence that would affix itself to his legacy the way "Give me liberty, or give me death" attached itself to Patrick Henry. Brewster had crafted the statement in advance, fifty-six words padded with throat-clearing.

"So in spite of my insistence on the limits of my official capacity," Brewster said, "I personally want to say that I am appalled and ashamed that things should have come to such a pass in this country that I am skeptical of the ability of black revolutionaries to achieve a fair trial anywhere in the United States." Gasps were heard in the hall.

"In large part," Brewster continued, "this atmosphere has been created by police actions and prosecutions against the Panthers in many parts of the country. It is also one more inheritance from centuries of racial discrimination and oppression." From there, Brewster appealed for calm. "The first contribution to the fairness of the trial which anyone can make is to cool rather than heat up the atmosphere in which the trial will be held," he said. Then he responded to demands that Yale address problems in New Haven ghettos. Although Yale couldn't "cure" injustices, it had a "responsibility to do what we can," he offered, inviting proposals. Brewster sat down to an ovation.

Later that night, Yale released a text of Brewster's remarks. The reaction was swift and sharp, focused entirely on the "skeptical" sentence. Even the word "skeptical" was trampled by the rest of the sentence.

"An awful letdown to the courts, the police and to the community," declared a prominent judge, Herbert S. MacDonald, in a public letter to Brewster. MacDonald—Yale class of 1929—accused Brewster of a double standard: Brewster wanted the Panthers presumed innocent, yet, in MacDonald's view, and in the view of other critics, Brewster presumed the court system guilty of being unable to conduct a fair trial before testimony had even begun in the Seale-Huggins case.

Connecticut Governor John Dempsey was similarly "shocked." As far as the critics were concerned, Brewster hadn't questioned whether black revolutionaries could get a fair trial. He declared that they couldn't. And to suggest that the criminal justice system dealt less than equally with notorious black defendants, in the view of the critics, was tantamount to treason.

"Dear Hub," Brewster wrote back to MacDonald, "I am sorry that my statement of skepticism . . . was so distressing to you. Of course I did not intend to disparage the legal system, or those who administer it." He noted that "racial minorities and unpopular radicals have found it difficult to obtain an unbiased jury . . . and a hearing free of extraneous passion and prejudice" throughout the course of American history. "The chance of fairness seems to me especially problematical at the moment because of a politically prodded backlash against both blacks and radicals." "To pretend" these problems don't exist, "or to conclude that it is cynical to take notice of them, seems to me wrong," Brewster concluded. "We badly need more willingness to admit the weaknesses of our institutions and a resolve to deal with these weaknesses."

Hub wasn't mollified. He continued blasting Brewster.

In the New Haven state courthouse, prosecutor Arnie Markle was steamed. Mayor Guida, too, saw Brewster once again putting Yale on the side of violent thugs bent on destroying the system. William F. Buckley resumed his campaign against Brewster, two years after running unsuccessfully for a seat on the Yale Corporation with the expressed purpose of trying to stop Brewster from opening Yale to blacks and women. Buckley penned a column called "The Metamorphosis of Kingman Brewster." "Mr. Kingman Brewster, the president of Yale University, is a prime example of what the mob can do to the leader," Buckley told the nation's newspaper readers. "The progression was like that of Marshal Petain, only it took Petain 24 years to go from '*Ils ne passeront pas*' at Verdun, to serving as quisling for the Germans in 1941."

Politicians, meanwhile, seized the chance to bludgeon an easy target, at least a target for the Nixonian "silent majority" of Americans soured on civil rights, radical protesters, and elite universities. U.S. Senator Thomas J. Dodd of Connecticut also attacked Yale's administration and students, claiming they were part of "a national conspiracy" to "wreck the legal process in the United States and to threaten the very existence of an American city and, indeed, of our whole American society." A New Haven politician named Ed Marcus, president of the Connecticut Senate, was making his big move at the time, seeking a U.S. congressional seat. Marcus, a Yale alum, called for a national poll of his fellow Yale grads to consider ousting Brewster. No matter that Brewster's speech featured a call for calm and nonviolence; the grandstanding Marcus tore into the Yale president for "serv[ing] to inflame community tensions and to encourage mob action. The flag of anarchy seems to be the new Yale mascot. With your statement, you have allied yourself with those forces that are coming to New Haven for the express purpose of freeing Mr. Seale from the jurisdiction of the State."

Finally, the country's highest-ranking liberal-baiter, Vice President Spiro Agnew, made a speech attacking Brewster. Echoing Marcus's call, Agnew said Yale alumni should demand "a more mature and responsible person" to head Yale. He parroted Brewster's skepticism about black revolutionaries receiving a fair trial: "I do not feel that students of Yale University can get a fair impression of their country under the tutelage of Kingman Brewster."

What would later come to be known as America's culture war opened a new front. Agnew's attack played well among the Florida Republicans to whom he delivered it. It resounded with the voters who would later earn the nickname "Reagan Democrats" or "red staters." The attack was part of the continuing battle between Main Street Republicans and old Yankee Republicans, between the old and the new establishments, between middle America and university, liberal elites.

Within hours of Agnew's remarks, 1,500 students signed a pro-Brewster petition; the number of signatures grew to three thousand the next day. The faculty presented Brewster with another petition containing more than four hundred signatures. Louis Pollak, dean of the law school, compared Agnew to red-baiting U.S. Senator Joseph McCarthy for promoting the notion that "constitutional rights are only for those whose politics are considered harmless by certain select wielders of official power."

Agnew's salvo also bombed with some influential editorial writers. The *Chicago Sun-Times* branded Brewster "an outstanding administrator" and Agnew "guilty of political petulance. . . . We submit that Agnew uses his mouth too much." *The Washington Post* gave Brewster "major credit for achieving a sense of unity, coherence and purpose out of seeming division and discord. Of course, he owes an incalculable debt to Vice President Spiro Agnew."

Letters poured in from around the world. Yale's administrators tallied popular sentiment: Of 1,513 letters and telegrams received over ten days, 1,012 expressed support for Brewster; 501 disapproval. Most of the mail came from alumni. Some did heed the call to push for Brewster's departure. "P.S.," added Henry H. Shepard of New York City. "I feel obliged to declare that in my Last Will & Testament prepared and executed several years ago, I included provision for the devolution of my residuary estate to YALE upon the decease of my wife, with the income payable to her during her lifetime. However, I have now determined to annul the disposition for YALE in view of the changed complexion and character of the University recently under your incombency [*sic*]."

By listening to students instead of reflexively fighting them, Brewster emerged as a translator for much of the middle-aged professional class outside university walls. People across the nation were genuinely confused. What were those privileged kids so upset about?

Some letter writers asked for copies of a well-publicized speech Brewster had given to newspaper publishers convening in New York on April 21, the night of the beating of the discombobulated graduate student at David Hilliard's Ingalls Rink appearance. "If the country does not rediscover its own sons and daughters, no amount of law and order or 'crisis management' will make much difference in the long run," Brewster informed the publishers. Students have lost hope in America, he argued. Why? He volunteered some "plausible explanations":

"The killing in Vietnam goes on without prospect of an end.

"The poor get poorer. Urban poverty, housing and health programs are curtailed. . . .

"The dedication to racial equality is pushed back to the inner limits of constitutional necessity."

The "younger generation" might feel less "dejected" if it saw "some indication that basic problems were being tackled or admitted," Brewster said. "It would be reassuring if it were felt, at the very least, that discussion of fundamental problems was welcomed."

Brewster was welcoming that sort of discussion at Yale, and all of America would see his progressive ideas put to a fateful test. May Day would test his alternative to the way that the Nixon administration, the Hoover FBI, and other university presidents squelched dissent. If New Haven blew up, hopes of a freer, more tolerant society could perish in the flames.

CHAPTER 15

Ball of Confusion

A BANK OF black rotary telephones—there must have been fifty of them—sat like silent soldiers awaiting the call to combat.

Sam Chauncey, Kingman Brewster's top aide in charge of preparing for the May Day weekend of protests, was inside Yale's Alumni House, a three-story wood-frame house on Temple Street, a block north of New Haven's Green. Chauncey monitored the phones with pride. He had transformed Alumni House into Yale's May Day command center. The beds, usually reserved for visiting alumni, would allow campus security officers to sleep in twelve-hour shifts; Chauncey wanted them staying nearby. The Green was visible from the second-floor window, where he would sit, monitoring the police radio. He would keep in touch with the masters of each of the twelve residential colleges, plus numerous other key people, on the fifty telephones.

Chauncey was showing the command center to Cyrus Vance, a Yale trustee, former secretary of the army, and regular passenger through the revolving doors linking the federal government and corporate boards. President Johnson named Vance his special assistant to investigate Detroit's 1967 riot; Vance headed a team of envoys and prepared a report. Kingman Brewster lured Vance to New Haven to help him and Chauncey contend with May Day. Vance imparted lessons from Detroit, including the need to stay in contact with the media when trouble starts in order to keep exaggerated radio or TV reports from inciting crowds.

Vance considered Chauncey's fifty phones.

"I'd like to hear one of those phones ring," he said.

Ring? OK. Chauncey called somebody up. He dictated a phone number and asked for a call back.

Rrrring! The call came. Chauncey and Vance stared at the fifty phones. They had no idea which one was ringing.

Chauncey ordered new phones. These had lights that flashed when a call came in. Chauncey still had time—a little time. May Day was fewer than forty-eight hours away.

IN THOSE WANING moments before May Day the White House was dispatching four thousand National Guardsmen to Connecticut. They would be reinforced by two thousand state troopers plus thousands of Marines and paratroopers on standby in neighboring states. Both Chauncey and Police Chief Ahern feared the troops would provoke violence more than prevent it. Ahern battled with the governor and state police chief to retain command of minute-by-minute deployments. Through Vance, Brewster and Chauncey made contact with emissaries whom the White House sent to New Haven, such as Assistant Attorney General William Ruckelshaus.

It was enough of a challenge for Ahern to prepare his officers, many of them working-class whites who resented the taunts and lawlessness of student radicals. He had sent teams to Chicago and Washington, D.C., to study police strategies for disturbances there. Ahern hoped to learn from their mistakes, especially those made in Chicago, where the cops started a riot by attacking unarmed hippies outside the 1968 Democratic National Convention. The "politics of confrontation" had failed in D.C., too, Ahern concluded. He rejected the D.C. police department's policy of making as many arrests as possible when crowds turn unruly. That only made crowds angrier, determined to avenge their captured comrades.

Understanding the challenge of breaking with such established patterns, Ahern struggled to dampen the hysteria generated by the FBI. The New Haven FBI office, pressured by J. Edgar Hoover for a continuous flow of information and evidence of action, was forwarding every drip of hearsay that came its way. Hoover had instructed the New Haven office, beginning on April 24, to file a daily report titled "Threatened Racial Violence New Haven, Connecticut; Racial Matters." Local agents had always collected the tidbits from the New Haven police department's wiretaps and vast network of informants. Usually, they were careful to distinguish the nuggets of reliable data from the mass of gossip, casual conversation, speculation, and misunderstood messages. Now, it all went straight to Washington, on to the president, as "definite" threats.

The New York police department passed along a lead, clearly identified as unconfirmed, that some Weather Underground members involved in prior bombings planned to hit "bank and commercial buildings only." By the time it reached the White House and the CIA, it had shed any trappings of doubt. The same was true of a report of a Yale SDS plot to trash a shopping center. Ahern recognized the report. It had originated within his own department. Sources said the radicals had merely mentioned the idea and then discarded it. The FBI version left that seemingly crucial part out. Ahern's crew had called New York bus companies to disprove a rumor that black militants there had reserved forty-five buses for May Day. Yet the FBI's report, conjuring visions of a race war, merely passed the rumor along as confirmed, just the way it did with a supposed "plot afoot to attempt the blackout of New Haven." Ahern had heard that same vague rumor surface before virtually every other major demonstration. (A New York Panther defense group's publication did advertise bus trips for the rally in a full-page ad headlined, "The People Charge Yale With Complicity in the Frame-Up of the New Haven 9.")

The FBI's exaggerations shook Ahern's faith in the quality of data on which the federal government based its decisions about the use of force. "Consciously or unconsciously," he would later write, "the publicly announced decision to move elite combat troops to within striking distance of the May Day demonstration had been based in part on a combination of deception and willingness to believe the worst."

Adding to the conjured hysteria were genuine fears and confirmed facts: the theft of eighteen rifles and shotguns from a Meriden sporting goods store; the theft of hundreds of bayonet-mounted guns from an unguarded truck; the disappearance of 140 pounds of explosive mercury fulminate, used in blasting caps, from a Yale laboratory; a suspicious fire in the Yale law school library's basement. "The current situation at New Haven is extremely volatile and appears to be building to an all-out confrontation between black and white extremists and supervisors with established authority," J. Edgar Hoover wrote to the agents in charge of all mainland FBI offices. "Assistance in the form of funds, arms and personnel may be requested from throughout the United States."

New Haven merchants feared random vandalism akin to what happened during the SDS "Days of Rage" the previous October, when white radicals ran down Chicago streets throwing rocks through windows; downtown business owners boarded up their storefronts and closed for the duration of the siege. Resentment coursed through New Haven's neighborhoods at the occupation of their city. Hundreds of Yale students had trimmed their hair, dressed neatly, and canvassed the neighborhoods to discuss the upcoming rally with New Haveners; they learned that white middle-class New Haven blamed them and the Panthers, not the police or the courts or the Man, for all this trouble.

Hardest to swallow for white radicals, eager conscripts in the war for black liberation, was the resentment of New Haven's black community. The Black Coalition, which had kept its distance from the Panthers but also raised money for their legal defense, was immersed in planning to help keep peace on May Day. It found time to write a devastating attack on "so-called allies of the oppressed," who claimed to pursue justice for the Panther defendants but truly sought the thrill of violent confrontation. "From their sometimes contradictory rhetoric and frantic posturing, blacks can see that the white radicals are only different in method from their daddies and granddaddies in the callous manipulation of the lives of black people," read the coalition's statement. "The truth in New Haven, as in most of the country, is that the white radical, by frantically and selfishly seeking his personal psychological release, is sharing in the total white conspiracy of denial against the black people."

Another group working in New Haven's poorer neighborhoods during the weekend, the Black and Spanish Community Control Network, directed its anger toward right-wing groups and people in power, rather than toward the radicals. "As the silent majority reactionaries arm themselves in panic, as irrational white crazies contemplate destroying this demonstration, as white hoodlums threaten to invade our neighborhoods, as local police refuse to legitimize our efforts to peacefully help prevent provocative situations, as federal troops and the National Guard-trained and not-so-trained killers mobilize around us . . . we Black and Spanish people can plainly see the threat to our survival."

Even if black neighborhoods weren't embracing the Panthers or their erstwhile student sympathizers, they were boiling with frustration. The zeitgeist was captured by an urgent, pulsating Temptations song about to burst its way up the charts, called "Ball of Confusion."

> *Segregation, determination, demonstration, integration,*
> *Aggravation, humiliation, obligation to our nation.*
> *Ball of confusion.*
> *That's what the world is today.*

Black Coalition organizers hoped to keep as much of black New Haven, especially young people, in the neighborhoods away from Yale and the Green on May Day—and to keep the largely white pro-Panther invaders out of the residential neighborhoods. Some of the marshals would stay by the Green, ready to intercede with any local people causing trouble, and would keep an eye on police brutality. Unlike the Panthers, whose core of local activists never numbered more than a couple dozen and rarely organized a sizable following in New Haven's black community (beyond the crowds of high school students lured to demonstrations), the coalition found neighbors eager to enlist in the cause of keeping the peace.

People like Sheldon Rhinehart made time to join the patrol. Rhinehart worked for the post office. He'd started as a clerk, then moved his way up in pursuit of a middle-class life that would eventually lead to a house in Hamden and serving as the area's first black postmaster. Active in the black postal workers' union, Rhinehart helped quadruple the number of blacks hired in New Haven by questioning the patronage system that reserved openings for the politically favored. Like the Panthers, Rhinehart came under surveillance for his activism. But he wore a jacket and tie to work, inviting taunts of Uncle Tom-ism from the Panthers. Rhinehart would get in arguments with the Panthers when they would crash a recruitment class Rhinehart ran in the Newhallville neighborhood that included teaching young blacks how to apply for jobs and dress for work. "Why are you doing that?" the Panthers would ask him. To which he'd reply, "If they're working, they won't rip my house off. If I can get them in where I can see them, then we're helping the neighborhood." The Panthers told him he was full of crap. The Panthers' presence in town did help him; when superiors at the postal service accused him of being too radical, Rhinehart could always point to the Panthers as a bigger threat.

TWO DAYS BEFORE May Day, riots erupted at Ohio State University. Guardsman and Columbus police shot hundreds of rounds of tear gas and pepper gas at students, trying to prevent students from gathering on the second day. Hundreds were arrested, scores injured.

From the Oval Office to Kingman Brewster's Woodbridge Hall, from dorm rooms to Middle American living rooms, foreboding, a sense of inevitability, loomed. Then, just hours before May Day, President Nixon went on TV to announce an expansion of the Southeast Asian battlefield. U.S. troops, he said, would invade Cambodia, until then neutral territory in the Vietnam War. "My fellow Americans," Nixon said, "we live in an age of anarchy, both abroad and at home. We see mindless attacks on all the great institutions which have been created by free civilizations in the last 500 years. Even here in the United States, great universities are being systematically destroyed." Nixon articulated a rationale for domestic and foreign policy that contradicted Kingman Brewster's vision to the core: "If when the chips are down the world's most powerful nation—the United States of America—acts like a pitiful, helpless giant, the forces of totalitarianism and anarchy will threaten free nations and free institutions throughout the world."

Behind the scenes, Nixon himself was moving toward what critics saw as the road to totalitarianism. Nixon's aides battled with J. Edgar Hoover's FBI to expand the massive illegal surveillance and disruption of domestic dissident groups. A White House aide introduced a plan to authorize the CIA and military intelligence to do what, unbeknownst at that point even to many insiders, the FBI was already doing on a wide scale under COINTELPRO: eavesdropping on people, opening their mail, breaking into their homes. The aide noted in a memo that the plan was illegal; Nixon still approved it. Feeling his turf threatened, Hoover fought back until Nixon cancelled the plan. Still, Hoover's number-two at the FBI, W. Mark Felt, believed, according to one later newspaper account, that he had to guard against encroachments by the Nixon staff, whom he likened to Nazis. (His concerns about Nixon's meddling in law enforcement for political aims, combined with anger over being passed over for promotion as Hoover's successor, would lead Felt to become the *Washington Post*'s "Deep Throat" source on its coverage of the Watergate scandal that prematurely ended the Nixon presidency.)

Even Felt—a supporter of Hoover and COINTELPRO who personally authorized illegal black-bag jobs on radicals—apparently concluded that illegal activities went too far within the FBI, too; he "had to stop efforts by others in the bureau to 'identify every member of every hippie commune' in the Los Angeles area, for example, or to open a file on every member of Students for a Democratic Society."

Within hours, Nixon's announcement about Cambodia would plunge universities across America into convulsions. Brewster and Chauncey heard from a Yale alumnus who was an active, moderate Republican; this alum reported that Nixon and Agnew wanted one university to explode in violence in order to fan hostility toward academia among the majority of Americans.

At the very least, Chief Ahern reasoned, Nixon knew the announcement of the Cambodia invasion would provoke outrage from the antiwar movement—at the very moment thousands of the movement's most devoted shock troops were streaming into New Haven. Whether or not Nixon wanted to provoke a battle, he had reason to anticipate one—hence all the troops he dispatched.

Word spread that the guardsmen had been told that, if they had to shoot, they would face no repercussion. More than six hundred credentialed reporters from around the world arrived in New Haven awaiting the bloodshed. Many checked into the Park Plaza Hotel a block south of the Green. Chief Ahern had someone surreptitiously photograph every hotel visitor. He told Sam Chauncey about one of the faces that appeared in the camera: White House Counsel John Dean. No one in Washington had said Dean was coming.

CHAPTER 16

Two Days in May

THIS TIME MARY Brewster spared the Cornish hen. She had another spread to prepare for one of Kingman's furtive get-togethers. This one was taking place after midnight, hours before the opening of the planned three-day pro-Panther May Day gathering. Kingman invited a motley group of guests to the two-story living room of the Yale presidential mansion on Hillhouse Avenue. Mary didn't particularly enjoy the company of some of these people. Fortunately, she wouldn't have to socialize. Kingman had important business to conduct with the middle-of-the-night guests; Mary gladly assumed the role of hostess. She put out beer, booze, and milk with cookies.

The guest list included Kingman's former Yale classmate and radical attorney William Kuntsler. Kuntsler was in town to join the Panther/Yippie brigade. Kingman fretted that the rally organizers had no handle on the details of the program they were running later that day. Confusion horrified him more than the most incendiary tirades.

Other organizers accompanying Kuntsler included David Dellinger, Tom Hayden, and Yippie Jerry Rubin, who'd been stretching his vocal cords in denunciation of Yale. Unbeknownst to the multitudes ready to congregate in protest hours later, these movement heavies were meeting with the avatar of Yale power and privilege. The protest leaders and Brewster got along like old college buddies. In these final hours, their agendas, even the police chief's agenda, had fully converged. The movement and the establishment—at least the New Haven wing—were on the same page. Brewster and Chauncey agreed with the protesters that Yale must do its best to keep gates open in the event of trouble and to try to move the invading army of guardsmen and state cops as far away as possible from contact with the hordes of ralliers on the Green. For their part, the radicals needed to hammer the nonviolent message home.

WHEN DAWN BROKE on May 1, people were still digesting the previous night's stunning news of Nixon's Cambodian invasion, as well as the breaking news of a police raid on Panthers in Baltimore. Even so, Bobby and Ericka would remain the focus for the day's outrage in New Haven. Visiting demonstrators, who were guests in the residential colleges, lined up for breakfast served by volunteers in the college courtyards. Other volunteers set up first aid stations. Vietcong flags filled the air; gas masks were distributed in anticipation of a repeat of the Guard's conduct at Ohio State. Slogans screamed from banners in the colleges, from graffiti, from bedsheets, from impromptu chants: "Seize the Time!" "Burn, Babylon." "End U.S. imperialism around the world!"

Tanks took up positions on the roads leading into New Haven; on the Green, a fresh coat of grease on the pole protected Old Glory from potential flag burners. The First Battalion of the 102nd infantry, based in New Haven, assembled for duty, joined by the Waterbury area's Second Battalion, the 192nd infantry's Third Battalion from Stamford and Greenwich, and the 242nd Engineer Battalion from Stratford. At a battalion meeting at the Goffe Street Armory, Guardsmen received ammunition, gas grenades, and a pep talk: Expect to see fifty thousand people out there on the Green. Don't worry if you feel a need to use weapons. "You will not be successfully prosecuted if you shoot someone while performing a duty for the State of Connecticut. There is nothing to fear concerning your individual actions."

Four hours before the scheduled start of the official rally on the Green, the protest organizers assembled in the Center Church for a raucous press conference. More than a thousand supporters packed the sanctuary. They whooped it up like students at a pregame pep rally. "Fuck Kingston Brewer!" Jerry Rubin led the crowd in chanting. He didn't mention his chummy visit with Brewster hours earlier. Dressed, according to an account by student chronicler John Taft, "in baggy, wine-colored pants and a tie-dyed tee shirt of yellow, turquoise and red," his long dark locks a multi-directional mess, Rubin screamed as he led the crowd in more "Fuck [Various Bad Guys]" chants for the TV cameras.

Though increasingly hoarse, Rubin kept up his tirade for over an hour. Along the way he managed to trivialize every last serious Pantherite complaint about genuine oppression with his caricature of privileged white whining. "The most oppressed people in America are white middle-class youth," Rubin declared. "We don't want to work in our daddy's business. We don't want to be a college professor, a prosecutor, or a judge. We're something else. . . . We ain't never, never, never gonna grow up. We will always be adolescents; we ain't never gonna be rational. . . . We are everything they say we are. I haven't taken a bath for six months."

A mostly white sea of disaffected American youth, peppered with young black Panther supporters, filled the Green for the noon start of the Big Rally, Day One. The half million hadn't materialized. The fifty thousand hadn't, either. The total was closer to fifteen thousand. Still, the Green felt like a liberated zone for New Haven's white radicals. They stripped down. They tossed Frisbees. They smoked joints. And they were not being arrested.

Battle-ready law enforcement officers and uniformed National Guardsmen remained just off the Green on adjoining blocks. They kept their distance as rock music blared from the stage. Local COINTELPRO chief Ted Gunderson had a dozen long-haired informants mingling in the crowd, with a phone number to call in case of trouble. He'd imported them from other cities. He and his fellow FBI agents were to be on duty for three twenty-four-hour days; they caught catnaps in the hotel room out of which they were working. They took photos of the crowd, including a clear shot of a naked male protester doing calisthenics. At one point an informant called with a sighting of a wanted Weatherman fugitive. By the time Gunderson's men arrived in search of the fugitive, he had disappeared.

The unkempt white protesters and fastidious black radicals converging on New Haven's Green presented just the image President Nixon and the FBI's Hoover wanted America to see. By provoking violence—through COINTELPRO's dirty tricks against the Panthers, through a militaristic approach to student demonstrations—the federal government led the white mainstream to view the hippies, the Black Power advocates, and the peaceniks and integrationists as dangerous threats to the American way. This would leave establishment-oriented liberal whites—the true threats to people like Nixon and Hoover—in an uncomfortable position.

In the wake of Alex Rackley's murder and the showdowns on the streets between protesters and government troops, Nixon, Hoover, and their horde of conservative pundits transformed the country's once-noble definition of liberalism by playing on white fears of the darker race. No longer did liberalism represent courageous advocacy of the rights of the minority or the oppressed. It was becoming a code word for cowardice in the face of demands by the black and the unwashed. To Nixon and his "silent majority," courage came to mean "standing up" to black demands.

The FBI kept intelligence flowing all day to J. Edgar Hoover, who then sent teletypes to the offices of President Nixon, the vice president, the CIA director, and the attorney general. Like a child's game of telephone, the information was distorted as it made its way up, down, and across the tangled chains of command. Facts mingled with rumors to convey imminent doom: "30 Weathermen Faction of SDS members were on campus with Abbie Hoffman." "Armed" Blackstone Rangers and Hartford Panthers were "attempting to secure trucks and buses to come to New Haven."

All the while, the neighborhoods stayed quiet. On the Green, speeches began around 4 o'clock. They went on for two and a half hours. A succession of Yippies resumed swearing at Kingman Brewster and, of course, the cops. Black Panther speakers decried the Seale-Huggins prosecution. While the rhetoric was militant, everyone kept true to their promises to Brewster and to each other. The speakers counseled staying calm, and the crowd was with them. Soon everyone dispersed for food, more speeches, and rehashed arguments in Yale's residential courtyards.

WARREN KIMBRO WATCHED all of the demonstrations on a black-and-white TV. At the direction of the corrections department, Warren and fellow confessed Panther felon George Sams were transferred from their cells in the Brooklyn jail to the state police barracks in eastern Connecticut for the duration of May Day.

A guard had come to fetch Warren from his cell, earlier after breakfast; he was reading. "They're here to pick you up," the guard said. Warren figured this had something to do with the rally. Reading his daily *New York*

Young Warren Kimbro on Spruce Street. FROM THE PERSONAL COLLECTION OF WARREN KIMBRO.

Warren and Sylvia
before the Revolution.
FROM THE PERSONAL
COLLECTION OF WARREN
KIMBRO.

Warren in Korea. FROM
THE PERSONAL COLLECTION
OF WARREN KIMBRO.

Young Veronica Kimbro.
FROM THE PERSONAL COLLECTION
OF WARREN KIMBRO.

Young Germano Kimbro.
FROM THE PERSONAL COLLECTION
OF WARREN KIMBRO.

Lonnie McLucas (at left) and Warren Kimbro (at right) at a "Free Huey" in downtown New Haven shortly before the murder of Alex Rackley. PHOTO COURTESY OF DAVID DICKSON.

Scenes from the New Haven Green during the Mayday protests. MANUSCRIPTS AND ARCHIVES, YALE UNIVERSITY LIBRARY.

Jerry Rubin at
Mayday protest.
Photo Credit: Yale
Manuscripts &
Archives.

Protesters on the New
Haven Green during
the Mayday protests.
Manuscripts and
Archives, Yale
University Library.

A March through downtown New Haven on behalf of Ericka Huggins and the other Black Panthers jailed for the Rackley murder. PHOTO COURTESY OF DAVID DICKSON.

Brewster faces the press
as May Day nears.
MANUSCRIPTS AND
ARCHIVES, YALE
UNIVERSITY LIBRARY.

Kingman Brewster (left) on
tranquil Hillhouse Avenue.
MANUSCRIPTS AND ARCHIVES,
YALE UNIVERSITY LIBRARY.

The National Guard and the local police were ready for war. MANUSCRIPTS AND ARCHIVES, YALE UNIVERSITY LIBRARY.

A fire broke out at the New Politics Corner across from the New Haven Green at Church and Elm streets. MANUSCRIPTS AND ARCHIVES, YALE UNIVERSITY LIBRARY.

Ericka Huggins right after being freed by Judge Mulvey.
PHOTO COURTESY OF HARTFORD COURANT.

Catherine Roraback, second from left, outside New Haven's courthouse with clients Frances Carter, far left; Margaret Hudgins, Rosemarie Smith; and fellow attorney L. Scott Melville. PHOTO COURTESY OF THE HARTFORD COURANT.

Dean Kimbro at
Eastern Connecticut
State University.
PHOTO COURTESY OF
THE KIMBRO FAMILY.

Dean Kimbro at
Eastern Connecticut
State University.
PHOTO COURTESY OF THE
KIMBRO FAMILY.

A new grandfather. FROM THE PERSONAL COLLECTION OF WARREN KIMBRO.

Warren and Beverly. PHOTO COURTESY OF THE KIMBRO FAMILY.

Sam Chauncey, circa 1995.
PHOTO CREDIT: KATHLEEN CEI
OF THE NEW HAVEN ADVOCATE.

Nick Pastore (center left) accepts an award from Warren (center right) at a Project
MORE ceremony. FROM THE PERSONAL COLLECTION OF WARREN KIMBRO.

From left: Warren, U.S. Sen. Joe Lieberman, and Germano Kimbro at an awards ceremony for Germano's male-involvement program. From the Personal collection of Warren Kimbro.

Times, *New Haven Register*, and *Hartford Courant*, watching the evening news, Warren had kept up with May Day. During her Saturday visits, his sister Betty told him she'd heard some kids planned to tear up the Green.

Warren followed the guard to the receiving area of the jail, where state troopers waited. Sams, whom Warren saw every day in jail, was there, too. The troopers cuffed each of them, in front rather than the usual, more humbling, rear position. Sams and Warren rode in separate state police cars, accompanied by two troopers each. Separate cars in front and in back formed a procession to the barracks. "What's this all about?" Warren asked the troopers in his car. They told him he was going to the barracks for his own protection. Officials feared the May Day protests might lead to a riot in the jails. They feared that the state's two key witnesses could become a target of rioters.

At the barracks, Warren got his own cell. He and Sams were the only prisoners there. Warren spent the day smoking cigarettes, drinking coffee, reading newspapers. The barracks had a cafeteria; the troopers asked him what he wanted to eat. Warren went through two cheeseburgers in a common area as he and Sams watched the news reports of May Day on TV. Warren looked at the masses of protesters, listened to the claims that there had been no murder, or if there had, that the Panthers had been framed.

"Do they really know?" he thought to himself. He remembered when he first went to jail, how he convinced himself of his own innocence, how he convinced himself the government somehow carried out this murder, even when he knew he himself pulled the trigger. Although he did agree that the government was framing Bobby Seale, Warren didn't see the point of the rally. And Abbie Hoffman and Jerry Rubin—what phonies they seemed to Warren, the kind of egotists who told kids to throw bricks they would never pick up themselves. It was all, Warren concluded, just another big show.

SCENES OF COMIC absurdity mixed with the fiery speeches in Yale's courtyards that evening. A knot of white visitors, frustrated at a Black Panther's exhortation to cut the talk of violence, shot back, "We're more oppressed than you are" because of "our long hair." Echoes of anarchist Emma Goldman's famous line—"If I can't dance, I don't want to be part of your revolution"—could be heard inside the common room of Timothy Dwight

College, where Chicago 8 coconspirator Lee Weiner addressed sixty people. "I want to make a revolution in this country. I want to destroy it," Weiner assured the group. "But my revolution's going to have to be fun."

The beat poet Allen Ginsberg recited a poem he had written for the occasion. In twenty-one lines, Ginsberg managed to pay homage to the rites historically performed on May 1 (before it became an international holiday honoring workers), the personalities, the national political currents, the holiday, countercultural aspirations, and even the New Haven landscape. No AP reporter on the scene could have crammed as much detail and color into so few lines. Ginsberg called the poem "May King's Prophecy."

> Spring green buddings, white blossoming trees, May Day picnic
> O Maypole Kings O Krishnaic Springtime
> O holy Yale Panther Pacifist Conscious populace awake alert
>   sensitive tender
> Children's bodies—and a ring of quiet Armies round the town—
> Planet students cooking brown rice for scared multitudes—
> Oh Souls all springtime prays your bodies
> Quietly pass mantric peace Fest grass freedom thru our nation
>   thru your holy voices' prayers
> Your bodies here so tender & so wounded with Fear
> Metal gas fear, the same fear Whales tremble war consciousness
> Smog city—Riot court paranoia—Judges, tremble, Armies
>   weep your fear—
> O President guard thy sanity
> Attorneys General & Courts obey the Law
> And end your violent War Assemblage
> O Legislatures pass your Creeds of order
> & end by proper law illegal war!
> Now man sits Acme Conscious over his gas machine covered Planet—
> Springtime's on, for all your sacred & Satanic Magic!
> Ponds gleam heaven, Black voices chant their ecstasy on car radio
> Oh who has heard the scream of death in Jail?
> Who has heard the quiet Om under wheel-whine and drumbeat
> Outside railyards on wire tower'd outroads from New Haven?

Around 9:30 P.M., a black teenager crashed the gathering in Branford College's courtyard. He claimed to be a Panther. He wasn't. Whom he truly represented, who sent him, no one would ever know. He shoved Jerry Rubin from a microphone to announce that police had arrested black men for entering the Green after dark. That, too, would prove a lie; no one had been arrested. The teen exhorted the crowd to crash the Green to confront the cops. "To the Green!" chanted motorcycle-helmet-wearing white youths from a militant outfit called Youth Against War and Fascism.

Rubin reclaimed the mike, channeling the spirit of the meeting with "Kingston Brewer." "Don't go down there!" Rubin yelled. Long after his midday rant, his voice still hadn't given out. "This is full of shit!"

Too late—the fragile peace was broken. Other provocateurs stormed a rock concert on the Old Campus. They brought the same false message to Stiles College, where Abbie Hoffman had just finished urging people to stay calm. A fired-up band proceeded out of Stiles. "The streets belong to the people," they chanted, and proceeded to smash the windows of stores apparently owned by non-"people" on Broadway.

By 10 P.M., the streams converged in a parade of more than one thousand violence-bent white people, many of them from out of town. They marched to the end of the Green opposite the courthouse. Hundreds of National Guard reinforcements arrived to supplement the four hundred who were already there from the afternoon. Walls of Guardsmen and local police fenced off the courthouse steps.

Calls for help went to the Panther Defense Committee headquarters. Doug Miranda raced all over, chasing after hot spots. He took the Old Campus stage and convinced crowds of protesters to remain in place. Then he sped to the Green. He joined teams of student and Panther monitors who fanned out and urged the marchers to return to campus. Throughout the center of New Haven, dozens of Panthers—one estimate ran as high as hundreds—worked the streets. After all the suggestions across the country of a violent Panther outbreak, coming from the Panthers and J. Edgar Hoover alike, the party had a chance to ignite Armageddon, to pull the trigger on the starting gun for the great Panther-hippie revolt in the streets. Instead, party members frantically worked to keep the peace in concert with every stripe of "pig" found in the Black Panther bestiary.

Most of the great May Day assemblage heeded their words. The hold-outs in front of the courthouse were determined to continue. They ignored the present and prior pleas of Panthers, the black and white Yale student monitors, and Bobby Seale himself. It didn't matter that a false rumor about Panther arrests, a call supposedly to defend the Panthers, brought them here in the first place. The out-of-towners, the hard-core thousand or so self-styled revolutionaries crashing New Haven, were in command now.

A bottle was thrown at the guardsmen and police. Bricks and cherry bombs followed. Finally, the police responded by shooting tear-gas canisters into the crowd. They pushed the demonstrators away from the Green. The demonstrators, still ignoring the marshals' furious pleas, regrouped a few blocks southwest, at Temple and Chapel streets. Through megaphones, marshals read a statement Bobby Seale had released through his wife, Artie; it called this kind of confrontation dangerous to the Panther cause.

Most of the demonstrators chilled out. A few resumed hurling bottles and rocks. Again, more tear gas. The police pushed them toward Phelps Gate, the Old Campus entrance planned to absorb crowds at moments of trouble.

Marshals formed lines to separate the holdouts who continued facing down the cops from the majority ready to retreat into the Old Campus. Just then, Sam Chauncey's longstanding order somehow got lost as an on-duty police officer started closing the gates. This was the nightmare scenario Chauncey and Brewster had worked so hard to avoid. Chauncey received a call at the command center on Temple Street. He furiously phoned the campus cops and ordered the gate opened. A statement from William Farley was read over a sound system telling the crowd it could find shelter inside Old Campus.

The majority of the protesters joined the rest of the assemblage in the Old Campus courtyard. Refugees from the clash washed their eyes at first-aid stations. Allen Ginsberg was at the microphone tapping universal Buddha consciousness amid the stinging cloud.

"Ommmmmmmmmmm," Ginsberg chanted, as he had done in the midst of the police riot in Chicago a year earlier. People dabbed at his eyes with wet towels.

Out on the street, holdouts refused to abandon their stare-down with Richard Nixon's National Guard. The guardsmen stood with bayonets pointed. More rocks and bottles flew. The guard set off thirty gas grenades; reporters and protesters struggled to breathe and see through the thickest, most debilitating gas fog they'd experienced yet in America's ongoing "youth rebellion." The reporters scurried to Crown Street, the last band of protesters to the Old Campus. Allen Ginsberg was still chanting; he paused only to blow accentuating notes into a harmonium. Some of the soaked, disheveled protesters chanted with him. Eventually, Doug Miranda took the mike and excoriated troublemakers. Out in the streets more gas was released. Students fled to residential colleges away from the Old Campus, seeking refuge on top floors where they could gasp more air.

Minutes before midnight, the clashes over, gas clouds still covering the blocks in and around the Green, a more peaceful assembly was breaking up four long blocks north. Rock bands had just finished playing for hundreds of May Dayers inside the Yale Whale, aka Ingalls Rink, site of the beating of the deranged Lebanese graduate student during David Hilliard's speech a week earlier. Two bombs exploded from the basement beneath the stage just as the last band finished packing up. The force was strong enough to blow out glass from both ends of the rink. The whale's ceiling arch cracked. Miraculously, everyone escaped serious injury.

Inside the Alumni House, Cyrus Vance's advice flashed in Chauncey's mind. He called the news desk at the local AM radio station. Chauncey knew the reporter on the desk, and he assured him that the situation was not nearly so serious as it may have sounded on the police radio. As emergency response personnel raced to assess the crowd and collect evidence, the story stayed off New Haven's midnight airwaves.

Investigators, combing through the wreckage, found no definitive signs of the perpetrators. Chauncey and Brewster wondered about the motive. Although no one could be sure, it seemed to them that the perpetrator had to come from the right; a bombing served the right's purposes, not the left's, by portraying the protest movement as violent and scary in the eyes of mainstream society. They suspected dirty tricks from the Nixon administration. They could never prove it. While the explosion would remain unsolved, Chauncey would never stop believing that it was the work of operatives from the Nixon administration.

May 1 ended with New Haven intact. On film, it looked like war in the streets around the Green. Thousands of participants certainly tasted the chemical air of catastrophic confrontation. Yet in the end, it was more of a full-costumed rehearsal, frightening and dangerous enough for those at the scene. A few windows were broken. Citywide, police made only twenty-one arrests all day, mostly on minor charges, some unrelated to May Day. Two police officers and a few demonstrators went to the city's two hospitals, which had geared themselves for massive emergencies. The injuries were minor, the victims released not long after being admitted.

OF COURSE, THE city couldn't relax yet; there were still two days of scheduled protests ahead. On the morning of the second day, Saturday, May 2, new rumors sent cops hunting for Molotov cocktails and other trouble.

Some young New Haveners, like attorney Hugh Keefe, found themselves in conflicting roles. Keefe represented two of the jailed Panthers, Landon Williams and Rory Hithe. He liked them. He had visited the New Haven Green on Friday and had a great time. It had felt like a party. An Irish-American scrapper recently graduated from the University of Connecticut's law school, Keefe spent months mastering the multistep Black Power handshake. The effort paid off on the Green, where he and the other lawyers spent what seemed like hours just shaking hands. Arriving home at midnight, Keefe got a call—from his National Guard sergeant, who'd been looking for him all day. Keefe reported immediately to New London to join his battalion. He caught a few hours' sleep in the armory there.

Before dawn on Saturday, the unit headed back to New Haven for another day of patrols, M16s in hand. The comments of his fellow guardsmen over the course of the day made Keefe shudder. Their ugly talk betrayed that they had no understanding of the protests, about the underlying complaints about the Panther case, about the war in Southeast Asia. Keefe thought back to comments he heard from recruits in basic training in 1967 about their mission to "fight and kill Commies." This sounded eerily similar.

As he drove the colonel's jeep around New Haven, Keefe feared the guard more than he feared the crowd on the Green. He took heart in his empty M16; Chief Ahern had insisted the Guard patrol without bullets.

In the afternoon the Panthers and the Yippies returned to the Green. The crowd had dwindled from the day before. A pilot made a peace sign in the sky; it reflected the tone of another day of celebratory, pacific protest, although it took effort to maintain high energy.

"Fuck Kingman Brewer—or whatever his name is!" proclaimed Jerry Rubin.

"Fuck Jerry Rubin!" some local protesters responded.

Artie Seale played a tape-recorded message from Bobby Seale about the injustices inherent in his trial. From the May Day stage came the first announcement of a nationwide student strike called for the following week, over the invasion of Cambodia. Doug Miranda offered a fiery call for disciplined revolution—organized resistance to America's racist power structure. He continued the theme of avoiding suicidal May Day weekend attacks on the cops. Then he closed with a reassurance to militants that the Panther hadn't lost its roar, that it'll strike, sure enough, once the time is right. He told the crowd that New Haven could still be "leveled at any time."

"All power to the people," Miranda called in his high-pitched voice. "And when the word is given, all power to the good shooters!"

The day ended with a speech by SDS leader Tom Hayden. He offered a remarkable synopsis of where he and other white leaders had taken May Day and the New Haven Panther cause, of what the murder of Alex Rackley had come to mean to the movement.

"Facts are as irrelevant in this case in Connecticut, as facts are irrelevant about Vietnam and whether the Vietcong commit terror," Hayden declared into the microphone. "If people are worried about these things, we should say one thing: the U.S. should withdraw its troops from Vietnam and from the ghettoes and let the people in Vietnam and the ghettoes of this country decide for themselves."

"A lot of educated people," Tom Hayden exhorted the crowd, "are going to have to be convinced that the facts are irrelevant!"

Hayden was one of the nation's preeminent student radicals. The New Haven event came at a turning point in Hayden's activist career and in the fate of SDS, his organization. SDS once drew tens of thousands of committed activists to organize thoughtful opposition to the war in Vietnam and support for civil rights. Then impatience, drugs, government infiltration, fatigue and frustration, and sectarian power struggles splintered the group into ever-smaller, warring factions. Some, like the Weathermen, went underground to plot bombings. Others drifted away from the movement. No one had the time or the interest or the energy to worry about facts any more.

In New Haven, they were even losing interest in the Panther case. There would be no Day Three to May Day weekend in New Haven. After Hayden's speech, organizers decided to cut off the rest of the gathering. Practically everyone was leaving town anyway. New conflicts beckoned elsewhere in the country; a new chapter was beginning in the war at home over the war in Southeast Asia. Even John Dean had seen all he needed to see. According to his account of his visit to New Haven, he spent an uneventful day "in the company of personnel from the FBI, the U.S. Marshals Office, local law enforcement and Department of Justice."

That night, another fire would hit a left-of-center target, a building off the New Haven Green housing a reform Democratic organization called the New Politics Corner. Investigators concluded that the fire was an accident, the result of a faulty oil burner. Inside sound trucks, Panthers shooed people away, branding the fire the work of provocateurs hoping to incite violence. Either way, it didn't cause much damage. The last remnants of the white militants did confront the guard and the cops, in smaller numbers, with fewer bottles and rocks. They got to taste some more tear gas; the guard had had enough.

"Send them back to Africa," remarked one guardsman.

"If they grab your weapon," a company commander instructed the troops on the way to this last confrontation, "break their fucking arms."

THEN IT WAS over. Call it luck. Call it brilliant planning. Call it a conspiracy between the Man and the Panther. Whatever the reason, death and destruction passed by New Haven.

America wouldn't be so lucky. As the National Guard battled the kids in New Haven, violence marked antiwar demonstrations at Oregon State and Hobart College in upstate New York. Stanford saw a window-smashing spree. New strikes were announced at Rutgers and Princeton in New Jersey and Temple in Philadelphia. Fifteen hundred students gathered to ransack an ROTC building at the University of Maryland.

Two days later, on May 4, National Guardsmen at Kent State University in Ohio, armed with the same weaponry and orders as their brethren in New Haven, shot into a crowd of unarmed student protesters. "Four dead in Ohio," Crosby, Stills, Nash & Young would sing of the victims.

Stunned, outraged, students poured out of dormitories coast to coast. The apocalyptic warnings of the violence-prone suddenly sounded true. Even Hillary Rodham's cautious classmates at the Yale Law School finally decided classes had to stop. They finished the semester protesting the war instead of studying for classes.

Even if New Haven had thwarted a desire within the Nixon administration for a bloodbath, the peace proved only temporary. Workers in hard hats beat demonstrators on Wall Street. Police shot to death two more students, black students this time, one a high schooler, during a riot at Mississippi's Jackson State College. Long-haired students were costarring with the Vietcong on middle America's evening news.

CHAPTER 17

Taking the Stand

THE MOVEMENT, OR its fragments, took a decided turn after those bloody, tear-gas-filled days in May. Some radical activists hardened their outlooks and their tactics. But many young people turned inward, reexamining their flirtation with risky protest outside the system.

The Panthers and their dwindling supporters had a seemingly endless string of court cases to deal with. Some would offer them an opportunity to make their case anew about injustices of the American legal system. Once the Rackley murder trial got under way in New Haven, the Panthers found one of their most visible and promising stages for that case.

THE MORNING OF April 13, 1971, brought a change of wardrobe for Warren Kimbro. He had a date in court on the witness stand.

The state needed Warren to look credible; he was the first major witness against the leading Panthers on trial for allegedly playing indirect but leading roles in the murder of Alex Rackley. The state wanted to kill national Chairman Bobby Seale. It also wanted to execute Ericka Huggins—a lover whose memory still accelerated Warren's heartbeat, still raced through his thoughts as he languished in his cell or pecked out embellished accounts of their sexual encounters on his Olivetti Praxis typewriter.

The state's claim was that Ericka and Seale had ordered less senior Panthers—Sams, Kimbro, McLucas—to carry out the murder of Alex Rackley. If convicted, Ericka and Seale would be guilty of a capital crime and, given popular sentiment, at grave risk of execution. Nobody had been put to death in Connecticut since 1960, when Joseph "Mad Dog" Taborsky was electrocuted for a string of murders committed in the act of robbing liquor and shoe stores.

Warren didn't want to see either of them die. But he was no longer on their side. He had pleaded guilty. He prayed for forgiveness for pulling the trigger that ended Alex Rackley's life. He wanted to serve the shortest life sentence in state history. He promised to cooperate with the state. He also promised to tell the truth, even if the truth left no one pleased with him.

Warren knew the prosecutor, Arnie Markle, wanted him to give up Bobby Seale. Sams claimed that Bobby Seale had given Sams and Warren the order to kill Alex Rackley. Warren knew that had never happened. Warren couldn't follow Sams's lead on the major evidence just because Arnie Markle had looked out for him. Markle's people were hoping for a Perry Mason–style moment when Warren took the stand. Warren knew they were disparaging him for refusing to put the murder order in Seale's mouth; they accused him of fearing Panther retribution. Warren didn't fear retribution. He didn't want to lie anymore—not to himself or to the jury.

And then there was Ericka. Warren told himself that he didn't have any information that could send her to the electric chair. That was only partly true, a rationalization. Inevitably, his choice to testify for the government, against Ericka, made it likely that he would help in the effort to convict her. Warren told himself that Ericka was just pretending that day at Ethan Gardens, just playing at being the tough revolutionary. Ericka hadn't been in the swamp. She hadn't told anyone to pull a trigger. Still, Ericka, unlike Bobby Seale, had been in the room at crucial moments leading up to the fateful car ride to Middlefield. She, like Warren, like McLucas, Williams, and Sams, had certainly played a role, whether voluntarily or somewhat under duress, in the events that led to Rackley's torture and murder.

It was quite a stretch for the state to argue that Ericka played a central enough role to justify electrocuting her. But the state, in the person of Markle, was making that stretch. There was no escaping that fact.

Warren had already testified in McLucas's trial the previous summer. That trial was a warm-up for the main event. And it posed no quandary for Warren. McLucas had ratted on him the moment he was arrested. Therefore, Warren felt fine returning the favor. Plus, there was no doubt that Lonnie McLucas fired that insurance bullet into Rackley's body. (McLucas charmed his jury. After a three-month trial, including the longest deliberation in state history, the jury convicted him of just one of four charges connected with the murder. Judge Mulvey gave McLucas the maximum twelve- to fifteen-year sentence.)

Three weeks earlier, Warren had also briefly taken the stand in this trial, in which the state was jointly trying Bobby Seale and Ericka. That appearance was cut short and Warren's testimony suspended until now. Markle had walked Warren through the initial events of the Rackley affair that day, including the torture. Warren had pulled back from identifying Ericka as a key player, as participating, for instance, in beating Rackley. He offered no evidence of Seale's involvement. Then an argument among the lawyers aborted his testimony. Markle prepared to introduce the tape recording, seized by police, of the Rackley interrogation; the Panther lawyers fought to keep it out of evidence for a while pending further argument. So Warren was sent back to the jail in Brooklyn while the trial turned to other witnesses. As the lawyers prepared arguments over whether the jury would hear the damning sounds of the torturers' voices, Warren waited to return to the New Haven court and finish with this ordeal.

Now that the court was ready for him to return, Warren was conflicted. "Just tell the truth," Warren's lawyer, Larry Iannotti, told him. "If you get on the stand and tell the truth, they can't trip you up." Warren repeated the words to himself like a mantra. He reached for other mantras, too, from the Guides for Better Living class, notably the "Serenity Prayer," borrowed from Alcoholics Anonymous: "God grant me the serenity to accept the things I cannot change; courage to change the things I can; and wisdom to know the difference." Warren needed all the mantras he could get to calm his nerves.

A guard took Warren to the property room to change from his khakis to the dark green Herman Pickus suit he stored there. Warren's brother-in-law Ernie had purchased a shirt and tie for him. Warren tied the knot; he thought it looked just right. The shirt was pressed. He looked sharp, though not as sharp as when he'd originally bought the suit and it hugged his 155-pound, six-foot-one-inch frame. Behind bars, Warren had lost ten pounds. Now the suit hung baggy, like it belonged to someone else.

The drive from rural Brooklyn to the New Haven courthouse took about an hour. As usual, a couple of troopers accompanied Warren in one car, escorted by state police cars in front and in back. The troopers were always friendly. "Thank goodness for you Panther guys," one trooper told Warren. "I'm going to have a good time this Christmas" because of all the overtime pay from the trips.

Most prisoners traveled to court appearances in a van. Warren always rode in this special caravan. At first, that was because officials wanted to thwart any escape plans the Panthers might have hatched for their arrested New Haven leader. Now they needed to protect Warren from Panther sympathizers.

The pro-Panther demonstrators held their signs in front of the courthouse steps as the caravan drove by. The crowds had diminished in the more than eleven months since May Day. Yale students returned to the classroom, the activists largely to protesting the war. Nevertheless, the few Panther supporters who showed up daily remained resolute and loud.

"Free Warren!" the protesters used to shout when Warren arrived for pretrial appearances. Then he pleaded guilty and became a state witness. Now, as the police cars rounded the corner, they pointed to Warren and yelled, "Pig!"

Warren closed his eyes and leaned his head back. Serenity; he sought serenity. He opened one eye a slit to see if he recognized anyone. No, no familiar faces today.

The troopers turned left onto Church Street. They pulled into the parking lot behind the white marble courthouse. They escorted Warren, handcuffed and shackled, to the basement lockup. Warren struggled for composure. "Let me get this fucking thing over with," he told himself. "Then let me do my time."

Before pleading guilty, Warren would spend hours inside the claustrophobic metal cages in the basement lockup on court days, just like the other prisoners awaiting their turns before the judge. Prisoners had two kinds of accommodations in the lockup: group cells in which prisoners squeezed together in open pens with a shared toilet in the rear and single closet-wide cells with no toilets. Once Warren went over to the state's side in the case, Warren was spared much time in the lockup and received better treatment. Days like today he made a perfunctory appearance in the basement, then was escorted upstairs to prosecutor Markle's first-floor office. His cuffs were removed. The state couldn't have Warren look like a prisoner, like a guilty man, when he took the stand.

From there, Warren was escorted through the hallway to Courtroom B. He held himself erect. He kept his head up. No matter how he felt at the moment, he didn't want anyone to think he was a defeated man.

Scowls greeted him in the hallway.

"Oh, he's nice looking!" a little girl exclaimed.

"Shut up!" snapped the adult holding her hand, presumably her mother. "He's the pig!"

"Pig!" echoed some white people nearby.

From another corner, Warren heard a black voice say, "We're with you."

AS WARREN PREPARED to take the stand on April 13, FBI staffers in Las Vegas prepared a memo for J. Edgar Hoover in the continuing quest to dream up extralegal plans to thwart the Panthers. The FBI was piling on the covert tactics, exploiting rifts among Panther leaders and instigating new ones. Cases like the one in New Haven had the Panthers on the run, fighting to survive amid recriminations and an exiled and jailed leadership. Eldridge Cleaver, in Algeria, was battling with Huey Newton, who was in Oakland; their factions declared war, and Panthers lost their lives. Somehow, those deaths didn't outrage the true believers demonstrating at courthouses like New Haven's.

The Las Vegas memo contained boilerplate suggestions. The office proposed sending an anonymous letter to the Vegas chapter identifying a local Panther as a police informant. Other suggestions: encourage First Western Savings and Loan to foreclose on the local chapter's building; "substitute names of members in good standing with the local BPP chapter for those listed on a recent flyer as having been expelled."

Though similar tactics had been used all over the country, including in New Haven, even after Alex Rackley's death, this time Hoover turned down the ideas. The "substitution" of lists "could be quickly determined and would, therefore, have little effect," Hoover wrote. The FBI would be embarrassed if evicted Panthers "took some action" against the foreclosed-upon building or against First Western in retaliation.

As for falsely identifying a Panther as an informant, Hoover offered this objection: "Such action could possibly result in a situation similar to that which occurred in Connecticut in May, 1969, when Alex Rackley was tortured and killed by BPP members, if the allegation was believed."

Hoover's hesitation clearly had to do with efficacy, not with moral or ethical concerns. Throughout the trial he approved continued FBI forgeries aimed at sowing the kind of suspicions and fights among Panthers that led to Alex Rackley's death. At one point the New Haven office sent the San Francisco office a letter to forward to Bobby Seale in the Montville jail. Seale had reportedly had a "violent outburst" the night before in his cell, "threw his TV set against the wall and for the remainder that night mumbled phrases such as, 'I am forsaken' and 'I have no support.'"

To further "drive a wedge" between Panther factions, the FBI letter (one of many secret documents that would come to light years later) appeared to come from a California Panther. "Dear Bobby," it read. "Blood, don't think for a minute that there isn't a reason for your sacrifice, but now that we have Huey, a beautiful man, you are not needed as greatly to lead the Party. We all say that you are right-on, but you understand the cause." Hoover approved this plan, which basically involved planting incendiary new disinformation with a man the government claimed was the murder-ordering capo of a violent criminal organization.

Hoover also OK'd the mailing of an anonymous letter to Eldridge Cleaver in Algiers. The approved letter, complete with "misspellings and punctuation errors" in order to add "authentic[ity]," reported on Huey Newton's visit to New Haven during the Seale-Huggins trial. Newton spent most of the time at Yale, including a three-day dialogue with Yale psychologist Erik Erikson.

"Brother," the script read before the further butchering of its spelling and grammar in its final longhand version, "as a dedicated Panther, I feel it necessary to come forth and rap to you about the happenings in New Haven. Thus, Supreme Commander has been here for a week and as yet has not related. Not to cry, but things ain't so well in New Haven. For some time the spot has been without heat and/or a toilet to use. Times are hard. Community is not as receptive as before, and the party here needs help. Supposedly help came when the man come to town. Yet, he ain't been to the community yet. That is not so bad, but he didn't even come to the spot and this went hard with the people. I'll follow the man but it's hard to convince the worker that he's concerned about us. Someone has to talk to him, and have him relate."

It was signed, "Brothers in New Haven."

Like the FBI, the city police showed no signs of letting up on extralegal efforts to monitor and thwart the Panthers. During jury selection, Police Chief Jim Ahern, disgusted with the state of policing in America, retired after only two years in the top job. In New Haven protesters saw him as head of an untrustworthy wiretapping police force. Nationally he emerged as a model of the liberal, enlightened cop who allowed room for social protest, who criticized confrontational tactics and the government's insensitivity to protesters.

In choosing Ahern's replacement, Mayor Guida, Irishman Dick Lee's successor, reached for a fellow Italian-American named Biagio ("Ben") DiLieto. That enraged the high-ranking Irish-American cops, partisans in the department's ongoing "Gaelic-Garlic War." They always worried about their own liability in the illegal wiretapping under Chief Jim Ahern. Now they no longer had one of their "own" to protect them.

In order to regain their sense of security, the Irish-American faction of the force set a trap for DiLieto. The illegal wiretapping operation had been halted. Steve Ahern, brother of Jim Ahern and mastermind of the wiretapping operation, pressed DiLieto to resume it. Ahern played on fears of new violence by protesters once the Seale-Huggins trial got underway

Nick Pastore, DiLieto's confidante, sensed the trap. He urged DiLieto to resist Steve Ahern's insistent demand.

One night Steve Ahern and DiLieto met over drinks at the Park Plaza Hotel to discuss the issue again. DiLieto asked his brother Frank and Nick Pastore to come along. The department won't be able to deal with this Panther problem without the wiretaps, Steve Ahern argued. The wiretaps work. Don't worry, Ahern reassured DiLieto: Ahern would take any heat; he had friends in the FBI and at the state level who could protect him. Besides, Ahern argued, illegal wiretapping had practically become a national pastime under President Nixon and FBI Director Hoover.

From DiLieto's body language, Nick could sense that Ahern was making progress. Ahern turned to Nick for affirmation. Yes, the wiretaps have produced good intelligence, Nick said. But they're illegal.

The foursome continued talking about the issue as they put on their heavy winter coats and left the Park Plaza. Ahern pulled DiLieto to the side. Nick saw Ahern bear down on DiLieto.

Not long after that night, DiLieto gave in. The police miscalculated the size of the crowd at a Panther demonstration. They expected many more protesters. They worried about violence. DiLieto issued the order; the four eavesdropping machines at police headquarters were cranked back into service to listen in on radicals' plans for future demonstrations.

As Warren's time to testify in the Panther trial arrived, Arnie Markle and Steve Ahern happened to be arguing over an unrelated murder case. Ahern demanded that Markle prepare a warrant for a suspect. Markle refused, saying he didn't have enough evidence. Frustrated, Ahern went to Chief DiLieto. He demanded that DiLieto publicly blast Markle for refusing to issue the warrant. DiLieto refused. So Ahern made a threat to DiLieto: Do it, or I'm exposing your involvement with the wiretaps.

DiLieto was beside himself. He had given in to Ahern on the wiretaps; now Ahern was turning against him. DiLieto summoned Nick to Kaysey's restaurant off the Green to talk.

DiLieto dropped an ashtray. The ashes fell on him, on Nick, on the table, on the floor.

"Why don't you calm down and relax?" Nick suggested.

They ordered drinks. DiLieto told him about Ahern's threat. "Steve Ahern gets mad and barks," Nick reassured him, "but he calms down. He's not going to do anything."

While illegal recordings may have become a sensitive subject in New Haven, and were on their way to making national headlines in Washington, it was the Panthers' voluntary recording of the Rackley torture session that would eventually cause debate on the day that Warren settled into the witness chair. Meanwhile, both sides rested in the "other" big Panther trial seventy-five miles south, in New York. Party members there stood accused of planning bombings in April 1969. The case, New York's longest state trial ever, had consumed more than a month just picking a jury; both sides weeded through 212 potential jurors to select sixteen (including four alternates). That was quick compared to the Bobby Seale/Ericka Huggins case in New Haven. Jury selection alone took seventeen weeks, the longest a Connecticut case had ever required; 1,034 potential jurors were grilled. Many expressed racist attitudes, anti-Panther biases based on the flood of pretrial publicity, or opposition to the death penalty. (Prosecutor Markle was determined that only death-penalty supporters sit on the jury.)

Despite the difficulty in finding unbiased jurors, Judge Mulvey insisted that the case continue. He didn't let death threats dissuade him, or a published caricature of himself as a pig riddled with bullet holes. He continued to walk his French poodle every night on the streets of New Haven's middle-class Westville neighborhood, where police protected his house around the clock. Taxpayers were paying for a fleet of overtime cops to guard people involved in the trial, from prosecutor Markle to the daughter of court reporter Walter Rochow as she rode the bus to school.

Mulvey, a conservative first-generation Irish-American machine politician who rose from city corporation counsel to state attorney general to superior court judge, resolved that he would disprove Kingman Brewster's skepticism. He was going to prove the Panthers wrong. Black revolutionaries would receive a fair trial in New Haven.

Despite his noble intentions, Panther sympathizers didn't trust that Mulvey could deliver a fair trial. Mulvey's private thoughts about blacks became public just in time for the trial. The thoughts qualified him more for a spot on *All in the Family* than for a seat on the bench of a Black Panther murder trial.

Mulvey thought he had a guarantee of anonymity when he made the comments in 1966 to a University of Connecticut sociologist conducting a government research project on politicians' racial views. The sociologist went back on his word years later, before the trial started. He released the transcript of the interview to the left-wing press. He defended the breach of confidence by arguing that he needed to save a man's life (Seale's) from a biased judge (Mulvey) bent on sending him to the chair.

In the interview, Mulvey blasted plans for racial integration in New Haven's schools. He contrasted the "fine" "Negroes" of an earlier time in New Haven with the new breed of public figures. "They were all church-going people. . . . Since World War II [an] entirely different group [emerged]—no respect for anyone—not even themselves. . . . So now there are some new leaders. I suppose there's a political leader. What's his name? He's the sheriff. He thinks he's the political boss up there. He's the boss of all these slobs that come up off the farm. Anyone who drives a

Cadillac has influence. Churches all vying. Bishop Brewer has a new beautiful church. New one, you know."

As a writer put it in a front-page report in a New Haven socialist paper, *Modern Times*, "The sentiments expressed in the interview would disqualify Mulvey from being a juror in the case, let alone the judge. It just proves what the Panthers have been saying all along: the courts and judges are stacked against them."

Judge Mulvey had similar distaste for the radicals protesting the Vietnam War. Two weeks before Warren's testimony, Mulvey, who had been a combat lieutenant in World War II, sent a telegram to President Nixon supporting Lieutenant William Calley, who was court-martialed for the murder of South Vietnamese civilians at My Lai. In Mulvey's view, the facts of the Calley case mattered less than the brutal realities of war, just as the facts of the Rackley case mattered less than the brutal realities of political warfare to pro-Panther protesters like Tom Hayden.

As the case proceeded, Mulvey surprised people. By the time Warren took his seat to the right of the fifty-six-year-old judge in Courtroom B, Mulvey's firm, patient presence on the bench had set a balanced tone. Mulvey's decisions rattled the prosecution as often as the defense. He denied Markle's efforts to have the case moved to the whiter suburbs; the defense wanted some blacks on the jury and succeeded in getting five. In return for Bobby Seale's promise of courtroom decorum, Mulvey made a point of responding to Seale's requests for fair play. After one court session, when Mulvey had already retired to his chambers, Seale called out to him. "Judge Mulvey! Judge Mulvey!" Seale hollered. Mulvey appeared at the entrance to his chambers to find Seale squirming in the custody of a guard leading him away. "They put on the handcuffs too tight! They're gonna break the skin." "Loosen the handcuffs," Mulvey ordered. The guard did. After that, Seale's escorts always kept the cuffs loose enough for comfort.

Beneath Mulvey's gaze, a drama was playing out between fiercely competitive legal teams. Mulvey calmly entertained their endless objections and kept them from pummeling each other. Witnesses called by the opposition were lucky to get in a full sentence before one of the lawyers, sometimes the prosecutors, sometimes Roraback or Garry, launched bitter, extensive objections.

The pugnacious prosecutor, Markle, was arguing the case of his career. Fiercely pro–law enforcement, Markle was also a white liberal. He believed he was avenging Alex Rackley's murder. He believed he was protecting New Haven's black community from the nefarious Panthers. He parried the Panthers' rhetoric by wearing a tie clip to court with a tiny pig figure displayed on it. A four-by-six-foot pig poster hung behind his office desk, framed by the Stars and Stripes on one side, a peace symbol on the other.

Markle's nemesis of the moment was Charles Garry, the flamboyant, jet-setting, West Coast Panther lawyer representing Bobby Seale. Garry crashed in a Yale law school office during the trial. He stood on his head on the Green for the cameras. He made exaggerated claims about government misdeeds in profanity-laced speeches outside the courtroom. In court, he objected loudly and often. In between the theatrics he left the real work of research, of preparing motions and arguments, to his fresh-out-of-Yale assistant, David Rosen.

They sat beside Ericka and her attorney, Katie Roraback, the careful, prepared, reserved Yankee trailblazer from an earlier feminist era. As the trial unfolded, Roraback found herself battling Garry as much as she battled Markle. She found Garry to be a male chauvinist who disregarded Ericka's interest as he pressed Seale's case. Behind the scenes, Rosen would have to mediate between the two.

CHAPTER 18

Betrayal

Warren settled into the dark oak witness box beside the judge. The box was set on a marble pedestal. He looked at Ericka and Bobby. He wanted to look Ericka in the eye, but she kept her head down. He wanted to make eye contact with everyone enclosed within the smoke-stained, marble walls. His father, Henry, always told him to eyeball people, lest they think you're lying.

Warren searched the faces of the jurors, the reporters, the spectators. He didn't recognize any of them. The crammed spectators' section seated only twenty-nine citizens. To the outrage of Panther supporters, Mulvey and Markle had the case heard in a small courtroom in order to limit the size of the crowd—and therefore the potential for disruptions. They were determined to avoid the theatrics of the Chicago Conspiracy trial, to maintain order in the court, even at the expense of a riveted public's right to see justice at work. As many as fifty people a day were turned away. Eight hundred and fifty people denied seats at pretrial hearings signed a petition in protest. The bulk of press slots were reserved for representatives of the establishment press; reporters from *Modern Times* or the Communist *Daily World* got seats some days, not others. Curiosity seekers traveled from other cities hoping to land a spot.

To his credit, Mulvey didn't allow his friends to pull strings to attend. Jack Keyes, a law student, accompanied his father, Tom, a close political ally of Mulvey, to the judge's chambers to request a seat. "Tom," Mulvey responded, "the rule is, they sign up; they get called. Everybody gets a day."

Warren spent the first morning on the stand listening to the lawyers cite case law to bolster their arguments about whether the tape recording of Rackley's torture could be played in open court. After a lunch break, Mulvey ruled in Markle's favor. The jurors would get to hear the tape.

Periodically the tape was stopped as Garry asked Warren to identify voices or to clarify garbled words. It seemed that Garry was trying to mitigate the damning power of the recording by interrupting it. Try as he did, the interruptions failed to blunt the horror felt in the courtroom by the sound of the interrogators' disembodied voices. Most jarring of all was Ericka's voice. It sounded cold, commanding, pitiless. The jurors saw her come to court carrying flowers, the model of earth-mother gentleness. Now her harsh rebukes flew at the ghost of Alex Rackley as he sat bound in the torture chair. "So we decided he was a motherfucking phoney," Ericka's voice declared, "that he was lying and that if he lied to us he lied to other party members and to the people. . . ." Ericka called Rackley a "disgrace to the people's revolutionary struggle." "Sit down motherfucker!" she snapped at him. "Keep still."

Then, the late Rackley's pained, frantic, desperate voice filled the silence of Courtroom B. When the tape completed, Warren braced himself like a patient in the dentist's chair for a root canal. Prosecutor Markle led him through the story of the murder of Alex Rackley. His body tense, Warren leaned forward as he answered questions, clearly distressed. "Another defeated black man in a suit and tie," wrote Panther loyalist Donald Freed.

As Markle elicited Warren's memories of the events leading up to Rackley's death, another figure loomed large: Landon Williams. Technically, Ericka Huggins and Bobby Seale were on trial. They were the ones facing the electric chair—not for killing Rackley but for supposedly conspiring to make it happen. They were the ones in the state's crosshairs. The defense, meanwhile, built its case on arguing that George Sams was the boss, the wild nutcase running the macabre show. Now, almost as an afterthought in the state's presentation, the name "Landon" kept appearing, referring to Landon Williams, the enforcer sent by the national party to the East Coast in April 1969 to whip local chapters into shape. The state was in no hurry to prosecute Landon Williams, and Markle did not pursue this evidence thread because it was Seale and Ericka that he was after.

According to Warren's testimony, Landon originally told him that Rackley was an informer. Landon had told the New Haven Panthers to tie Rackley more firmly to the bed. Landon insisted that Rackley be kept tied. Landon, as much as or more than George Sams, gave orders as they prepared Rackley for his ride to the swamp. Dress in dark clothing for the mission, Landon had said. "Landon again reprimanded George for not having Alex ready to take out," Warren testified, "and told us to get Alex ready to take him out." Landon led Rackley and the others out the back door. Landon handed Sams the murder weapon.

Now Markle produced the .45. It was the first time Warren had seen the weapon since the murder. He had hoped never to see that gun again. Markle insisted that Warren hold the .45. Warren didn't want to. Silently, Warren resorted, as he usually did in tense situations, to comedy. "I should pick this up and point it at someone," he told himself.

MARKLE: What, if anything was said [as Landon ushered the other Panthers to the car and they prepared to drive off without him]?

WARREN: Landon said something like 'Right on, all power to the people.'

MARKLE: Then what, if anything, happened?

WARREN: We said right on.

There was no equivocation in Warren's description of Landon Williams's role—no anger, no hesitation, just damning facts. These facts collected on the courtroom floor thick as leaves in autumn. Markle didn't seem to care at all about Landon. He cared about Bobby Seale. Warren had nothing of value to report about Bobby Seale. Even the most skeptical, anti-Panther observer couldn't help wondering: Why is Bobby Seale even here?

Ericka was another matter. No definitive evidence emerged regarding the most severe charges. But as Warren continued recounting the story, figurative blood seemed to accumulate on her hands. In addition to her role in the Rackley interrogation, she was present at key moments, overheard crucial conversations, and watched as Rackley was escorted from the house for the last time.

As Markle wrapped up his case, Ericka's lawyer, Katie Roraback, knew she could dampen the effect of the most damaging testimony—until Charles Garry, a lawyer for the defense, got his crack at Warren. Garry recognized how helpful Warren's testimony had been—for Garry's client, for Bobby Seale. At no important moment did Warren, one of the state's only two cooperating eyewitnesses, place Seale near commission or even discussion of any crime. Garry decided to drive that point home. He walked Warren through some of the same scenes Markle had just traversed.

Seated beside Ericka, Katie Roraback couldn't believe what she was watching. Surely, Garry knew he was endangering Ericka by walking Warren back through the story. Still, Garry pushed on, following up on Warren's initial description of discussions that took place right before Rackley was taken out in the car—a period in which Bobby Seale was out of town.

> WARREN: . . . Landon said, 'Take him out and take care of him.'
> GARRY: Landon said that to you?
> WARREN: Yes.
> GARRY: All right. When did Landon tell you that?
> WARREN: When we was in the house. . .
> GARRY: And who was present when Mr. Landon said that to you?
> WARREN: George Sams was, Ericka Huggins, myself, Lonnie McLucas, Rory Hithe, Landon Williams.

Ericka, once again, was placed at the scene at a crucial moment. The interrogation continued.

> WARREN: We couldn't find a car, so then Landon said to use my car. So Ericka said, 'No, don't use his car. Warren's car is too well known,' so I called to get another car.

This, too, was new—and far more damaging for Ericka.

Warren didn't think he had made any kind of significant statement. He didn't think he had crossed a line. He was just telling the truth, as he remembered it. He didn't realize he was remembering the truth differently from the way he'd remembered it for two years running.

Warren, Ericka's former lover, the man Ericka trusted, had delivered a bombshell that for the first time showed Ericka directly conspiring in the plan to have the killers elude the police as they drove Alex Rackley away to be "taken care of." Warren's allegation showed Ericka directly participating in, even directing, a murder conspiracy.

Not once did Ericka have any noticeable reaction. No shock, no tears, no glaring reproaches. What else could people do to her now? She'd been arrested, locked up, vilified, isolated within the prison walls, and targeted for death by the state. Her husband had been shot, her baby grabbed by police; her friends were arrested, killed, or revealed as probable traitors. She was numb in the face of this betrayal. However, Roraback was not numb to what Garry had just managed to do to her client.

He had jeopardized Ericka's life just to pile on a point already in his favor. By this point, Garry didn't give a damn what happened to Ericka. Roraback would stop talking to Garry—again. From a distance they appeared to be a team defending two Panthers jointly on trial; in practice, Roraback saw Garry working against her as often as with her.

Roraback hurried to even the score. She was withering when her turn came to cross-examine Warren. She confronted Warren with the original statement he gave Sgt. DeRosa of the New Haven police, back when Warren decided to plead guilty. She pointed to where Warren said a different Panther, not Ericka, had discussed whose car to use. She reminded him that he had testified at Lonnie McLucas's trial months earlier—and said nothing about Ericka making such a comment then, either.

RORABACK: This is the first time you said it, is that correct, Mr. Kimbro, when you testified here in the last several days?

WARREN: The first time I said it here, yes.

RORABACK: And this is approximately two years after this alleged conversation took place?

WARREN: Yes.

RORABACK: And approximately fifteen months after the first statement you gave concerning—

WARREN: Yes.

RORABACK: And approximately nine months since you testified in the McLucas trial, is that right?

WARREN: Yes.

RORABACK: And you are claiming that your memory is better today, Mr. Kimbro, than it was seven or eight months after the incident?

WARREN: Somewhat, yes.

RORABACK: Who has refreshed it for you, Mr. Kimbro?

WARREN: Myself. Two years going over and over and over and over and over.

RORABACK: And adding and adding and adding and adding and adding?

Roraback had succeeded in planting doubts, in poking holes in Warren's tale. Everyone—Ericka, Roraback, Warren—left the room in weaker shape than when they'd entered. Warren stumbled back to the police car, back to Brooklyn. He wouldn't have to return to face Ericka. He wouldn't have to face the Panther lawyers anymore. The FBI was pleased with Warren; following his testimony, the New Haven office sent a memo to J. Edgar Hoover stating that it had deleted Warren from the "Agitator Index." (Pending a subsequent interview, he remained on the bureau's "Security Index.")

George Sams confronted Warren in the cell block after dinner that night. The guards expected a confrontation. Warren's testimony had been all over the news. Sams was proud of being the star witness, and Warren had undermined him on the stand.

Sams pushed his chest out as he approached Warren.

"Brother Warren," he seethed, "you messed up. You were supposed to say—"

Warren cut him short.

"George, get outta my face."

Warren was used to Sams trying to provoke fights only to have them broken up before they started. In fact, the guards had previously called Warren to talk Sams down when Sams butted heads with other inmates.

Sams stood his ground. He leaned into Warren.

"George," Warren said, "your fists are no bigger than your brain."

They walked away from each other. The confrontation—and Warren's active role in the case—was over. George Sams still had a star turn awaiting him.

CHAPTER 19

The Unraveling of Dingee Swahoo

THURSDAY, APRIL 22, 1971, was George Sams's twenty-fifth birthday. His present was the opportunity to begin a three-day stint in the spotlight in Judge Mulvey's Courtroom B. At long last, the witness on whom so many hopes rested took the stand. Prosecutor Arnie Markle hoped for the conviction of a lifetime. Sams was the key to bringing down the chieftains of the notorious Black Panther Party. Ericka Huggins and Bobby Seale hoped to escape the electric chair.

ATTORNEY CHARLES GARRY: Would you tell the court and jury what names you have been known as? . . .

GEORGE SAMS: I have nicknames, like Crazy George, Madman, Detroit George—several names. I had the name Dingee Swahoo, which was an African name.

JUDGE MULVEY: Dingee what?

SAMS: Dingee Swahoo.

JUDGE MULVEY: All right.

SAMS: It's an African name. And I had the name that Chairman Bobby and David Hilliard gave me, which was Madman No. 1, which was in San Francisco. This is what we had. These are the names that we had, just like *you* have a nickname, Mr. Garry. You know, people call you a nickname, basically.

GARRY: What else?

Sams: They call *you*, Mr. Garry, "Fat."

Garry: What other names have you been known by?

Sams: That's about all I can recall. No, lately I have been called
     No. 1 Agent. I have been called Rats, Snitch. . . .

Sams had seen all that happened to Alex Rackley. He pleaded guilty to his role in conducting the torture and orchestrating the murder in the swamp. Sams was practically all Markle had. Warren had corroborated parts of the story, but not the important parts dealing with Bobby Seale. The only other major witness was New Haven cop Nick Pastore. Nick testified that he saw Seale walk into the Panther headquarters following the speech, whereas the defense claimed that Seale merely stood out on the stoop. Even if Nick did see Seale walk in, Nick was watching from a distance. He couldn't claim to have heard Seale give the murder order.

For their part, the Panther attorneys, Charles Garry and Katie Roraback, had to do more than strafe holes into Sams's already-flimsy tale. They had to destroy his credibility. Other witnesses had offered verbal glimpses into how Sams terrorized the women, terrorized everyone, with beatings and erratic threats and orders. The lawyers now had to reveal for the jury more fully, more viscerally, the George Sams on whom the entire prosecution scenario depended. They had to keep him on the stand until he cracked, until the legitimate, sane witness Markle presented to the jury dissolved into a babbling, explosive, demented mastermind of murder, bent on revenge against Bobby Seale, capable of orchestrating the entire Rackley affair on his own, whose violent unpredictability rendered Ericka, among others, helpless to resist. They had to give flesh to the nicknames that followed George Sams throughout his career as an itinerant ne'er-do-well.

Before they got their chance at Sams, Garry and Roraback had to sit through Act I, Markle's gentle stage direction of his star witness. As Markle built his case against Ericka Huggins and Bobby Seale, the name of Landon Williams kept squeezing them out of the picture. In Sams's telling, Williams was letting people know right away that he considered Alex Rackley a spy to be watched. It was Williams who asked for tapes and reports on Rackley's captivity; who identified Rackley, erroneously, as Alex McKiever, the indicted New York Panther who fled to Algiers; who ordered Sams to beat Rackley with a stick soon after Landon and Sams arrived in New York. Of course, Williams would later deny Sams's story.

Markle steered Sams away from Williams toward the prosecution's targets. Sams delivered two blows to Ericka, one practically casting her as a madam corrupting teenage girls into sex slaves. Without fully absolving himself of a role in having a fifteen-year-old Panther sleep with Rackley in order to seek a spy confession, Sams brought both Landon Williams and Ericka into it.

"Brother Landon asked Sister Ericka, did she have a sister that would probably, you know, be able to get some information out of Alex. . . . And she informed him, 'Yes,'" Sams testified. "We both, Ericka and I, talked to Maude. . . .

"So Sister Ericka began to talk to Maude, and asked her to check Brother Alex out, and to seduce him if she thought she could get some information from him, and I told her not to, if she didn't think she could get some information. If she could, so go ahead. So they went to bed."

Sams also alleged that, during Rackley's torture session, "Ericka brought down the first bucket of hot water," which was eventually poured on Rackley's body. He also claimed that "we all participated in disciplining Alex Rackley," including Ericka. "Some stomped him, he was on the floor, some beat him upside the head. We have what you call a 'mud hole.' That means that all the members participate wholeheartedly in disciplining a member."

Sams had an even bigger accusation against Seale, of course. It was the biggest single piece of evidence against Seale. To consider finding Seale guilty, the jury would have to believe Sams's account of what happened when Seale briefly stopped by the Orchard Street Panther headquarters after his speech at Yale's Battell Chapel the night of May 19, 1969. According to Sams, Seale walked into the room where Alex Rackley was tied to the bed. According to Sams, Warren, Landon Williams, and Ericka, among others, were there, too.

Chairman Bobby walked over and looked at Rackley, and Landon took all the gags out of his mouth and the tape and stuff off his face, and he asked Rackley, was he a pig. So Rackley said, "No, sir, I'm not a pig."

So he began to check the clothes hangers that was around his neck and the tape and all the stuff that was on Rackley, and he walked over toward the back of the room, and Brother Landon went over and asked him, what was we to do with him.

Chairman Bobby seemed to get an attitude. "What do you do with a pig? A pig is a pig. Do away with him. Off the motherfucker."

Then, Sams continued, "He went out and used the bathroom for about, I guess about ten minutes. And he came out and told everyone— Landon ordered everyone to get rid of the fingerprints in the bathroom, anything that Chairman Bobby had probably touched, and we all went downstairs."

On his way out, Seale had parting words for his old nemesis, Sams, according to Sams. "He began to tell me how I was a field Negro."

After the lunch break, Garry got his crack at the star witness. He started slowly, covering Sams's experience as a prisoner cooperating with the state in this case. He began to build the case for Sams's resentment toward Seale. Garry's goal was to show how a vendetta could have motivated Sams to come forward with this incriminating, uncorroborated story. By Sams's own acknowledgment on the stand, Seale once kicked him out of the party for stabbing another Panther in the leg.

Drawing out the interrogation into Friday morning's court session, Garry finally started getting to Sams. In the face of Garry's pestering jabs, Sams could no longer hide the depth of his fury against Seale and the Panthers. Sams unraveled slowly. First, Garry provoked a protest from Sams when he asked the name of a woman who accompanied him on a failed marijuana-buying mission. Sams protested Garry's questioning.

SAMS: Mr. Garry, you want to pretend everybody had their own piece in the crime, and everybody was following orders, and that's just what I was doing, Sister Ericka was doing. Chairman Bobby give the orders, and we follow them. The Central Committee gave the orders, we followed them. . . .

Like they tell you to don't smoke weeds. And Chairman Bobby drinks Cutty Sauce [sic] all the time, and the members smoke weeds, and they tell the society they don't do these things.

Garry seized an opening to ridicule Sams, to confuse him, to prod him along on the Seale rant, then step out of the way.

GARRY: You say Bobby Seale drinks 'Cutty Sauce'?

SAMS: Man . . .

JUDGE MULVEY: Cutty Sark?

SAMS: He constantly—

GARRY: He said, 'Cutty Sauce.'

SAMS: Cutty Sauce, liquor. He drinks all the time. He was drinking when he came to the rally at Yale. Warren Kimbro tells the Chairman to put away the liquor. And do you think he put it away? This man tell the members not to drink, and he drinks all the time. He does the same thing. And if you do, he gives—he's on the stage at the rally hollering about members smoking weeds, and he's drinking Cutty Sauce, the liquor in the bottle, and I don't think that's fair, Mr. Garry.

GARRY: He was drinking Cutty Sauce?

SAMS: Because all the time he drinks like Cutty Sauce, all the time.

GARRY: When did you see him? When did you see him?

SAMS: I see him all the time. Every time I seen him. There wasn't a time he wasn't drunk. Sometimes you have to hold him up on the stage.

GARRY: When did you hold him up on the stage?

SAMS: I hold him up on the stage at the 'Free Huey Rally,' when 10,000 people were there. He was drunk.

GARRY: Where was this 10,000 people?

SAMS: Right there in San Francisco, May 1st rally, Mr. Garry.

GARRY: What day?

Until now there had been months of staccato courtroom dialogue—of witnesses speaking a word or a line or two at a time, inevitably interrupted by lawyers' objections and motions and procedural debate. Now a witness was veering off into an uncharted rant. And, except for an occasional prod from Garry, the witness kept going, on and on. Even stern Judge Mulvey, who customarily insisted on adherence to procedure, allowed Sams to babble on in answer to questions no one was asking him.

Prosecutor Markle, usually a bulldog ready to bark at any potentially damaging sentence, watched his star witness unravel. Out went Markle's meticulously prepared script as the soul of George Sams escaped from the prison of its coached witness persona. A bubbling stream of consciousness, equal parts resentment, bravado, revenge, and outrage gushed from the witness stand.

> SAMS: May 1st, on the rally in San Francisco, in front of the courthouse at the "Free Huey Rally," he was drunk. He was drunk. He always drunk. . . . This is the whole argument between Eldridge Cleaver and Bobby Seale. They break their own rules and regulations. They break them, you know, and you are here trying to paint people as—the black man is dead, I'm not denying it. This man gave the order to kill that man, and that's the simplest—this is as plain being, like, as I can.
>
> What you want to do is paint me as a monster, and every member dies in the party. The party put them in the paper and say they are agents, and there ain't a member ever resign at the party. That person just do not go out of the party and nothing said about it. Every member who go out of the Black Panther Party, something is wrong of some kind. He's an Uncle Tom, a sick nigger of some kind, an agent, and there ain't a member that can resign without being intimidated by the people in the black community, you know, for lying, Mr. Garry.
>
> You know the party is lying. You're lying. I just—I'm not going to be no martyr. I'm not going to be no martyr for the party. I have never been a martyr. I just speaks my own mind.
>
> Bobby don't like it. When I first came to San Francisco, he tells me, he says, "Who are you? What are you here for?" I said, "I am here to see Don Cox." He says, "My name is Chairman Bobby. You supposed to see me," and because I refused to see this man, he got the attitude, he wants to move on, and he called me a East Coast nigger . . .
>
> I happen to be one that survived and not to get killed in the Black Panther Party, and I have made up my mind I am going to expose the truth to everybody, and if I have to, if I

have to, I can prove the fact that you are on the Central Committee. You are part of the same Panther party that goes around promulgating and using the blacks and whites, and I would do it, Mr. Garry, and this is a fact, and you are wrong.

GARRY: Why don't you go ahead and do it?

SAMS: Well . . . You are the lawyer of the Central Committee of the Black Panther Party. . . . You got on the David Frost Show and said the police killed the Panthers. You know the Panthers killed some of the Panthers. John Huggins. What happened to John Huggins? What happened to Brother John—

That was enough for Katie Roraback, John Huggins's former lawyer, now his widow's lawyer. "Your Honor," Roraback interjected, "I object. . . ."

"You object?" the judge asked Roraback.

"I object."

"It's about time somebody did, or we would be here all day," Mulvey said. "All right Mr. Sams, there is no question pending. . . . It's all very interesting. But it is not pertinent to this case."

With the freewheeling monologue halted, Charles Garry returned to pertinent information. Sams admitted he would have shot Warren Kimbro if Warren hadn't shot Rackley in the swamp. Next, Garry meticulously walked Sams through all the "reefers" he smoked. Tempers cooled. Garry brandished page 5 of the statement Sams gave the cops after his arrest the previous August and page 1,291 of Sams's testimony in the Lonnie McLucas trial. He thrust the papers at Sams, asked him to look them over. A debate ensued over the text.

GARRY: You did tell Mr. Landon Williams . . . that Alex Rackley had lied 3,000 motherfucking times, isn't that right? . . .

SAMS: That don't say "motherfucker" there, does it?

GARRY: What does that say?

SAMS: I say 3,000—"He lied three thousand fucking times."

GARRY: And your original statement said "3,000 motherfucking times," didn't it?

Proper Katie Roraback wasn't one to say "motherfucking" in court, if she could help it. When her turn came, she visited the question with more decorum. Sams, too, was more polite. Even so, the result was just as devastating, one final hole in Sams's credibility.

> Roraback: Didn't you say to Landon Williams that you thought that Alex Rackley had lied some 3,000 times?
>
> Sams: Yes, ma'am.
>
> Roraback: And that statement wasn't true, was it?
>
> Sams: Yes, it was true.
>
> Roraback: You thought he lied 3,000 times?
>
> Sams: Yes.
>
> Roraback: But you thought he told the truth?
>
> Sams: Yes, to some degree.
>
> Roraback: I have no other questions.

Neither did the jury, at least when it came to Bobby Seale's guilt. Ericka's fate, on the other hand, remained unclear. Unlike Seale, she had been placed at several incriminating scenes; more than one witness had offered damaging testimony. And that voice of hers on the interrogation tape hung in the air, clinging like the aged smoke stains to the courtroom's marble walls.

CHAPTER 20

Ericka's Gamble

My advice to black students is to study
Shakespeare rather than Huey P. Newton.
—EARL I. WILLIAMS, PRESIDENT, NEW HAVEN NAACP

THE TWO DOZEN Panther supporters lucky enough to gain seats in Courtroom B watched Ericka drift through the door to the defense table. She brought books by Herman Hesse to court. Some days, she might have a band in her hair. With a smile, she would acknowledge the raised-fist power salutes of her public. Upon his daily entrance, Bobby Seale acknowledged the salutes with a raised fist of his own.

On his way to his seat at the defense table, Seale, his face fixed in determination, passed Walter Rochow and Arthur Moan, the straitlaced, middle-aged white court stenographers who lived in suburban Hamden. "Good morning, Walter," Seale greeted Rochow quietly, amiably. "How's everything?"

When Ericka passed by, she leaned over to the court stenographers with her own sotto voce greeting: "Motherfucker, drop dead." Then she took her seat, tender smile fixed on her face.

As the case against Seale disintegrated—his lawyer concluded Seale didn't need to testify to counter any remaining crumbs of evidence—the court contest came down to the clash between the two Ericka Hugginses. Was she the cold-hearted interrogator heard on the tape of Alex

Rackley's torture? The party's "black widow"? The high-ranking, scheming evil seductress who lured well-intentioned, impressionable black people like Warren Kimbro into a brutal criminal enterprise?

Or was Ericka the railroaded dreamer, the sensitive poetess portrayed by her attorney Katie Roraback? Was she the serial victim of violence and state oppression and male chauvinism, forced at gunpoint to launch the interrogation of Alex Rackley? The beautiful, innocent, idealistic young woman who might now lose her life? The low-ranking Panther who had nothing to do with the crazy plans of male party members?

Ericka herself needed to convince the jury which of those identities to embrace. Roraback and Ericka decided that Ericka would have to take the stand.

Roraback and Ericka spent three weeks preparing her testimony. While Roraback planned to portray Ericka as a victim, as less of a leader, more of a follower, she could go only so far. There was no denying, in the face of testimony, in the face of that tape, in the face of her very essence, that Ericka Jenkins Huggins was a forceful person. Rather than deny it, Roraback and Ericka had to harness that strength and twist it to their advantage.

They felt besieged, the two of them, from all sides. By the state, of course. By former comrades like Warren. By their own team's fellow attorney, Charles Garry. Neither Garry nor the state had informed Roraback when two other important Panther defendants yet to stand trial in the Rackley murder, Landon Williams and Rory Hithe, had been extradited to New Haven from Denver. Roraback discovered Hithe's presence in the courthouse just as he was negotiating with a New Haven detective to testify in Ericka's case—testimony that could help Seale but destroy Ericka. Garry knew about it. That's why he encouraged Hithe to testify and didn't let Roraback know. Once Roraback discovered what had happened, she convinced Hithe not to testify, in order to protect Ericka's life.

Roraback went tens of thousands of dollars into debt preparing Ericka's defense. She was mugged walking home at night from a meeting with her team of Yale Law School volunteers; her pocketbook turned up days later at the police department with all her scribbled notes neatly pressed and folded. Ericka had lost her husband, her baby, her freedom.

Both she and Roraback, like most radicals in 1971, had good reason to distrust the government, to believe it operated in violation of rules and laws, that it was determined to kill movements, to kill leaders, by any means necessary.

At the time, Roraback got wind of the fact that a fellow inmate at the Niantic prison convinced Ericka and the other Panther women to join her in a jailbreak. She consulted other attorneys for advice. Then she told Ericka: Don't do it; it's a bad idea. Ericka agreed, then talked the other Panthers out of it. The woman escaped alone, out of a window where the screen had been left open. She was returned to jail.

Ericka figured at first the woman really wanted to escape. She penned a tribute, "for who ran from the camp / and was eventually caught" ("if it is true that they / have stifled your attempt / to breathe air and see / life and be part of the / chaos that is the streets / then I cry inside. . . "). Then something strange happened. The captured escapee contacted Katie Roraback. She asked Roraback to visit her at Niantic right away. Roraback agreed. At the jail, the woman, unnerved, told Roraback a wild story: The woman had come from Boston to New Haven for a pro-Panther rally. The police arrested her and other Panthers for driving a car rented on a stolen credit card. On her way to jail, she was asked to keep an eye on the Panther women. The FBI said it had a mission for her. Eventually, she was asked to enlist the Panthers in an escape attempt through an open window; a car would await her and return her to jail, no questions asked. The woman ended up escaping alone, perhaps to preserve her cover once Ericka's group dropped out. Now she feared that the government had abandoned her. She had a date in court. She thought she wasn't supposed to go to court. No one was helping her.

Roraback asked her to write out the whole story. The woman did. Roraback informed her she couldn't serve as her lawyer because that would present a conflict of interest with her representation of Ericka. Roraback said she could show up in court the next day to offer informal advice.

She did show up at court the next day, and there was no sign of the woman or her case. It didn't appear on any court record.

Roraback had no doubt: the FBI, or other authorities, planned to shoot Ericka as she tried to escape. She couldn't prove it. The arrest of the woman who had called her for help was public knowledge. Boston's Pan-thers did develop questions about whether the woman was a government agent. Whether or not the escapee's story was true, it very well could have been. The FBI and local police agencies *were* up to deadly dirty tricks. The police had shot Chicago Panther leader Fred Hampton to death, for instance, as he lay asleep in his apartment, in a raid the FBI helped orchestrate. Informers and agents provocateur were everywhere. The fact that you could never be sure who they were, could never avoid suspicion and paranoia, was part of the point of hiring them.

In a world where almost everything was questioned, where virtually no one could be trusted, there was not any one who questioned Ericka's honest dedication to the Panther cause. Of those Party members in New Haven, she alone seemed beyond suspicion. She wore a long green dress for her first day on the stand, Tuesday, May 11. Taking note of her black shawl, homemade necklace, "beautiful skin and hair," one of her admir-ers, Professor Donald Freed, wrote that Ericka "could have been Pak-istani or Hindu and at the same time someone in a nineteenth-century photograph."

In a low, soft voice, Ericka followed the lead of Katie Roraback's opening questions about her life. She spoke of working with underprivi-leged children at a community center in her youth, of studying for a ca-reer in special education to help children with disabilities. She recounted the horror of her husband's murder and her subsequent arrest on charges of conspiracy to commit murder. The unspoken point: the L.A. affair was an echo of trumped-up charges in this case.

Judge Mulvey beckoned Roraback to the bench. Somehow he had learned that the L.A. police had arrested—and charged—Ericka's three-week-old baby when they busted everyone the night of John Huggins's murder. Outside of the hearing of the court reporters, of the other partic-ipants, the judge told Roraback, "I don't want you to put in anything about the arrest of that child."

The story then moved to the minefield of New Haven. Ericka and Roraback stepped gingerly through the details of the visit by Alex Rack-ley and the other New York Panthers. Ericka spoke "slowly and calmly, her tall thin frame almost motionless in the witness chair," as a *New York Times* reporter put it. She identified Sams as the one telling her that Rackley, "that Maryland farmer," was an informer.

Ericka did raise her voice, incensed, when Roraback asked her if it was true, as Sams had alleged on the stand, that she told a fifteen-year-old girl to have sex with Rackley in order to obtain secrets.

"I most definitely did not!" Ericka declared.

Sams did order her, with "force in his voice," to ask the girl to get information from Rackley, "or else," Ericka testified. "She looked at me very puzzled and asked me, you know, what did I mean? And I said, 'Well, you know, find out where he is from, just talk to him.' Then I—that was all I said, really."

Similarly, Ericka didn't throw a book of Mao's military writings at Alex Rackley when she came downstairs the next morning to find him dozing. No, she insisted. She "gave" it to him.

And during that horrid interrogation captured on tape, she feared for her life, under threat from George Sams to narrate the opening part of the proceedings.

Ericka recounted horror stories of her time with George Sams. She portrayed herself as practically a hostage to his violent eruptions and bone-chilling rants. She spoke of how Sams vowed to kill his mother, to kill any woman who miscarried his baby. "He described to us how [his mother] supposedly threw him to his father when he was very young in a bar one day in the South. Then he described how he had been shot by some black policemen and he described how the bullet entered and exited. And he told us he had a plate in his head."

Her tales built on previous testimony by Panther women called by Roraback; they had told of Sams ordering them, at gunpoint, to carry out orders or face death, of how he vowed "to get even one day" with Bobby Seale. One witness, Shirley Wolterding, claimed that Sams punched her in the face when he returned to New York following Rackley's death; when she cried, he told her, "'You should have seen Alex's face. Bang. Bang. You should have seen that motherfucker's face. . . .' He said that he offed him because he thought he was a pig, and that he would off me as well."

Sams was an easy target. A trickier challenge was separating Ericka from association with the top echelon of national Panther leadership, and from her own role as driving force behind the New Haven chapter. Ericka testified to Roraback that she had met Bobby Seale "just once" in Oakland before his New Haven visit on the fateful weekend of Rackley's

murder. She had talked to him "not really more than two or three minutes." She portrayed herself as a bystander, continually frightened, during the frantic events leading up to Rackley's death.

Only once did she feel safe enough to speak up, Ericka testified: on a
drive to the post office with Warren Kimbro following the torture.

"I looked at him," Ericka said, "and I asked him: Why did all that
have to happen? And he looked at me very confused, and didn't answer.
And there was no more said."

CHAPTER 21

The Cut-Off

Woman is the nigger of the world.
—JOHN LENNON

ARNIE MARKLE WASN'T buying Ericka's testimony. The pugnacious prosecutor knew that Roraback had coached Ericka to downplay her role in the party. He jumped at the chance to set the record straight when his turn to cross-examine Ericka came toward the end of her first day of testimony. He continued through the following day, then all the morning of Thursday, May 13.

Markle reminded Ericka, in front of the jury, of her every step, every remark, during the assault on Alex Rackley. He asked her to elaborate on the phrases she used on the tape, such as the "discipline" Rackley received and the "cowardly tendencies" Rackley showed. He parroted her mocking words of how she saw Rackley "whimper and moan." She said now that she was forced to utter those words; Markle wanted to make sure everyone kept in mind how she sounded.

> MARKLE: You stated on the tape that the reason the stick was taken to [Rackley] was because he was acting like a "coward" and a "non-Panther"?
>
> ERICKA: That's what I said on the tape, you know.

Markle: That's on the statement. And that's the way you felt
   that Sunday, when you made the tape?
Ericka: No.
Markle: That's not the way you felt? And so that was untrue?
   That's the reason the stick was taken to him?
Ericka: That's the way George Sams felt about it. . . .

They went back and forth on the question, on and on. Ericka was
made of stronger stuff than George Sams. Markle couldn't crack her. In
the face of Markle's "grueling" probes, observed *Hartford Courant* reporter Stan Simon, Ericka "never flustered. She took long pauses and
replied carefully to questions, most of which Miss Roraback had antici-
pated and prepared her for."

Still, Ericka had some difficult explaining to do. Even weeks of prepa-
ration could produce only mediocre answers to some of the questions.
Ericka described herself in a "detached" state of mind during the Rackley
affair, depressed. She said "a feeling of futility" "forced" her to "withdraw" from her surroundings.

Markle walked Ericka through all the times she had been in the presence of Warren Kimbro, Landon Williams, and Bobby Seale in the days
leading up to Rackley's death. At each point, he asked her, did she speak
up about "what had happened to Alex Rackley?"

"Well, I didn't feel like I could talk to anybody," Ericka said.

Markle: Was there something about Mr. Seale that prevented
   you from talking to him at that stage about Mr. Rackley? . . .
Ericka: I didn't know him, and at the time I wasn't—I guess I
   wasn't thinking, you know, of ways in which to approach
   anyone about it, you know.
Markle: Well, now, this—
Ericka: And I felt that I wouldn't—I just didn't feel that I could
   say anything, you know. I just didn't feel that way.
Markle: How about Landon Williams, an old friend from
   Oakland? You had seen him here? You had talked to him?
Ericka: I—I—you know, Landon Williams is my brother, you
   know, one of my brothers in the party, but he wasn't an
   old friend.

MARKLE: Well—

ERICKA: And I didn't feel I could talk to him either.

MARKLE: In point of fact, didn't you feel that Landon Williams was in charge of the situation, as far as Rackley was concerned?

ERICKA: No, I didn't.

MARKLE: You didn't?

ERICKA: No.

MARKLE: But you didn't feel you could talk to a brother about what happened at that apartment that made you nauseous?

ERICKA: Well, you see, it's very hard, first of all, for a woman to be heard by men.

The moment Roraback had hoped for. The trap she and Ericka had set, to turn one of their greatest weaknesses around on Markle. Roraback knew Markle wouldn't let slide the contention that Ericka was a low-ranking bystander in the Panther hierarchy. There had been too much testimony to the contrary. They knew he wouldn't accept the notion that Ericka felt inhibited in speaking her mind.

Instead of avoiding the question, they decided to throw it back at him, so he would claw and claw away—so harshly, they hoped, that he would lose the jury's sympathies, especially the sympathies of the female jurors. Roraback hoped to turn Ericka into the target of yet another male's badgering. They prepared for Markle to challenge the story of the men cutting off Ericka when she tried to speak—then, they guessed, he would proceed to cut her off himself and therefore prove her point. Roraback and Ericka practiced the line about women having trouble being heard by men. After all, what female juror wouldn't have experienced the same thing?

Markle walked right into the trap. While Roraback silently celebrated, Markle pulled in closer for the kill, sarcasm dripping from his voice.

"So what you are telling me," Markle persisted, is "that you did not tell anybody about what had happened to Mr. Rackley is because you were a woman?"

"That's part of the reason," Ericka responded, "yes."

Markle pushed ahead, refusing the answer he had been given. Again and again, he put Ericka in the presence of important Panthers. He

returned to asking about what happened in her apartment a few hours
before Chairman Seale's speech, when important Panthers were sitting
around.

> MARKLE: During that time, did you say to Mr. Seale or Mr. Hithe
> or Mr. Williams or Mr. Hilliard or Mr. Brothers or the un-
> known male [present] that there was a brother who had
> been tortured against party rules and regulations and that
> he was being held at the Kimbro apartment?
> ERICKA: I tried.
> MARKLE: Who did you try to tell?
> ERICKA: I tried to speak to someone, but there was a conversa-
> tion going on, and I got cut off, and I didn't try again.
> MARKLE: You mean this man was being held there in this
> condition, and you tried to say something, and you got cut
> off? And you let it go?

Charles Garry objected: "That's argumentative." Judge Mulvey sus-
tained him. Markle pressed on.

> MARKLE: Who did you try to talk to?
> ERICKA: Well, I tried to say something to Chairman Bobby.
> MARKLE: What did you try to tell him?
> ERICKA: You want to know what I was thinking to say? Because
> I never got it out.
> MARKLE: I want to know what you said.
> ERICKA: I said, "There is a brother. . . ."
> MARKLE: That's all you said?
> ERICKA: Yes.
> MARKLE: And you were cut short?
> ERICKA: Yes.

To Markle, the point was self-evident, Ericka's version preposterous.
He still didn't recognize the pit into which he had fallen and continued
to bury himself, regardless of the facts.

As Roraback had calculated, Markle, like most forceful males of his
era, was unfamiliar with the lessons the women's movement was teach-

ing about how men ignore or discount women's voices. Markle was too preoccupied with the point that Ericka was shading the truth of her close relationships with top Panthers. Markle knew something the jurors didn't. In the previous trial in this case, Lonnie McLucas's trial, Bobby Seale had testified that he "talked to Ericka a lot. . . . At the time I came here, the only person I related to most directly was Ericka Huggins."

Once Ericka was done testifying, Markle could ask Bobby Seale questions to elicit the same statements when he testified in this case. Then the jurors would see how credible Ericka's story was.

There was one problem, though. When it came time to call Bobby Seale to testify in his own defense, Charles Garry had a surprise. He wasn't going to call Seale, after all. Why should he? It made more sense to let the state's evidence—or embarrassing paucity of credible evidence—speak for itself. Now the jury would never hear why Markle spent so much time getting Ericka to testify that she barely knew or spoke with Bobby Seale.

After Ericka's testimony, Markle had one last chance to salvage his case: final arguments, which consumed most of Tuesday, March 18. Actually, Markle had two chances. He was permitted to present the first closing argument. Then, after the defense's summation, he could finish up with a second closing argument.

The setbacks suffered during Ericka's testimony only doubled Markle's ferocity. He was not prepared to give up on the case of his career. In his appeal to the jurors, the prosecutor zeroed in on the image of Ericka as the "black widow." He cited Ericka's admission, in response to his questions, that she took her baby to Panther headquarters in the presence of the wild man George Sams. Markle argued that there could only be two explanations: Either Ericka was a bad mother, or she didn't truly fear Sams as she said.

"I'm going to ask you, when you get in that room, when you start your deliberations, if you really want to believe that kind of story, that she was terrified at that time, listen to the tape. And listen to her tone of voice." Details of the torture followed. Ericka "started it." "She's there throughout the torture."

Markle, like Roraback, appealed to jurors' views of what it meant to be a woman. "All the milk of human kindness, all the nurturing that womanhood is taught," he said of Ericka confronting Rackley about his inability to read. "She cuts it right out." He railed against "the callousness, the unruffled nature of this woman." The torture session "didn't faze her one bit, not one iota"; when it was over, she proceeded to make a previously planned trip to the post office.

The prosecutor reestablished his argument on firm ground by pointing out that Ericka, whatever her explanations of her role, was present at just about every incriminating moment in the saga save for the murder itself. "If you can tell me in truthfulness," Markle argued, "that someone could close their eyes to a man being led out by a wire hanger, with his hands tied behind him, barefoot, and didn't know where he was going—having gotten the clothing for him, having heard the interrogation of him, having partaken in the torture of him, having seen him tied up—then there's got to be something wrong."

Markle tackled the charge that this was a political case prosecuted in a government effort to slay the Panthers. He said that this case wasn't about politics; rather, it was about Alex Rackley, an innocent man savagely executed.

"He is the only person that was politicalized here. He was killed over petty policy. Demolished for no reason. Wiped out without any dignity. Because people had no concern for their brother man. People had no compassion for a man that had every right to live." The murder in the swamp, Markle claimed, also "wiped out what potentially was a good, good, fine leader, Warren Kimbro. . . . He had potential, and now he's a convicted murderer."

After Markle concluded his remarks, it was Katie Roraback's turn for sarcasm. She was not about to let the prosecutor characterize Ericka's lover-turned-semi-accuser into a noble victim. "Warren Kimbro, you must remember, is also one of those who was down in the cellar. He was also one of those who, even in the living room, took that stick that he had gotten and beat Alex Rackley. He got some of that boiling water and poured on Alex Rackley. . . .

"This lovely fellow, Warren Kimbro, is the same Warren Kimbro who a short ten years before had been found guilty of two aggravated assaults here in the city of New Haven. . . . Oh, and one other thing. Of course, Warren Kimbro is the person who actually did kill Alex Rackley."

Roraback ensured that Warren wasn't winning any votes in the jury box today, but he wasn't on trial; Ericka was.

The climax of Roraback's closing argument was, of course, Arnie Markle's chauvinism. "Arnold Markle would have you believe she should have rallied to go back to the house to free this man," Roraback told the jurors. "This group of men, she got cut off in. Maybe this seems unusual or impossible for Arnold Markle. But, then, he is a man. And perhaps a few of the women in the jury will know just how easy it is to have that happen."

In one last burst, one last cry for outrage, for justice, Markle lifted his final appeal to the jurors beyond the assassination of Ericka Huggins's character to the brutality, the tragedy, of the murder itself. He made one last stand in the name of Alex Rackley.

Even animals don't treat their own like that I know of. But here we've got human beings. . . .

Rackley was expendable. He was a man who could be used.

They didn't care what happened to Rackley.

Who's going to raise a hue and cry about a man from Florida, the poor man that comes from Florida and been in the party eight months?

Did you hear one voice say, "Don't do it. Stop. Help him"? Not at all. There was no voice. Because they didn't care what happened to Alex Rackley. They were in the pack, and they were after Rackley. And they used him and they tossed him away all in the name—and that's what makes it so, so deadly, so sad—all in the name of something that could have been decent.

They say to you, they say, "The establishment is what creates Rackley." That's not true. Alex Rackley is a product of our environment, there's no question about it. And if anyone should have had compassion for Alex Rackley, it should have been the people that were holding him, because they should have understood all of what had contributed to his makeup.

Spent, Markle, like Roraback, had summoned the fullness of his convictions and legal training. The jurors heard all there was to say. Now they had to decide.

CHAPTER 22

Days of Decision

THE JURORS TOOK up the matter of Bobby Seale's case first. After two hours, they voted. It was unanimous: not guilty. The trouble started when they moved on to Ericka's case.

The five black jurors believed her innocent. So did a white twenty-six-year-old graduate student named Marilyn Martino. In her prior days as a social worker in black New Haven neighborhoods, Martino had developed convictions about the system's racist abuses. She was determined to free Ericka.

Conversely, Barbara Foy—a forty-two-year-old white woman—was equally determined to find Ericka guilty. Foy declared that she was withdrawing her vote to acquit Bobby Seale unless Ericka were found guilty. She felt she "owed" that to the prosecution. Foy was the one hard-core pro-Markle juror. During jury selection, Ericka had sensed it; she asked Katie Roraback to use one of her challenges to dismiss Foy. Roraback disagreed and held onto the challenge for someone else.

The deliberations stretched out over five days. They grew increasingly tense as positions hardened. Screams could be heard in the adjoining courtroom. Most of the white jurors wanted out. Some feared retribution, the protesters.

Juror Marilyn Martino met privately—and illegally—with the other pro-Panther jurors at night to plot the next day's strategy. At one point during deliberations, Martino ordered a black juror to sit in a bathroom to cool off; Martino feared people might discover the juror's pro-Panther leanings, which had gone undetected in jury selection. It turned out the juror's daughter even belonged to a pro-Panther group.

Martino was able to coax all but two of the white jurors into acquiescence. The foreman, a white former Scoutmaster, concluded, as he would later tell *Hartford Courant* reporter Stan Simon, that even though Ericka had probably done something wrong, prosecutor Markle had overplayed his hand. He felt Markle charged her with more than her crimes, "spread her case too thin."

Meanwhile, Barbara Foy dug in, becoming angrier and angrier. Another white juror asked to hear tapes of the testimony. This juror, honestly unsure about the case, was losing sleep, wrestling with the details. He and Foy became the last holdouts. Martino led a fight to prevent him from re-hearing the testimony. When he tried to talk, Martino shouted him down. For days he pleaded to hear tapes. Their arguments came to a head the morning of May 22, when, as Stan Simon would later write, the undecided juror "shouted, slammed his fist on the table, kicked a chair against the wall."

A doctor was called. Barbara Foy erupted. "The heck with you all," she told the other jurors, according to the *Courant* account. "They're guilty on all charges, both of them." More yelling ensued. The doctor arrived to examine the juror. The diagnosis was an upset stomach. The doctor prescribed medication and a day of rest. At 10:32, Judge Mulvey sent the jurors home the rest of the day.

On May 24, after five days of haggling, after they listened to a tape of Warren Kimbro's testimony, the foreman sent Judge Mulvey a note at 11:15 A.M.: "Your Honor, we feel we have not and will not reach a decision on either case on all charges."

Give it another try after lunch, Mulvey said.

The jurors tried again for another ninety rancorous minutes. "Your Honor," read the foreman's next note to Mulvey, "we still feel we are deadlocked on all nine charges. We feel that it is in vain to continue deliberating." Mulvey declared mistrials in cases No. 15681, *State v. Ericka Huggins*, and No. 15844, *State v. Bobby Seale*.

As he dismissed the exhausted jurors, Mulvey admonished them: Don't say a word about this case to anybody. That would jeopardize the defendants' chances for a fair hearing if the state tries them again, Judge

Mulvey declared. He wanted to see all the lawyers and the defendants at two o'clock the next day. The courtroom cleared.

Marilyn Martino, the jury's leading pro-Panther strategist, immediately ignored Mulvey's order. She met with attorney Charles Garry and revealed all that had gone on in the jury room.

Based on that information, on the jury's initial decision to acquit Seale, Garry's assistant, David Rosen, came to the next afternoon's meeting in Judge Mulvey's chambers prepared with a motion to dismiss the case. Katie Roraback had a similar motion. She planned to argue, once more, that all the publicity prevented the Panthers from receiving a fair trial, even with a new jury. Prosecutor Markle came prepared with a motion of his own—not just to have another trial, but to have it moved outside New Haven.

As they prepared to move into the courtroom, Garry asked permission to make his motion first. He needed to catch a plane to California.

As usual, he and Roraback were working at cross-purposes. Roraback pleaded with Mulvey for time. She needed days to prepare her motion, she told the judge, to accumulate the evidence of damaging anti-Panther publicity.

Don't worry, Judge Mulvey told her. "I think I can take judicial notice of that."

They convened in open court at 2:21 P.M. Mulvey allowed Markle to go first. The prosecutor asked for a new venue for a new trial.

"Deny your motion," Judge Mulvey responded.

David Rosen went next, then Roraback, asking for dismissal of the charges.

Mulvey listened as Markle made one last plea. "These people can get a fair trial," he said. "We can get a jury."

When Markle finished, Judge Mulvey turned to Katie Roraback. "Anything further?" he asked.

"No," Roraback responded.

At that point, the judge reached into his robe. He retrieved a piece of paper. It turned out that, before they all gathered in his chambers, he had already considered the arguments and handwritten a decision.

"I have been involved in these cases and related cases," Mulvey told the courtroom, for something approaching two years. I have, by that happenstance, gained a rather wide knowledge of the factual situation and, indeed, of the defendants themselves.

Mrs. Huggins has been confined for more than two years in this state. Mr. Seale has been confined in this state and other states for at least that amount of time. He is also faced with the problem in the State of Illinois that involves confinement. I have observed a rather remarkable change in the attitude of these defendants during the time they have been before me, and I don't think it is feigned.

I am advised by the clerk of this court that the array of jurors for this court year is practically exhausted and that the possibility of drawing a panel for these cases is practically nil. The new array will not be available until September. . . .

The state has put its best foot forward in presenting its effort to prove its case against these defendants. They have failed to convince a jury of their guilt.

With the massive publicity attendant upon the trial just completed, I find it impossible to believe that an unbiased jury could be selected without superhuman efforts, efforts which this court, the state and these defendants should not be called upon either to make or to endure.

The motion to dismiss is granted in each case, and the prisoners are discharged forthwith.

Shock swept the courtroom. Livid, Markle sputtered a request for a new trial. Mulvey denied it. The two law-and-order men, who had begun this case as affectionate partners, left on bitter terms, their friendship permanently riven.

And that was it. Ericka was free.

The conservative judge—the target of Panther protesters who argued that his previous private antiblack statements should have disqualified him from hearing the case—had not only dismissed the jury. He ended the case. No new trial, no more charges. He even went so far as to praise the defendants. Incredibly, the judge later revealed to the *Courant*'s Stan Simon (the star reporter at the trial, who earned every side's confidence) that although he believed that Seale and Ericka were guilty of at least some charges, he felt they had served enough time.

Furthermore, Mulvey came around to the view that had so infuriated him and Arnold Markle when the case began. He agreed with Kingman Brewster. After his determination to spend years proving that the system worked, he now declared that, at least in this case before him, two black revolutionaries could *not* receive a fair trial in this country.

Bobby Seale was ecstatic. Sure, he'd lost years of freedom, and marshals were about to return him back to custody to face charges in Illinois. But he'd won a round against a government determined to convict him. He escaped, at least temporarily, the threat of the electric chair. Seale turned to the people next to him, the court stenographers, Walter Rochow and Arthur Moan. Seale clasped their hands warmly. Then he hugged his lawyers.

Ericka was at least equally ecstatic. Joy burst like a sudden sunrise on her face as supporters prepared to usher her through the crowded hallway onto the Green. She hugged Roraback. Around her, people were crying; so was she. On her way out, Ericka, too, turned to the court stenographers Rochow and Moan: "You haven't died yet, motherfuckers." Rochow and Moan celebrated the case's end, too. Thanks to all the overtime they'd made, they bought new Cadillac Coup DeVilles. They would drive those cars for the next fifteen years.

Moan bought a dark blue model. He named it "Bobby." Rochow named his car "Ericka." It was bright yellow.

Part III

CHAPTER 23

Time Out

ON JUNE 23, 1971, Warren returned to Courtroom B to be formally sentenced on his second-degree murder charge. The charge carried a life sentence.

Warren's lawyer, Larry Iannotti, prepared a motion asking Judge Mulvey to suspend the sentence and release Warren on probation. A letter pleading Warren's case came from his old boss at West Shore Cleaners. His fellow antipoverty workers testified to Warren's heroic work in the community and his gift for reaching troubled kids. They all characterized his Panther period as an unfortunate, short-lived aberration from which Warren had recovered. Remarkably, this group of supporters included a former supervisor whom Warren had branded a "back-biting motherfucker" (at a community meeting called about whether to fire him). The CPI bosses even said they would hire Warren again.

Making his pitch to Judge Mulvey, Iannotti invoked the ghost of Alex Rackley. "One of the tragedies here is that Alex Rackley has been mourned really, it seems to me, by really very very few. And outside of his immediate family, I think one person who has mourned him has been my client, Warren Kimbro. That has been lost sight of in all of the fanfare that surrounded these proceedings, and I hope Your Honor recognizes this remorse, this contrition."

When Iannotti finished, Warren declined, on Iannotti's advice, a chance to address the court. Iannotti saw no sense in jeopardizing a script that appeared tilted in Warren's favor.

The prosecutor, Arnie Markle, and Judge Mulvey took their turns speaking. Markle used his opportunity for rebuttal instead to continue the tribute to the reformed Warren. Markle mentioned encountering Warren in the pre-Panther days, when Warren would try to negotiate second chances for his charges at the Residential Youth Center. "I don't think that I have ever been impressed more with someone," Markle gushed. He spoke of the "proper adjustment" Warren had undergone in prison since the murder. He spoke of how the Black Panthers "used him and threw him away."

"This man is truly contrite. I think that there is very little that prison life can do for him," declared the same prosecutor who had fought so hard to have Bobby Seale and Ericka Huggins executed on the flimsiest evidence. "I know that [Warren] took a life. I think that nobody knows it more than he does. But, on the other hand, I think he tried to repair many lives and will continue to, and I think if there is any merit to our system of justice, that some place along the line the state will be able to extend some consideration to him."

"He has purged himself," concurred Judge Mulvey. "I think he has come to a full realization as to what a terrible thing was done, and he wants to clean himself. I think he has, to a large degree."

Under the law, Iannotti's motion notwithstanding, Mulvey said regretfully, he had no choice but to sentence Warren to life in prison. Markle agreed—and promised that he would speak up for Warren if he should choose to seek a pardon.

Iannotti knew all along that his motion was a long shot. Still, he needed to have it placed in the record for that next step—which Warren fully intended to take. He still hadn't given up on the goal he'd chosen in the prison Guides for Better Living class.

Even though Warren's attorney was building a persuasive case for giving his client a second chance at freedom, there was also a measure of justice in the fact that the Panthers remaining in prison for the long haul were the three who gave the order and fired the shots in the swamp, George Sams, Warren, and Lonnie McLucas. Like Iannotti, McLucas's lawyer had a plan for springing him early: he filed a writ of habeus corpus based on the fact that evidence used against McLucas was in part the product of illegal wiretapping conducted by the local police department.

The state would have to choose between producing embarrassing evidence of its illicit methods or allowing McLucas to go free. The state eventually chose the latter.

Meanwhile, a jury in New York City found all the Panthers on trial innocent of the charges connected to the supposed 1969 plan to blow up department stores, the case that set in motion the paranoia and events culminating in Alex Rackley's fatal trip to Connecticut. The trial produced revelations of undercover agents and informants being mixed up, too mixed up, in plans that the real Panthers—whoever one can assume them to have been—might never have cooked up on their own.

Even with party members winning their freedom in New York and New Haven, the Black Panther Party had been crippled by the internal fighting, the trials, and the raids in cities around the country. Followers would still emerge from time to time in New Haven, but the party had seemingly petered out. Loyalists to Huey Newton gathered in Oakland to remold the party as a bipartite entity. One part came aboveground. It registered voters, ran candidates for office (Bobby Seale's respectable showing in a campaign for mayor laid the foundation for the election of Oakland's first black mayor the next time around), worked with churches, ran a school. Ericka threw herself into the latter project. The other half of the party Newton modeled on the mafia: overseeing rackets, carrying out beatings and murders.

Back in the turn-of-the-century red-brick schoolhouse-looking jail in rural Brooklyn, Connecticut, Warren wanted to put not just the case but the party behind him. Of the fourteen Panthers arrested, the only ones whose cases remained open were Landon Williams and Rory Hithe. Soon these two were also on their way to freedom. When they appeared in court on November 19, the state no longer had the energy to conduct any more Panther trials—even though one could reasonably argue that the evidence at trial had pointed a far more damning finger at Landon Williams than at Bobby Seale or Ericka Huggins. Nevertheless, Prosecutor Markle allowed Williams and Hithe to plead guilty to conspiracy to murder-related charges in return for twenty-nine-month suspended sentences, covering the twenty-nine months they had already served. The sentencing judge suggested that as part of their release, Williams and Hithe should agree to go straight to the airport in New York, fly to California, and never return to Connecticut. At this point, Williams and Hithe would probably have agreed to any terms. They were happy to leave the State of Connecticut.

Maybelle Kimbro, on the other hand, was happy her son was still in Connecticut, where she could at least visit him in prison.

"Your son turned around. He's a new man," people told Maybelle Kimbro when she visited Warren in prison.

"No, he's the same man," Maybelle replied. "He's just being himself now, what he was raised to be."

Whether reborn or reverting to his true self, Warren continued racing down the road to redemption. His attorney's strategy paid off in October 1971, when the state pardon board did what Judge Mulvey and Prosecutor Markle wanted to but felt they couldn't: it reduced Warren's sentence to four years, an unheard-of act of lenience in Connecticut.

That meant Warren had less than two years left behind bars, assuming he maintained his exemplary record. Warren walked through prison hallways with his head high, whistling. He was determined not to jeopardize his release. Observing the other inmates marking off each day on their calendars until their release, Warren repeated his mantra: Don't count time. Make the time count.

It hurt to keep silent when he saw problems that, on the outside, he would have spoken up about. When he overheard guards badmouthing inmates or saw one guard waiting for a female visitor to see her incarcerated boyfriend then asking her out, Warren chose not to say a word. No, he wasn't happy being in prison. Yet he was determined not to let prison make him unhappy, even though he desperately missed his freedom and having privacy.

The warden eventually allowed Warren to begin taking weekend furloughs. The first furlough was for Thanksgiving, 1971. Warren's brother-in-law Ernie drove his Audi up to Brooklyn in a snowstorm to bring Warren home for Thanksgiving dinner.

The meal was a disaster, the tension between Sylvia and Warren thicker than the cranberry sauce on the table. Even though his children desperately missed him, Warren chose to spend the second night of the furlough at Ernie and Betty's house. He filled the time with visits to old friends and relatives who asked to see him.

Germano and Veronica were starting to get into serious trouble at school and in the neighborhood. At Sylvia's request, Warren did make time during his Thanksgiving visit to pull aside Veronica, at the threshold of adolescence, for a birds-and-bees talk.

Sylvia and Warren decided it made sense to proceed with a divorce Sylvia had originally sought, then dropped, back in '69. Sylvia had a job with the state's social-service agency. And she had a new man, Bobby, who worked at the local rifle plant. During a visit home, Sylvia and Warren agreed that Warren would break the news of the divorce to the kids. Veronica was crushed.

Once back behind bars, Warren worked hard at his studies, hard enough that he earned a spot in Eastern Connecticut State College's honors program. In early '72, the warden allowed Warren to start traveling to the campus to take courses.

Most mornings an English professor who lived nearby picked Warren up. Warren soon developed a close bond with his new acquaintance. The professor, Carl Meigs, who taught English, chauffeured Warren even on days when the professor didn't need to go to campus. Meigs ran an honors English program in which Warren enrolled and in which he took a strong interest.

Each day they drove seventeen miles past woods and sun-sparkled lakes, dotted by the shacks and rundown homes of the rural Connecticut "Swamp Yankees," who relied on wood stoves out of fiscal necessity, not a thirst for quaintness. The ride along the bucolic roads to campus seemed endless. Warren was eager to interact with people other than inmates. He felt like a kid wondering, "Are we there yet? Are we there yet?"

Talks with Meigs helped pass the time. With his moustache and low Southern drawl, Meigs reminded Warren of Tennessee Williams. It impressed Warren when he'd see Meigs finish the *New York Times* crossword in under an hour. The two would pick up coffee at Dunkin' Donuts, light up cigarettes, and engage in long conversations about the history and development of the English language. They talked music; Meigs, who played around on the piano, adored Scott Joplin.

In school Warren focused on sociology and English. He maintained an A-minus average. He also resumed his pursuit of the opposite sex, in the form of an undergrad named Janice. People called her "J.J." Twenty years old, eighteen years younger than Warren, she followed Warren around when he first appeared on campus, a magnetic celebrity with a fearsome rep and a disarming manner. At first Warren kept his distance;

he feared that romantic involvements with students could jeopardize his eventual release from jail. But he couldn't help noticing her wide hips, her bright smile. J.J. was flattered when this older man started paying her attention. She didn't date much; she was attractive, but shy when it came to romance. With Warren, it was different. J.J. drove Warren back to jail at night and spent weekends with Warren on furloughs at Warren's friends' homes.

One of the old friends Warren would see offered a more lasting ticket out of jail. Warren's old boss from the Residential Youth Center, Ira Goldenberg, had left his professor's job at Yale for a post at Harvard. He was part of a new program called Clinical Psychology and Public Practice. It aimed to attract students with real-life experience in community work. Goldenberg decided that Warren belonged in this Harvard program. So what if Warren never graduated high school, if he was in jail on a murder conviction, if he was taking undergraduate courses at a second-tier state college. Goldenberg recommended Warren for admission to the Harvard program, through the Graduate School of Education. Warren was accepted.

One problem: Warren couldn't get to class. The prison system refused to grant him permission to travel out of state to Harvard's campus in Cambridge, Massachusetts. A corrections worker who was pursuing a doctorate at Harvard offered to drive Warren to school each day. Denied.

Warren's lawyer appealed to the state corrections department to release him. Counting the years Warren spent in jail before his sentencing, plus time he'd earned for good behavior, he'd already served the minimum four years of his newly reduced sentence. Even the FBI was through worrying about Warren. On May 12, 1972, the New Haven office informed J. Edgar Hoover that it was deleting Warren from its "Agitator Index." As a memo four days earlier noted, Warren "has alienated himself from the BPP [Black Panther Party]. . . . He is no longer in a position to influence others and to engage in acts inimical to the national defense. KIMBRO is not likely to furnish financial aid or other assistance to revolutionary elements and is not known to have any revolutionary sympathetic associations nor ideologies at this time. . . . KIMBRO has undergone a complete change since his involvement in the RACKLEY murder case."

Despite support from brass at the Brooklyn jail, corrections department officials refused to accept Warren's math. Warren was technically serving a life sentence for murder. They wouldn't count his two years of incarceration prior to his sentencing. They couldn't start subtracting earned good-behavior time until four years after his sentencing, or until June 1975.

Warren's attorney filed suit to challenge that decision. The attorney, Larry Iannotti, appeared before Superior Court Judge Anthony E. Grillo.

"Do you mean to tell me, Mr. Iannotti," Judge Grillo asked him, "that I should let loose someone who killed somebody, so he can go to Harvard?"

Well, yes, Iannotti responded. He claimed society received its retribution by jailing Warren for his crime and that Warren reformed himself while incarcerated. The community would benefit more from his release, from the work he would do, than from keeping him locked up. Furthermore, Iannotti argued, Warren was entitled to release based on the time he served before his sentencing. Judge Grillo decided, like the corrections department, that under the law Warren had to serve at least four years from his sentencing. The state legislative record made clear lawmakers' intent. Whatever the legal merits of Iannotti's argument, whatever impressive strides Warren had made behind bars, whatever anguish he suffered for his misdeed, it was hard to summon sympathy for Warren.

The Harvard angle intrigued others besides Judge Grillo. "Panther Sues to Leave Prison for Harvard," read a *Washington Post* headline. Many people were understandably wondering how a high school dropout and convicted murderer earns his way into Harvard. One of the many intrigued parties was David Susskind's television producers in New York. They invited Warren to appear on Susskind's syndicated show. Warren was reluctant, as Susskind had a reputation for skewering guests. Warren's lawyer suggested an appearance could help Warren's cause. Warden Hills at the jail encouraged Warren, too. His model prisoner would make the prison system look good. Indeed, the same prison system that decided Warren couldn't travel out of state to attend Harvard classes had a change of heart when it came to driving out of state to TV studios in New York.

Upon arriving, Warren was ushered into the studio before the hour-long show's taping. A platter was set up with salami and corned beef.

Warren, rail thin and adorned in loud multi-colored polyester, wearing his Afro large, couldn't keep still. He wondered if Susskind would make him look like a fool.

The white-haired host appeared in a wrinkled suit. He grabbed a hunk of cold cuts and quickly scarfed it. "We're going to ask you a series of questions," Susskind told Warren as they sat down. "The producers have them for me on a card."

Warren fidgeted in his swivel chair as the interview began. He bobbed about as nervously as he had in the witness chair in Courtroom B.

Susskind wasn't in attack mode. Still, Warren couldn't settle down.

"Please have Mr. Kimbro sit still in the chair!" the producer called to Susskind at the first break.

"Be calm," Susskind implored Warren.

The producer spoke again to Susskind. "You're not asking the questions we gave you," he said.

Warren wondered what those questions were.

"These questions are ridiculous," Susskind declared. "I'm not going to embarrass him!" Then he tore up the card. Warren wondered if it was a trick.

As the hour-long show progressed, Warren finally relaxed. Susskind asked about Warren's life, his goals, how he got into Harvard. At a break, Warren told Susskind how the cops had known all about what was happening with Rackley, how the police could have prevented the murder if they chose. Warren wholeheartedly believed these things, but he didn't want to repeat them on the air.

And then it was over. Nothing but softballs. Susskind asked Warren to let him know if anyone tried to prevent him from getting out of jail. "When you get up to Cambridge," he said on the way out, "have a good time. That's where I went to school."

Warren returned to his studies at Eastern. He and Sylvia had been divorced for a year now, and that marriage seemed like ancient history to Warren. Meanwhile, young J.J. offered the promise of something new, a fresh start. They soon began talking about marriage. Warren didn't sink to his knees to propose, but they agreed at some point after his release from jail they would make the relationship official and legal. Warren gave J.J. money to buy a diamond ring, which she did. In between furloughs and campus visits, they kept up a passionate correspondence. "I miss you precious. I don't know if I miss you more than I love you or love you more than I miss you," Warren wrote. J.J. addressed one card to "my sweet ebony man—knowing that you are mine makes my heart sing, my body dance and it makes words hard to find. I love you, I love you, I love you!"

Warren's reputation as a smart guy with a social gift, more pussycat than Panther, spread beyond the pages of his correspondence with J.J. and even beyond the campus confines. Rich Singleton, a New York idealist running a drug treatment program called Perception House a few blocks from Eastern, heard about Warren from student workers. Singleton, who wore sandals, psychedelic shirts, and a "WASP 'fro," planned to leave his job to attend social work school. He encouraged Warren to apply to replace him as head of the organization. The Perception House board liked the idea. Warren could serve as a role model for those looking to turn their lives around. Moreover, he was tough enough to handle the ex-cons who worked at Perception House. Warden Hills liked the idea, too. He knew it was a bold step to allow Warren to take the job while remaining a prisoner. Hills also knew it would offer more good publicity for programs that rehabilitated, rather than merely warehoused, inmates.

"Murderer in 1969, Counselor Today," marveled a *New York Times* headline. The article described Warren's journey from high school dropout to Panther (in a "reported love affair with Mrs. Ericka Huggins"), to murderer, to prison counselor and award-winning newspaper editor, to $12,500-a-year director of Perception House. (Warren only kept $27 a week as the rest of the money went to the state for his room and board and child support to Sylvia.) The article quoted Warden Hills saying that Warren "earned whatever he has. He worked hard for it." The article also quoted Henry Karney, Warren's previous warden at the Montville jail. Karney's words dispelled any doubts about which side of the system this former Panther now inhabited, whose agenda he promoted. "He got the militant young blacks he knew were going off in the wrong direction and got them re-directed," Karney said. "He did all this voluntarily; we didn't brainwash him."

While clearly no longer a barricade stormer, Warren did still challenge the status quo at Perception House. He disagreed with the "hard concept" approach he inherited at Perception House. Counselors berated addicts and humiliated them. The addicts wore large signs reading, "I'm a junkie dope fiend drug addict." They got to take off the signs when they performed community work. Why, Warren asked, if we don't want to shame them out in the community, do we shame them inside the agency? He worried that the approach lowered expectations and reinforced poor self-esteem. Doctors on the board of directors agreed with him. The signs shrank in size. The terminology changed to describing people as *acting* like junkies.

One of Warren's first tasks was to fire two ex-cons who had been accused of having inappropriate sexual relations with female clients. One called him an Uncle Tom.

"What do you know about being a drug addict?" the other challenged him.

"I know something about running an agency," Warren responded.

J.J., who was still in school, dutifully picked Warren up from jail and drove him to work at Perception House. At first they used a '69 Cougar borrowed from Wes Forbes, Warren's buddy from antipoverty agency days. (Forbes was another standout community worker whom Ira Goldenberg recruited to the Harvard graduate program.) Then one day Warren spotted a '72 sunburst gold MGB GT. He wanted that car. He had saved enough money to make monthly payments. He bought insurance from a part-time agent in town who happened to be a state cop. After a while, Warden Hills even let Warren drive himself to and from work. He knew Warren wouldn't jeopardize his pending release by sneaking in liquor or drugs. He understood Warren had a mission.

Warren knew he was pushing it when a guard noticed the sparkling new sports car in the lot. "Whose car is that?" the guard hissed.

Warren made up a story on the spot. "I'm using it," he said. He usually drove the older Cougar, but it broke down one day when J.J. was driving it, Warren claimed. Warren pretended his mom lent him this one. Warden Hills, in earshot, kept mum.

Hills recommended Warren for an "Outstandingly Meritorious Performance Award." Corrections Commissioner Manson granted it, cutting Warren's sentence by another three months. On December 12, 1973, the parole board considered Warren's case again. This time Warren got a break. He wouldn't have to wait until the middle of 1975 after all to be released on parole. A new date was set: January 17, 1974. Just weeks away.

CHAPTER 24

BMOC

FORMER INMATE 24835 was an Ivy Leaguer now, and he determined to dress the part. The leather jacket of his Panther days gave way to a corduroy coat and, on other days, a grey and black herringbone tweed jacket, with grey wool flannel pants or houndstooth-checked Pendleton-Mills slacks. While the schlumpy look was de rigueur for many of Cambridge's privileged students, Warren preferred to walk out of a J. Press catalog.

Sartorial enthusiasm notwithstanding, his Crimson loyalty had limits. When Warren and his old buddy Wes Forbes went to Cambridge's Soldier's Field for the annual Harvard-Yale football game, they sat among their fellow Harvard students. But Warren rooted for the Bulldogs, the way he had since his childhood days at the Yale Bowl. (Yale, undefeated all season, lost to Harvard that day.)

On campus, Warren caught the eye of Professor Charles V. Willie. Dr. Willie, as he was referred to, noticed the clean-cut older student in his graduate education class on an upper floor of Harvard's Guttman Library. He noticed how Warren spoke up often in class, how much he had to say, and how his real-world perspective added to the discussion.

Warren noticed how Dr. Willie dressed, too. Dr. Willie wore a shirt and tie to class, neat, ready to teach. Warren's other professors more often looked as if they'd just rolled out of bed. Warren admired Dr. Willie. Like Warren, Dr. Willie was black, a product of modest circumstances. Dr. Willie's father, a sleeping-car porter in the era of A. Philip Randolph, and his mother, a schoolteacher, put five kids through college. Warren liked addressing his professor as "Dr."

Warren devoured the material in his classes on statistics and on moral development, but he cherished most of all Dr. Willie's course on families, class, and race. The black family was a hot topic on campuses amid America's morning-after reexamination of the '60s. Liberal academics and civil rights activists were furious at Daniel Patrick Moynihan, a Harvard-educated future U.S. senator, for a prominent report he authored on the breakdown of the black family. Moynihan pinned much of the blame on the absence of black fathers. Supporters credited him for telling painful truths. His critics accused him of blaming victims, of providing cover for racial discrimination.

Moynihan's critics included Dr. Willie, who considered Moynihan's research second rate and his conclusions short sighted. Dr. Willie reported to the class on the distressingly high number of single female-headed black households in America, the same trend that concerned Moynihan. Dr. Willie also presented statistics showing that, in a majority of cases, the men in those families had died prematurely, from cancer, hypertension, heart attack.

"What's the issue?" Dr. Willie asked his students.

Warren listened to black women in the class trash "these brothers" for abusing drugs and alcohol and shirking responsibilities. He raised his hand. "Dr. Willie," Warren said, "that seems like a public health issue to me." Yes, Dr. Willie said, it seemed that way to him, too.

At no time during the discussion did Warren's mind turn to the single-female-headed household from which he'd been absent, to his own two children, who were getting into increasing trouble at school and in the neighborhood. This was about statistics. This was about drug and alcohol abuse. This wasn't about him.

Warren immersed himself in his course work. He was drawn, as always, to new ideas, and new faces. He hadn't even finished his undergraduate work, and he was already pursuing his master's degree at the country's most prestigious university, while holding a job and embarking on a new marriage. Somehow, he managed to find time for everybody in his immediate orbit, from J.J. to students to old friends. His friend Wes, whom Ira Goldenberg had also recruited for the Harvard program, was struggling. He didn't know if he could keep up with the demands of raising five children, holding a full-time job, and pursuing a graduate degree. Warren talked him out of dropping out.

Each day Warren drove to classes in Cambridge from the apartment he and J.J. had in Willimantic, Connecticut. He taped his professors' lectures and listened to them again on his way back to Connecticut. He drove to the Eastern Connecticut State campus, where he now pulled down a paycheck as a consultant for student activities. He was the administrator that students saw when planning campus activities; they also started showing up for general life advice. Warren was tired by the end of the evening, eager to get home to J.J. Students kept him on the Eastern campus late into the night. They talked to Warren about school, about careers, about their love lives—everything except the Black Panthers. They knew he listened to them. He had good advice. They called him by his initials, "WAK."

Warren earned his Harvard degree in June 1975 at forty-one years old. That fall he earned a promotion to assistant dean of student affairs at Eastern Connecticut State. The job paid $14,000 a year (about $50,300 today). The university's president at first hesitated to promote Warren. After all, Warren had only a year and a half earlier been released from prison, a notorious murderer. Ultimately the president figured that Warren could reach the kids. It would not be long after Warren's promotion that he delivered. Students planned a sit-in to protest the slow pace of construction on a new student center. They told the former Black Panther of their plans.

"Look, kids, I've been through this," Warren said. "You don't want to take this over. It's only going to delay it. If the cops have to pull you out, the place will get more trashed and take even longer to fix up."

The sit-in was called off, much to the pleasure of the administration. The center did get built—with an upstairs office for Dean Kimbro.

A smiling Warren grabs a rope in a game of tug of war in a photo in the November 24, 1975, issue of *People* magazine. Another photo beside it shows "Dean Kimbro" making a point to a table of Eastern students as they "rap" about "issues ranging from student government to a Hula Hoop tournament." Warren's old, unsmiling, police mug shot nestles between the two photos, beside the celebratory article's headline: "A Black Panther Who Murdered Salvages His Life and Becomes a College Dean." The article describes Warren's "great rapport" with the students and the long hours he worked. It credits his continued determination to address injustice, this time by peacefully seeking "lasting change [that] starts with education."

In spite of the media's continuing fascination with Warren, his brand of advice initially disappointed student body president Joel Ide. Ide, an Air Force vet, turned radical before entering college at twenty-three. He protested against the war in Vietnam. As he sought to stir the activist cauldron at Eastern, he figured he had an ally in the former Panther dean. When he encountered Warren in the student union one day, Ide told him of plans to organize a protest against an administrator with a reputation for sexually harassing female students and faculty. Warren surprised Ide by urging him to proceed slowly, through proper channels. He warned Ide against making claims if he didn't have female victims willing to testify publicly.

"This isn't how you *used* to do things," Ide thought.

Another time Ide listened as Warren talked him out of fighting with a student government member over how to spend student activity money. Warren walked Ide through Robert's Rules of Order to settle the dispute in a less confrontational way. Ide followed the advice and prevailed in a public vote. Gradually, Warren convinced him of the possibility of working within the system for change.

"Where did the *other* Warren go?" Ide took to teasing the tamed Panther. The affectionate tone reflected Ide's respect for Dean WAK.

WARREN ALSO TRIED to intervene in the lives of his own children; he had less success there than at Eastern. His ex-wife Sylvia was having trouble with both of them. Veronica, thirteen, was skipping school and smoking cigarettes. Warren had recently given up his smoking habit on his doctor's advice. Sylvia struggled to earn the rent and to keep strong for the kids. She found it hard to talk with them about what was going wrong; getting through the day and keeping the home together proved enough of a challenge. By this time she had learned she couldn't count on Warren.

Warren pressed Sylvia to allow the children to move in with him and J.J. in Willimantic. Veronica came up for the fall of '75. She wanted out of Sylvia's house. While Warren was happy to see Sylvia with a new mate (mostly he was pleased not to have to pay any more token alimony, just child support), he worried about the children's reaction. Indeed, like many children of divorce, Veronica and Germano resented the new adult in the house. They wanted Warren, not Bobby, to be their father. So they refused to allow Bobby to play the role of parent. His attempts to discipline them led to shouting matches and a continuing standoff.

In Willimantic, Veronica resented J.J., too, at first. J.J. was so much younger than Warren. Veronica felt lonely sitting on the couch while J.J. and Warren snuggled on their big black bean-bag chair. Veronica wanted to be the one snuggling with her father. She decided J.J. was simple minded—although she couldn't deny that J.J. loved Warren. She also appreciated the fact that J.J. cooked his meals and kept the house clean.

After being absent from Veronica's life for years, Warren thought he could now assert himself, set limits. He grounded Veronica after she was caught smoking at school. One day Veronica wanted to go to the library with a friend to work on a term paper. Warren said OK. He warned her to go straight to the library, then straight home. As it turned out, Veronica's friend, who delivered newspapers, needed to pick up a check first at the newspaper office. Then she stopped by a store to buy cigarettes. As they walked on Willimantic's main drag toward the library, she asked Veronica to hold the pack in her pocketbook. Veronica agreed.

Just then Warren happened to pull up to mail a letter at the post office. He spotted Veronica. "I told you go to the library," he fumed. Veronica's friend was smoking; Warren demanded that Veronica open her pocketbook. There Warren found a pack of cigarettes. "They aren't mine," Veronica insisted; she said they belonged to her friend. Warren wasn't buying it. Warren took her home.

It was the first spanking Veronica had received in years. Warren whipped her butt with a belt; J.J. watched, horrified. Veronica fumed for weeks and never did finish the term paper. At Christmas time, Sylvia's sister drove down from Boston to pick up Veronica for a New Haven visit with her cousin Cece. Warren didn't want Veronica to go until she finished the term paper. "She's not going to *nobody's* house," Warren declared, "until she does that."

Veronica couldn't believe it.

"You should let her make the decision," Sylvia's sister said.

Warren turned to his daughter. "Veronica," he said, "let me tell you something. If you leave, you're not coming back. When I put you on discipline to do something, you can't keep running."

"Oh daddy," Veronica responded, "Cece needs somebody to play with over Christmas." And she left.

After the holidays, Sylvia called to ask whether she should send Veronica back to Willimantic by bus. "Don't send her on nothing," Warren responded. Either he was raising the kids, or Sylvia was. Warren recognized after a while that he had made a mistake, that he could still assert authority over Veronica even if she made occasional trips back to New Haven. Indeed, Sylvia wanted Warren to straighten out Veronica; Sylvia felt overwhelmed trying to balance her work (now with the state social-services department) and two troubled teens needing an absent father. But Warren was too proud to revisit his ultimatum.

Warren didn't get even that far with Germano. Eleven months older than Veronica, Germano had fallen into deeper trouble than the occasional cigarette. With his father/coach in jail, Germano stopped playing sports. His friends introduced him to marijuana a couple of years later. He liked getting high, liked the acceptance he felt from his new group of friends. He started hanging out on Winchester Avenue, the beaten main drag of New Haven's Newhallville neighborhood, where jobs at the Winchester arms plant had once kept thousands of black migrants from the South employed.

The sharp-dressed drug dealers on Winchester Avenue, always flush with cash, replaced his dad's revolutionary pals in Germano's pantheon of role models. By thirteen, he was selling, too, starting out with marijuana. He also began hanging out at some less than reputable pool halls. As his dad earned his Harvard degree and took his post at Eastern, Germano only occasionally attended classes at Wilbur Cross High School, eventually dropping out altogether.

His father had dropped out of high school, hadn't he?

Come up to Willimantic, Warren pleaded over the phone. Germano said he couldn't. "Somebody owes me $20," he said.

"I'll give you the $20," Warren said.

"No," insisted Germano. "It's the principle." The principle, clearly, had more to do with Warren, with the hero who disappeared from his life, than it had to do with any deadbeat friends.

Warren kept asking why he couldn't come. Germano invented reasons. He didn't tell his dad how busy he really was, working. Black neighborhoods in postindustrial cities like New Haven, while bleeding manufacturing jobs, were emerging as destinations for a booming illegal drug industry, the heartiest legacy of the '60s cultural revolution. The bigger dealers were always on the lookout for talent. It wasn't long before they gave Germano larger supplies of marijuana, then speed, THC, and cocaine, to move. Germano hired a crew of kids, also under the age of sixteen, to help him. They wore wide-brimmed hats. They coined names for their crew and for other loose collections of dealers they formed with other friends: "The Macks," "The Ville," and "The Dogs." Germano might not have been a revolutionary the way his father was, but he had the guns to be as big and bad as any Black Panther. Everyone saw promise in the young teenager they called "Malow"—a bastardization of "'Mano," itself short for "Germano." Germano liked the anonymity his nickname offered, the cloak from the previous world that had fallen apart since his father's arrest.

WHILE GERMANO WAS fast acquiring a past, Warren worked to transcend his own. Back in New Haven, a community group called Project MORE, which helped ex-offenders rebuild their lives after jail, gave Warren an award for his turnaround.

Still, the past hovered around Warren's successful new life. One story gnawed at Warren over the years, practically asking to be discovered. The story had something to do with a tragedy in his father Henry's distant past. The grown-ups would whisper about it when relatives visited Spruce Street in the 1930s and '40s; they always shooed the children from the room.

One day in 1976 Warren learned the details during a phone conversation with a relative, Henry Kimbro's daughter from a previous marriage in Philadelphia. It happened that Henry grew up in rural Goochland County, in the hill country between Richmond and Charlottesville. Lynchings shaped the world around Southern blacks of that time. More than a thousand blacks, virtually all of them men, perished this way during the 1890s, while Henry Kimbrough (as his last name was spelled then) was entering manhood.

Henry's younger brother Walter became one of those victims. When Henry and his older brother John heard of Walter's fate, they took action.

They tracked down the ringleaders of the lynching party. The details wouldn't survive, but this much is known: Henry and Michael John killed at least one white lyncher.

This put their own lives at risk. The Kimbrough brothers beat a path out of Virginia. Henry fled to Kentucky, then to Delaware, then north to Philadelphia. Henry raised a family there, then skipped town and left them behind. He landed in New Haven—and covered his tracks, beginning by dropping the final three letters from his last name.

So, Warren learned, his father, too, had murdered. His father, too, had abandoned a wife and children. In their murders, they both were making efforts—one clearly retributory, the other misguided—to resist the racial order of their time. Like his father, Warren was also able to build a new life from the rubble of tragedy, self-inflicted and otherwise.

Warren's more recent past caught up with him in June 1976. That month Warren and J.J. finally got married. They'd been engaged for four years, living together for two. Warren didn't propose. Instead, they were about to move, and J.J. suggested that if they move together again, they should do both—settling in a place, taking vows—at the same time. J.J. wanted to marry more than Warren did. Her parents made it clear they considered them to be living in sin. She also figured he might start to trust her more if they married. OK, Warren said; we'll get married. J.J.'s father was pleased. Warren and J.J. walked down the aisle to a recording of Roberta Flack's "The First Time Ever I Saw Your Face."

It was also graduation season. Warren accepted an invitation to speak at commencement exercises at Fitch High School in the town of Groton, home of the Electric Boat shipyard, builder of nuclear submarines for the U.S. Navy. Parents protested. Warren got hate mail. Groton's Republican mayor, Donald Sweet, called Kimbro's invitation "the goddamnedest thing I ever hear of. If Kimbro isn't a Communist, I don't know what is." A violent right-wing group issued a threat.

Still, the senior class stuck by its invitation. Warren delivered his ten-minute address. It failed to fulfill Mayor Sweet's Communist expectations (although Warren did, in an act of sartorial irony, wear red pocket-squares on his jacket). Warren stuck to standard-issue pomp and circumstance rhetoric. He chose responsibility as his theme. "Success is achieved by those who keep trying," he told the seniors. "As young adults you will be held responsible for your actions whatever they may be." His script was straight out of Guides for Better Living. The supposedly dangerous radical also offered a few conciliatory words for Mayor Sweet: "I think young people are easy to influence, and I agree with Sweet and others who are concerned over the choice of speakers for events like this."

A state cop, part of beefed-up security, joked with Warren about how the policeman's job had changed. "One time we were guarding against you," he told the commencement speaker. "Now we've got to guard *you* against these nuts out there."

CHAPTER 25

Coming Home

By THE MIDDLE of the "Me" decade, the '60s were a distant memory. Radicals had dropped out of protest movements to enter academia, or they had cut their hair and taken conventional jobs, bought homes, and started families. Soul and protest music were gone from the airwaves; the radio played disco and Bread and Loggins and Messina. *Laugh-In* went off the air. President Nixon resigned amid the Watergate scandal. The bunker mentality of the Nixon White House gave way to the laconic, uneventful Ford presidency. The harsh tactics of both sides in the domestic war over dissent became subjects of revelation and study, not action. The U.S. Senate's Church Committee held hearings on COINTELPRO and other widespread FBI and CIA misdeeds and delivered. Participants in the bygone era's battles gobbled up the revelations. The attention of society at large turned away from politics and demands for change—except to begin to beat up on liberalism.

To his friends and to colleagues at Eastern, it appeared Warren was settling into a stable, middle-class existence. He thrived in his job. The slow pace of Willimantic was a tonic after years of turbulence, a peaceful, distant planet on which to rebuild a life. Warren and J.J. seemed as close as they had ever been. In June 1976, they married. They bought a raised ranch on North Ash Street. But Warren wasn't really home. In prison, he had written to J.J., "I think we can name our baby hope—whenever it comes around." Now that they were free to build a nest, Warren balked at having kids. J.J. was crushed; they fought about it. Their relationship lost its spark. They started to grow apart.

J.J. watched the gentle Warren, the steady mentor to Eastern students and Perception House addicts, turn into a violent control freak at home. They were far apart in age, and Warren had played the role of older man who set the terms from the start. As in previous relationships, Warren occasionally fell into fits of jealousy. As in his Panther days, as in his youth, he failed to control his temper. J.J. came to fear his violent outbursts. One outburst came the day Warren came home to find J.J.'s car outside, the door to their home chain-locked, and J.J. sitting on a couch with a longtime male friend. (She had absent-mindedly locked the door.) Warren demanded that she open the door. When she didn't comply fast enough, he screamed and shoved at the door—and broke it down. During other arguments he slapped her hard across the face.

J.J. grew frightened for her safety. Yet she told her therapist and her friends that the problems were her own fault. She told them, she told herself, that she was lucky to be with someone who helped so many people. She was lucky to meet so many of his interesting friends. After a fight, he would rub cocoa butter on her scrapes. He would profess his love for her. She wished she could figure out how not to ignite his rage. It would take years for J.J. to stop blaming herself and settle into a more stable marriage. In the meantime, her relationship with Warren crumbled.

For Warren, home would always be New Haven, and no matter how hard he tried, he couldn't make it in Willimantic with J.J. He started showing up in New Haven on weekends, thanks to his old friend and boss Ira Goldenberg. Leaving Harvard to head a small college in New Hampshire, Goldenberg launched yet another idealistic, nontraditional experiment for which he considered Warren an ideal participant. The experiment's acronym was FRED. Officially, it meant Franconia Education Degree; unofficially, participants called it the "First Radical Education Degree." Goldenberg wanted to find a way for hard-working blue-collar people to earn bachelor's degrees on weekends by having their real-life job experience count toward academic credits. He opened a satellite office just over the New Haven border in Hamden, where paraprofessionals and poverty-program workers enrolled in classes. Most weekends the faculty would drive down from New Hampshire; one weekend a month, the students would travel to the Live Free or Die state, black ripples in the region's white demographic stream.

Goldenberg convinced Warren to start teaching at FRED in 1979. Once he started coming to New Haven on weekends, Warren found reasons to spend more and more time there, less time in the static environs of his domicile with J.J. Once recharged, refocused, Warren hungered for the stimulation, the intellectual currents, the bustle, the daily challenges, the action of his hometown. Eastern wasn't Yale. Ash Street wasn't Spruce Street.

His peaceful, bucolic new start in Willimantic wasn't turning out as planned; Warren's real ties remained in New Haven. Thankfully, the polishing of his criminal record did proceed as planned. On April 26, Warren received a letter notifying him that the state had discharged him from parole; his murder sentence had formally ended. The parole board decided to end Warren's parole early. His record spotless, Warren, the board concluded, no longer posed a threat to society. The final report on him described him as a model parolee.

Warren found an office worker at Ira Goldenberg's FRED program harder to impress than the parole board. Her name was Beverly Moore. She ran the program's finance office. Warren met her early in his tenure at the program, when he drove over to the Hamden office in his sun-gold MGB to submit a travel bill. J.J. wasn't on Warren's mind much these days; she was back in Willimantic, while he made longer and longer trips to New Haven. At FRED, Warren was the hotshot new instructor, the ex-Black Panther, the strutting hometown celeb.

"Who's that?" one of the office workers asked, looking out the window. She thought the new guy looked handsome.

Beverly glanced out the window, then returned to work. "I don't know," she said. And she didn't care. She was busy.

It was Warren's first day. His friend Wes Forbes, now head of the Hamden campus, accompanied him. Forbes introduced Warren to Pat Little and Beverly.

Warren's travel bill was based on a special arrangement he had worked out with Ira Goldenberg. The salary at FRED matched Warren's Eastern salary; Warren said he needed more. That posed a problem for Goldenberg. As at RYC, Goldenberg promoted an egalitarian environment, so he couldn't pay Warren more salary than the other instructors. So he found a way to conceal a higher payment: As part of his deal with

Goldenberg to teach five courses, Warren could pad his travel expenses to add to his salary.

Warren handed Beverly his travel expense voucher.

An expense voucher on his first day? Beverly was suspicious. How could he have run up expenses already?

As he handed over the voucher, Warren noticed Beverly—attractive, skinny, with a bright smile. Given New Haven's small-town familiarity, Warren knew of Beverly; he was friendly with her brother.

"This isn't right," Beverly said, examining the bill. "You didn't travel this much. You can't get paid for this."

"Ira told me to put in for this extra travel."

Beverly didn't budge. She called Ira on the phone. "Let it go, Beverly," Ira said. "I approve of it."

Reluctantly, she handed over the check to Warren. "I don't know how you got this," she said.

"It's one of my fringe benefits," Warren responded. "By the way, you're another one of my fringe benefits."

Beverly shot him a scowl. She complained to her brother about his friend the rude, presumptuous instructor. "Well," her brother said, "just don't become a fringe benefit."

Even if his initial overtures were not particularly smooth, or at least not particularly well received, Warren wasn't about to give up. Now he had a challenge. He tried again one night when, after classes, FRED staffers retired for drinks to a bar called the Spirit Locker.

Wes Forbes invited Beverly to sit at a table with Warren. Warren chatted her up. She remained unimpressed.

"I'm married," Beverly informed Warren, who was barely tasting his Harvey's Bristol Cream.

"Oh, I didn't know that," Warren said. "Where's your husband?"

"We're separated."

"You're separated?"

"Yeah, I gave him a year to straighten up, or we're going to get a divorce."

Professor Kimbro slid into street mode. "You tell that nigger," he said, "his year is up."

Beverly looked at him, startled. "What did you say?"

"You tell him his year is up!"

Another night, over drinks with the gang from FRED at a watering hole called the Robin's Nest, Warren invited himself back to Beverly's place. "Don't you want to ride home in a sports car?" he asked. She took the invitation. As they arrived at her home on Diamond Street in New Haven's middle-class Beaver Hills neighborhood, Warren asked, "Don't you want to fix me breakfast?"

"You better go to the all-night drive-in if you want breakfast," Beverly snapped.

"You may not be cooking me breakfast now," Warren said, "but you'll be fixing me breakfast later."

He leaned over for a kiss. Beverly turned away, bade him good night.

Warren was undaunted. He couldn't stop thinking about her, and he was convinced that Beverly was softening on him. He bought her an orange rose. Then red roses started appearing at work, along with love poems.

When Beverly went to the closet to grab her coat at lunchtime, she noticed that Warren had wrapped the arms of his own coat around hers. "He's after you, Beverly," remarked her coworker. This man, twelve years Beverly's senior, was courting hard. Meanwhile, Beverly's friends urged her to give him a chance.

One Friday, he earned a ticket inside Beverly's door. He learned that a bunch of FRED people were going to her house to watch a Sugar Ray Leonard boxing match on TV. Warren picked up the phone. "How come you didn't invite me?" he asked Beverly. "Can I come over, too?" Yes, she said, he could join the group.

Warren was still in Beverly's home after the rest of the group went home that night. This time Beverly was open to the idea of making him breakfast, even though she hadn't even planned on inviting him to the party in the first place.

As they started dating, they grew comfortable together. Beverly liked the bond she saw developing between Warren and her only son, whose father had dropped out of his life.

Technically, Warren was crashing at a FRED building in Hamden. Technically, he still lived with J.J. in Willimantic. In truth, he was spending most of his time on Diamond Street in New Haven.

Warren began drawing closer again to his daughter, Veronica, after learning how much of her life he was missing. She was pregnant with her first child, staying in California with her uncle. Warren hadn't known. Just days before her delivery, a relative told Warren the news. He was disappointed but not mad. He sent her roses. No one had ever sent Veronica roses before, certainly not the man who had impregnated her and was staying in New Haven, where he was busy making babies with other women.

Warren also sent Veronica a plane ticket home. He and Beverly rented a station wagon and picked her up at JFK. Beverly drove back to New Haven, while Warren, swooning, held baby Imani in his arms in the front passenger seat.

Warren asked Veronica not to mention Beverly to J.J. It was obvious that J.J. and Warren's life together in Willimantic was winding down, but Warren wasn't ready, or forthright enough, to fess up to J.J., to reveal the details of the new life he was building in New Haven.

Veronica went to live with J.J. in Willimantic. Warren was rarely around. In his absence, Veronica and J.J. became friends. As Veronica stumbled into unfortunate relationships with other men, Warren stood by her. She was on her way to raising five children whose fathers disappeared. Warren, not the fathers, would drive Veronica to the hospital, buy the diapers she needed, and, more important, stay in the grand-children's lives. He called Veronica regularly to hear how the kids were doing. He advised Veronica on important decisions, and he scolded the kids when needed. He was "Poppa."

Warren and Beverly both filed for divorce. By 1982, their divorces were completed. Beverly and Warren liked the rhythm of their life together. Unlike J.J., Beverly knew how to negotiate Warren's moods. She had a mature strength from being out in the working world and from having survived a marriage. And she liked cooking, especially for Warren, who was an appreciative diner. When she sensed Warren getting upset, she prepared his favorite dish, spaghetti with pepperoni and meat sauce. Beverly's cooking was the closest to his mom's that Warren had ever tasted. Warren was gaining weight and starting to feel settled. Maybelle approved of Beverly; she made a point of complimenting a blue-and-white striped dress Beverly wore with a sailor collar with little red stars.

Again, Warren didn't drop to his knee to propose; the idea of marriage became inevitable during cozy conversations on the couch of Beverly's Diamond Street home. "I hope you get it right this time," Maybelle told Warren. "You have a good woman."

The morning of October 15, Warren and Beverly went to watch Beverly's son play football. That afternoon they got married in front of some fifty friends and relatives at a sprawling Colonial owned by Beverly's friend Mary Mitchell. For the first time since his days on Spruce Street, Warren was back home.

As Warren's life with Beverly was coalescing, his professional life at FRED was beginning to unravel. Warren and Ira Goldenberg had always been fighting friends. They loved each other and argued virtually without end. Warren accused Goldenberg of lowering standards for the students, especially when it came to writing. It didn't help students to give them passing grades in courses when they could barely write, Warren argued. Goldenberg beefed up writing training. He insisted the students deserved their passing grades.

Before long, they agreed they should part professional ways. Beverly was fired as part of the dispute because of her relationship with Warren. An attorney offered to sue FRED over the firing; he felt confident enough of winning that he was willing to take the case on contingency. But Beverly, who by nature preferred to avoid conflict, turned him down and found a job at her old employer, Yale University. Warren ended up all the way home, back in the Hill neighborhood, doing the precise kind of work that he had originally done in Dick Lee's antipoverty programs before joining the Black Panthers. The job was with the struggling young outfit that had given him an award in 1976, Project MORE. The acronym stood for "Model Offender Reintegration Experience." The program helped people leaving prison get back on their feet and find jobs, apartments, training, counseling. The previous director had left the job after police arrested him on drug charges. When Warren started work on March 8, 1983, he found lax systems in place—sloppy books, employees taking their paychecks days early. He needed to clean house.

More and more young people in the city's poor neighborhoods, especially males, were landing in jail, then returning to the streets with nowhere to live, no skills for legitimate jobs. A counterrevolution had broken out in cities across the country against the idealistic social experiments of the '60s. Around the time of Alex Rackley's murder, with a law-and-order Republican elected to the White House, America gradually turned away from seeking to address the root causes of crime and poverty and toward locking up the visible symptoms of urban poverty. After 1970, the number of Americans locked up in jails exploded. About 200,000 people were in prison or local jails in 1970, the level it had been for decades; three decades later the number would leap to close to two million. The majority of these inmates were blacks and Latinos under forty. They would emerge from jail back into their communities less equipped than ever to find work and lead stable lives. When Warren assumed the Project MORE post, he stepped to the front lines of resistance to that counterrevolution.

Warren was the ideal person to tackle that challenge. He had landed in a spot where he would stay and grow for decades, well past retirement age. His star was rising again in New Haven and throughout Connecticut. He even returned to Courtroom B as a regular visitor, as part of an alternative-to-incarceration program Project MORE was pioneering.

Warren built a staff in the image of the Residential Youth Center: street-savvy people from different backgrounds who could connect with people on the street as well as navigate through the bureaucracies of social services and local government. Soon Project MORE had a dynamic team in place and was operating new programs at the cutting edge of criminal justice reform. Warren recruited talented outreach workers like Gaspar Ortega, a former professional boxer and Mexican immigrant, and Joseph Caccone, an Italian-American social worker born in New Haven and now living in neighboring East Haven. They helped Warren boost Project MORE's employment rate for clients referred to the agency from around 25 percent to 80 percent. Before job interviews Warren gave the clients pep talks. He taught them about selling themselves, dressing well, acting polite, checking their egos at the door.

Warren set down rules for staff and clients alike: No swearing. ("Swearing is a strong way to express a weak mind," his father, Henry, used to say.) No blaming race for failures in the job market. (Warren crafted a motto: "Don't let racism be your excuse or reason why you can't. Let it be your motivation why you can and will succeed.") And no cash gifts to clients. Staff members like Caccone would be inclined to fish a few bucks from their pockets if a client said he was hungry. Buy him the meal instead, Warren said, so the money doesn't go to drugs or alcohol.

Project MORE blossomed into a stable, important force in the community as the staff of about half a dozen grew tenfold. Warren interacted with people from all levels of society. The agency held an annual awards program for politicians and other big shots; Warren knew how to cultivate the support of community leaders, who in turn could open the spigots of government money. One of the first politicians to pick up his framed Project MORE certificate, in front of the press at a ceremony at the downtown Chamber of Commerce office overlooking the Green, was Ben DiLieto—the former police chief who had once ordered illegal wiretaps of the Panthers. DiLieto had resigned as chief in 1977 after *New Haven Journal-Courier* reporter Andrew Houlding broke the story about the wiretap scandal. Two years later, DiLieto was elected mayor, propelled by a backlash among conservative white voters tired of Panthers, tired of liberals, tired of black people.

DiLieto showed up at Warren's Project MORE event and graciously accepted his award. DiLieto's City Hall, previously leery of Project MORE for hiring Warren, now supported the program. It helped Warren open a halfway house on Baldwin Street, one of the toughest stretches of the Hill, for prisoners released before the end of their sentences—prisoners like Warren's own son.

CHAPTER 26

Footsteps

W<small>ARREN AND</small> B<small>EVERLY</small> took the elevator to Flemming Norcott's court-room at the new courthouse on Church Street. The courthouse was a bright, sterile, glass-and-concrete tower looking down, a block away, upon the old squat, gloomy, marble courthouse, marked by its discolored wall and grand statues and frescoes of ladies and lions, where Warren and Ericka and Bobby Seale had been judged twelve years earlier. So many years later, Warren was back in the courthouse because he had an ap-pointment to see his son, before he vanished into the bowels of the prison system for an extended stay. Germano had done stints behind bars before. Now, at twenty-three, he had been prosecuted on drug-related burglary and larceny charges. The case was handled by the state's career criminal division, which was created to build cases against persistent felons, to make sure they enjoyed long taxpayer-paid vacations behind locked gates.

Warren knew Judge Norcott, a rising legal star in New Haven's black community on track to a state supreme court judgeship. He knew Tom Ullmann, the idealistic young public defender representing Germano. They'd arranged for Warren to meet with his son, in Ullmann's presence, in an anteroom before Germano's case went to trial.

Warren was angry. He was angry at Germano and angry at himself for his failures as a father. He didn't know what to do. His frustration ex-ploded when he walked into the anteroom to see his son. Germano looked hardened, like a gangster, nothing like the child who once showed promise with Dad on the ballfield.

If Germano wanted to play tough guy, then Warren would show him tough. Warren slapped Germano's check. He struck the son against whom he had rarely raised a hand growing up. The smack was so loud the sheriff in the courtroom heard and rushed in to investigate. Germano barely flinched. He glared at the father he'd never forgiven for disappearing from his life. "Maybe," Germano told him, "you should have done that earlier."

When Germano saw his father, feelings of insecurity wrestled in his soul with the last reservoirs of confidence, of manhood, with the conviction that to be a man meant concealing fear, meant standing up to take his punishment. At first he wanted to proceed with a jury trial. Then, partway through, he faced reality, pleaded guilty, and prepared for sentencing. The toughness Warren saw on his son was a facade. Germano resolved to change his life.

It wasn't Warren's slap that awoke him; rather, it was Tom Ullmann's writing assignment. The state labeled Germano a career criminal. At trial, the prosecutor called him "incurable," with no hope of ever leading a responsible life. Ullmann was convinced otherwise. For the sentencing, he asked Germano to write a sketch of his life to prove it. Once Germano started writing, he couldn't stop. In the days leading up to the sentencing, he stayed awake in his cell at the Whalley Avenue jail, the same lockup outside which he had ridden his bike in 1969, shouting his father's name in the hopes of telling him about his batting average. Torrents of memories now poured out, filling fifty handwritten pages. He reflected on the life into which he had descended and the thug he had become.

For the first time he traced the route that had lead him to this day. The route ran smack down the center of the expressway of the country's late-'70s drug explosion. New drugs like Orange Sunshine and THC hit the street when "Malow" was building up his weed-peddling crew on Winchester Avenue. Around 1978, more and more cocaine entered the mix. The profits were good, and so, Germano thought, were the drugs.

Deep down he always knew he was heading for trouble and occasionally toyed with the prospect of going straight. Too angry to approach his father for help, he had turned to an auto mechanic in town, Carlton Heath, who preached for the Nation of Islam. Heath, the father of one of Germano's friends, took an interest in the lost boys of Newhallville.

He ran a Getty gas station in Hamden, where he paid Germano to pump gas, learn to fix cars, and help manage the business. Germano worked hard—too hard, it seemed, for $3 to $4 an hour, compared to the $100 an hour he collected moving drugs on Winchester Avenue. Still staying up long past midnight drugging and gambling with his buddies, Germano soon stopped getting up early for work at Getty. He resumed his night job.

While the money did flow steadily, the job had its risks. These risks generally came in the forms of police officers and rival hustlers. One time, during Germano's eighteenth winter, he discovered four pounds of marijuana missing. A supplier had given him the marijuana to sell; Germano stashed it at an uncle's house where he crashed. Someone broke into the house and stole the stash. For weeks he tried, without luck, to recoup the lost profits to pay back his supplier.

Desperate to meet the debt, Germano hooked up with friends, stole a car, selected homes in nice neighborhoods to burglarize. They had just finished cleaning out a house in the Beaver Hills neighborhood around dinnertime when a police officer spotted their stolen car on Whalley Avenue. Germano's crew sped away toward the Southern Connecticut State University campus, past the city dog pound, over into Newhallville. The pursuing officer radioed for backup. More police joined the chase. Germano and his friends ditched the car and ran through backyards of side streets. Germano came upon an open back-porch door at the house of one of his friends. Germano slipped into the hallway and caught his breath. The police were in the backyard looking for him. A young boy in the house—the brother of Germano's friend—went outside and told them where to find Germano. The officer who had initiated the chase, a man known for brutality, grabbed Germano by the collar and dragged him to the front of the house. He slammed Germano against a wall and searched through his pockets.

Germano went to prison upstate for more than three years. He spent the time working in the kitchen, making homemade wine, drinking some of it, trading some to other prisoners for the weed procured from visitors or guards. Inspired by fellow inmates from New York, he shaved his Afro in favor of the low-cut "Caesar" look.

When Germano was released in 1982, he visited Carlton Heath's new repair shop on New Haven's Dixwell Avenue, amid much of the drug trafficking. Germano again tried an on-the-job-training gig with Heath, but he kept running into his old friends. As soon as a friend slipped a package into his hand, Germano was back in business. Cocaine was the hot commodity now, both on the job and after hours. Germano's friends were smoking it, and he was fast developing an addiction of his own. As quickly as the money poured in the street, it went up even faster in smoke.

He avoided his family. He also avoided developing long-term relationships with women. All the women in Germano's life were as much business partners as girlfriends. They drove to New York together to pick up product. They sold stolen clothes on the street. He grew close for a while to a particularly adept shoplifter named Robin. They purloined a bunch of Botany 500 suits. They went to Congress Avenue, the Hill neighborhood's main strip. It was near the corner of Baldwin Street—where Warren ran Project MORE. Germano encountered his dad.

How's it going? Warren asked. Germano asked him his suit size. He remembered how his dad loved good clothes. Here was a chance not just to make money but impress the hero he otherwise couldn't bring himself to face.

I can get you a good deal on a nice suit, Germano said.

Not interested, Warren said. They parted ways, again.

During the summer of 1983 Germano's hustling days were hurtling toward a crash. He lost $3,000 in a dice game at the Red House, an after-hours club on Dixwell Avenue near Henry Street. He fell $2,000 in debt at another joint called the Jai Alai. Increasingly reckless in his search for money, he was now the one slipping into fellow dealers' stash houses to steal as well as regularly breaking into homes in the Prospect Street area, the mansions where lawyers and Yale professors lived.

Around this time, Germano went on a coke-buying run to Harlem with a white friend who had a rental car. In Harlem, their contacts introduced them to a new brand of heroin known for its purity. Macho jokes circulated about heroin; guys Germano knew claimed that it gave you an erection that lasted all night. Germano took a small sample for the car ride back.

It knocked him out. Germano was still sleeping when his friend pulled home and went into the house. Germano awoke to banging on the window.

Cops. They were looking for a stolen car.

"Get out of the car!" shouted an officer who had chased Germano in the past.

"He's a runner," he called to his cohorts as Germano stumbled out of the car. "Watch him." The cop jammed a gun into Germano's back. "Go ahead," he said. "Run if you want to." Even if he'd wanted to, Germano was too doped up to try.

It turned out the police had previously picked up a sixteen-year-old with whom Germano had been burglarizing all of those Prospect Street homes. The kid gave up Germano for their previous robberies—which is how Germano ended up in Judge Norcott's court, staring at more years in prison than he cared to count. The fifty pages of writing released years of emotion. He looked at how he was conditioned, from an early age, to disrespect authority, to rebel. He had always considered the police the bad guys. His own actions he had never considered bad.

He expected a ten-year sentence. Norcott surprised him: He sentenced Germano to eighteen years, suspended after thirteen. With good behavior, some breaks, Germano could theoretically get out earlier, but not much earlier. He'd followed his dad's career path, but he wouldn't enjoy the same breaks. The system no longer encouraged favors for prisoners who discovered get-out-of-jail goals in Guides for Better Living Classes. It was 1983. Germano wouldn't taste freedom until well into the '90s.

CHAPTER 27

Second Chances

Having lost a son to his own neglect and the lure of the street, Warren latched on to another: Beverly's boy, Arthur, aka "Little Butch." As Beverly and Warren grew closer, so did Warren and Butch. Butch was as young as Germano had been when Warren disappeared from his life; now Butch's father, "Big Butch," was disappearing from his life. When Big Butch didn't show up with a promised Dallas Cowboys jacket, Warren made a last-minute Christmas Eve run to Sears. He taught Little Butch how to ride a two-wheeler.

Warren, the errant father, had a second chance.

"Watch him strike out," a nervous Beverly said to Warren in the bleachers at Davis Street School as Butch walked to the plate. It was the final inning, there were two outs, the bases were loaded, and Butch's team was down by three runs.

"Shug, don't say that," Warren remarked.

Beverly hollered encouragement at her son. "Don't holler at him," Warren said. "Let him do it."

Butch delivered a deep drive to the outfield. Grand slam.

Each fall, Warren returned to the Yale Bowl, his childhood haunt, whenever the Bulldogs had a home game. Beverly accompanied Warren and Butch at first. They packed fried chicken coated in flour and crushed potato chips.

Warren always made a point of wearing something blue to the games, in honor of Yale's official color. Butch sometimes wore his Cowboys jacket.

As a proud New Havener, Warren felt loyal to Yale. He'd always gone to the games as a kid. He had to avoid the Yale Bowl during his Panther period, of course; rooting for Old Eli would be a bourgeois error of high magnitude. Back home, freed from Panthermania, freed from jail, freed from the metaphorical prison of life in Willimantic, Warren could resume his Bulldog revelry.

As Butch entered his teens, Beverly stayed home from the football games. The two male buddies developed a halftime routine. Warren would give Little Butch money. "Get me two hot dogs." Butch would buy a hot chocolate for himself, a Sprite for Warren. Eventually Butch started taking longer and longer to return. Scanning the crowd through his binoculars, Warren discovered Butch chatting up some girls.

Far be it from Warren to object. But he was hungry. "Look, Little Butch," he told him upon his return. "From now on, I give you money. You do your thing. I'll go out and get my own hot dogs."

More than just spare change for the occasional hot chocolate, Warren threw himself into Butch's life, compensating, somewhat, for those lost years with Germano. They went out to McDonald's on weekend mornings; they'd order Egg McMuffins or pancakes, bring some back for Beverly. Warren taught Butch how to tie a tie. When Butch had a school assignment on Greek columns, the two walked around Yale's campus taking pictures.

With so much strong support from Beverly and Warren, Butch did well at school. Warren and Beverly wanted something better than New Haven's public high schools for him. Butch gained admission to the elite Hopkins private prep school. His old friends called him a sissy; Butch wanted to return to public school. Beverly and Warren found a house in a middle-class stretch of the otherwise wealthy white town of Woodbridge, to New Haven's west, so Butch could attend the suburb's respected Amity High School.

Butch knew about Germano from overhearing Warren and Beverly. Germano, who was in his mid-twenties, could sense the respect in Butch's voice when Germano would call from prison. Butch was eleven years younger than Germano. When Warren wasn't home, Butch accepted Germano's collect calls (despite Warren's edict to the contrary). They grew closer through their talks; Germano appreciated having someone accept his collect calls and listen to him. He also appreciated it when Butch patched in third-party calls to a girlfriend who couldn't afford to pay bills for collect calls.

Even without Germano, Butch had plenty of his own friends to run with. One of these friends, from Amity, was behind the wheel the night of Friday, October 17, 1987, when Butch and some of his New Haven friends went for a drive along Downs Road, a narrow, twisting street running along a reservoir. Some of the kids may have been drinking. The driver lost control of the car. The car flew into the air right where the reservoir dropped down over a waterfall. It flew 120 feet across the water; the car was traveling fast enough to chop off the tops of trees along an incline. Then the car plunged seventy feet down into the water.

The driver escaped from the car, swam to safety, and flagged down a trooper. Butch could swim, too. But he was sitting in the back seat. The kids in the back, trapped, never got out. They were two miles from War-ren's and Beverly's home.

Near midnight, Beverly awoke to the sound of a siren. She got up from bed and checked Butch's room. It was empty.

She went downstairs to look up the phone number of one of Butch's friends, then walked back upstairs to dial the friend's family's number. A knock on the door interrupted her.

It was a Woodbridge police officer. He informed Beverly that her son had been in an accident. She needed to go to St. Raphael's hospital. The officer mentioned having woken up the school superintendent to learn Beverly's address, since Butch had a different last name.

Beverly woke Warren. He drove them to the hospital, trying to stay calm and strong for Beverly. "I'll bet he cracked his tooth again," Beverly thought to herself. A question interrupted her efforts at positive think-ing: Why didn't they just ask Butch himself what his address was?

"I am the mother of Arthur Moore," Beverly announced to the woman at the hospital front desk. She asked Beverly to have a seat. "I want to find out how he is first," Beverly said. "I'm not going to sit down."

Just then another Woodbridge police officer walked by. She held a folder reading, "Fatal accident on Downs Road in Woodbridge." Beverly saw the folder. "I'm glad it's not them," she told herself. She tried to ask what was happening.

The officer snapped at Beverly. "I already have one dead at Yale-New Haven Hospital. I'm trying to see what's going on over here."

"I am the mother of Arthur Moore. I'm also trying to find out how he is."

The nurse behind the desk observed the exchange. She took Beverly to a side room and told her the details of the accident. Little Butch's heart was beating at the scene but had stopped on the way over. Now the doctors were trying to revive him.

The nurse returned soon after. "He didn't make it," she reported.

Warren heard. He collapsed on the floor, screaming. It was Beverly who found herself charged with keeping control. She phoned Warren's nephew Joseph; he rushed over, took Warren outside to calm him. Beverly's ex-husband arrived. Beverly couldn't bring herself to identify the body, though. Her sister and ex-brother-in-law did it for her.

Beverly asked Warren to be strong for her at the funeral. Warren shielded Beverly from having to answer too many people's questions. Neither Warren nor Beverly shed tears.

The tears waited until a trip the two took to Washington, D.C. On the way home, Willie Nelson was singing on the radio.

> *Maybe I didn't hold you*
> *All those lonely, lonely times*
> *And I guess I never told you*
> *I'm so happy that you're mine*
> *Little things I should have said and done*
> *I just never took the time*
> *You were always on my mind*
> *You were always on my mind*

The tears had been there all along, waiting. Now they finally poured out. They returned unannounced another day when Warren and Beverly drove by a basketball court. Some boys were playing. Warren and Beverly had to pull over. Warren, too, felt he had lost a son. He had taught Butch to ride a bicycle, to shine his shoes; he hadn't had the chance to do that with Germano. Warren was crushed; Butch was such a good kid, so respectful, so full of promise. Warren felt the loss as deeply as any parent.

Tragedy drew Warren and Beverly together. Beverly lost her sister the next month. Warren lost a sister and a brother. Beverly was diagnosed with breast cancer; she survived. So did their relationship. Warren had finally found a match, just as he had finally found a job, that fit him, that could last for decades.

Warren couldn't bring back Butch. He failed to become part of Germano's life again; Germano was still too hurt to respond to Warren's calls. Instead, Warren focused on the teens in his program, some of whom were estranged from their own fathers. Peter Cox called him "Pop." Cox's father and Warren were friends. A troubled adolescent, Cox found it easy to talk to Warren. As a young adult he traveled south and ended up serving ten years in a Georgia prison for armed robbery. He acted out in jail, so much that he spent seven years in solitary confinement. His solace came in the form of a monthly letter from Warren. Warren urged him to change his life. Develop patience, Warren advised. Be careful how you deal with people. Exert control over your life. I did it, Warren told Cox; you can, too.

Once freed, Cox returned north to New Haven determined to follow Warren's path. He struggled. His mother and stepfather had continual, ugly battles. Cox had a gun; he resolved to shoot his stepfather. He went to see Warren first. Warren sat with Cox and talked out the problem. Warren usually asked questions in such situations rather than tell people what to do. He did convince Cox to dispose of the pistol instead of shooting his stepfather and destroying his life. Instead, like "Pop" Warren, Cox enrolled in college courses. He found a job. He worked his way up to a manager's post at a local oil company. Although he was earning $50,000 a year, Cox didn't enjoy the job. Again, he went to talk to Warren. "It's not about money," Warren told him. "You can always replace money, houses and cars. You can't replace time." You have to make the time count by doing meaningful work, work you enjoy, Warren advised. Again, Cox took the advice—and a $20,000-plus pay cut. He became an outreach worker at New Haven's Columbus House shelter, helping homeless ex-cons find not just a temporary roof but permanent homes and job training or substance-abuse counseling. Cox started speaking to inmates at prisons. He told them about his past and how close he had come to throwing his life away.

Warren's own transition to upstanding member of New Haven's community continued with an appointment at police headquarters on February 24, 1990. Nick Pastore was calling.

The police force had come far since the time Nick encountered Warren in the lockup the night of the Rackley murder. The city built modern headquarters south of downtown, a block from the Metro-North train station. Nick, like Warren, had come far since those days. Nick, too, was shaking off old ghosts, reflecting on past police mistakes, trying to do better. Like Warren, he had been branded a traitor by former comrades in arms.

When the police wiretapping scandal became public, Nick drew the ire of some by testifying during hearings of a government investigatory commission. He laid out the details. He advocated reforming the way that the police did business. New Haven's high-ranking Irish and Italian-American cops finally found a common cause—hating Nick Pastore. Life at the department became a daily battle, as his once meteoric rise through the ranks halted. Inside the confines of the modern new building, the department remained stuck in dirty old tactics, brutalizing citizens, harassing and entrapping gays, excusing—even promoting—cops sued for brutality. Violent drug gangs were out of control; since the local police force was known for beating up people, the public didn't trust them enough to feed them enough information to help put the leading dealers away. A vanload of cops known as the "Beat-Down Posse" roamed black neighborhoods, stopped at street corners when they saw black kids hanging out, then pummeled the kids. The one-time Model City had a new national distinction: one of the country's highest per capita murder rates.

Nick took a disability leave. He dabbled unsuccessfully in real estate. He opened an ice cream parlor. And he kept abreast of changes happening—elsewhere—in policing. Then, in November 1989, New Haven's voters threw out the corrupt patronage crew that had cemented its power after Dick Lee's death. They elected the city's first black mayor, John Daniels, on a reform platform. Both Warren and Nick were old friends of Daniels. They both worked for his election; Nick met secretly with Daniels every week to craft his central campaign plank: an overhaul of the police department, to make the force an ally of the community. The plan went under the umbrella of "community policing."

Once elected, Daniels startled the city, and disappointed some of his black campaign supporters, by selecting a white police chief: Nick. Nick proceeded to turn the department upside down. He pushed the high-ranking white proponents of military-style policing into retirement. All but one went willingly. Nick reassigned the holdout—by coincidence, the same officer who had chased and roughed up Germano Kimbro that day in Newhallville—to oversee the dog pound; Nick declared he couldn't trust him to deal with humans. (Eventually the exiled cop landed a job as chief of a suburban police force notorious for racism and brutality.)

Nick quickly moved to dismantle the Beat-Down Posse. He recruited and promoted record numbers of black, female, and gay cops. He opened neighborhood substations to base neighborhood police and community programs. With the help of citizens in poor neighborhoods, the local po-lice force developed intelligence on the heads of drug gangs and sent them away for long sentences. New Haven's murder rate plunged. The level of violent crime in New Haven eventually fell to the lowest levels since President Lyndon Johnson's first term, setting the stage for a renais-sance in New Haven. Nick joined with Yale to develop a program—later copied nationwide—linking beat cops with psychiatrists to help children who witness violence.

Some of the dealers who were put away for a decade or more on Nick's watch used to run the street with Germano as part of the Macks pack or the Ville or the Dogs. They beckoned for him to join them back in the game; they'd advanced to the trade's higher echelon. But Germano was determined to straighten out, just as Warren had. Germano began trying to go straight in jail, beginning with creating a black history program. He was released in 1990 to Project MORE. He emerged from the pro-gram ready to turn his life around. Germano battled his drug problem. He relapsed a couple of times, but picked himself back up each time. He worked his way from barbering jobs to the social-service sector.

Warren's mission at Project MORE fit like a glove onto Nick's new softer hand of law enforcement. That's why Nick invited Warren up to his third-floor chief's office for a chat. Nick recognized the publicity value, the message he could send about the new era in New Haven. "Former foes join forces to push alternative to jail project," read a headline the next day at the top of the front page of the *New Haven Register*. There in the photo, on the chief's couch, sat Nick and Warren, the one-time Panther and the one-time "pig," "talking over old and new times" and discussing plans for a 110-bed center for drug treatment on demand.

Warren held no grudge against Nick and didn't mind being trotted out for the press. He welcomed any publicity that could potentially be used to help ex-offenders. That was the focus of their discussion—what to do next. Warren didn't like to talk about "old times," at least not his life as a Panther. He wanted to move on. Nick felt the same way, even more so. "Let's forget the past," Nick said to Warren that day. "It's over."

Nick liked to think everything that happened was buried, along with all the untold secrets. Warren was less sure.

CHAPTER 28

Arts & Ideas

In June 2001, the Panthers returned to New Haven's Green. There were no frantic meetings behind closed doors, no desperate phone pleas for the National Guard. This time no one was scared. In fact, official New Haven, which had barricaded itself against the Panthers three decades earlier, invited the Panthers this time. The Panthers were welcomed as stars, larger-than-life characters from a great historical moment. For days, in church halls, Yale spaces, office buildings in and around the Green, they were invited guests of New Haven's International Festival of Arts & Ideas.

Arts & Ideas, an annual event spawned by civic and corporate leaders and City Hall, represented New Haven's renaissance in the twilight of the twentieth century. Modeled on an annual event in Edinburgh, Scotland, the festival brought theater troupes, musicians, intellectuals, and newsmakers from around the globe to performance spaces and lecture halls throughout downtown and Yale's campus. The city enjoyed weeks of plays, forums, and concerts, many of them free, many right on the Green.

Each year the festival chose themes for its "Ideas" events: human rights, globalization, urban renewal. This year, a central "Ideas" theme revisited Panthermania—the rise of the party in New Haven, the murder, May Day, the trial, the legacy.

With the passing of time, the trauma had drained out of the episode. To the kind of New Haveners who would have left town on May Day weekend in 1970—in some cases, who did leave town—the affair assumed a romantic echo of a time when people actually took to the streets in American cities, when they took risks, when they acted on their dreams and visions of a better world. Three decades later, the National Guard's tear gas no longer burned the eyes. It lingered in a nostalgic mist amid the relandscaped Green and refurbished downtown commercial buildings. New Haven was safe now, especially downtown; Nick Pastore's community policing had accomplished that, even, to some extent, in poorer neighborhoods. Even though the city's industrial base was shot, Yale was growing. More important, the university made a decision to start investing in the city, in attracting high-tech businesses, in working with neighborhood groups.

The city that spent more money than any other in the country to help the poor retained persistent pockets of poverty and struggling schools. The roots of the problems appeared to be national in scope, beyond the ability of one city to tackle alone, exacerbated by the get-tough criminal laws that swept the nation in the decades following Alex Rackley's murder and the Panther implosion. Thanks to long sentences for nonviolent drug offenses, cities across the country saw the emergence of "million-dollar blocks"—where so many people are in jail that the annual cost of incarcerating them, taken together, reaches seven figures. Thirty-five of those blocks could be found in Brooklyn, New York, alone. New Haven continued to have some of the nation's highest concentrations of subsidized housing and therefore of poverty; the effects weren't as extreme as in other cities, thanks to the presence and expansion of a major unionized employer, Yale, which couldn't be tempted out of town by the lures of global capitalism.

Despite the challenges of entrenched poverty, New Haven had awakened from the gloom, from the stifled energy and development, that marked the years following the Rackley case. New Haven was trying again. Compared to many cities with similar challenges, it was a kinder place.

A kinder and perhaps less passionate place. It was distinctly devoid of heroes in June 2001. So, at a series of festival events, the Panthers would have to do.

History repeated itself in one crowded hall, the sanctuary of First & Summerfield Church at the northwestern corner of the Green. The mostly white, Yale-affiliated young audience cheered a panel of former Panthers and Panther supporters as they presented a portrait of a heroic party destroyed by an evil government. One young woman, a pacifist, dared to ask whether advocating violence was a wise strategy. Tension swept the room; the other "questions" had simply exalted the Panthers.

Ericka Huggins wasn't there this time, but the other panelists repeated her approach to the skunk at the Bethesda Lutheran Church garden party in 1969. They attacked the questioner, who was white.

Only white people would worry about black people with guns, snapped one panelist—as though black-on-black crime hadn't destroyed hundreds of lives in New Haven since the Panther era, as though New Haven's black community itself hadn't opposed the Panthers' violent rhetoric back in the day. The speakers turned the crowd against the young woman, who was duly shut up.

Another evening, Bobby Seale himself arrived at the United Church on the Green to appear on a panel. Nick Pastore, the cop who arrested Seale and testified in an effort to send him to the electric chair, joined him on the panel. They got on like old friends. Sam Chauncey, the Yale official in charge of May Day, was another panelist. Catherine Roraback, Ericka Huggins's radical lawyer, was there, too. She agreed to attend on one condition: that Warren Kimbro *not* take part. Decades after Warren cooperated with the government and testified against Ericka, Roraback refused to sit anywhere near him. The organizers assured her that it would not be a problem. It's not like Warren was itching to speak before a crowd about the Rackley murder, anyway.

Hours before the event, Warren was at the New Haven Savings Bank office tower at the northeastern edge of the Green, signing a line of credit for Project MORE. He entered the elevator for the ride down only to encounter Bobby Seale, who'd been visiting the Arts & Ideas office on an upper floor. They greeted each other warmly. Seale brought up that evening's forum.

"You've gotta come out here to support me," Seale said.

Warren was noncommittal. "Why do I want to get involved in this stuff?" he thought. Later, he talked it over with Beverly. Why not go just to listen? Beverly suggested.

So Warren drove to the Green. He was early. He took a seat in a pew near the front.

At the last moment, a panelist dropped out. Seale suggested bringing Warren up. The Arts & Ideas organizers forgot their promise to Roraback. They asked Warren. He had reservations, but he had little time to weigh them. After all these years, he still found it hard to resist a request from the chairman.

Roraback was civil. At a dinner after the event, she was downright friendly.

Two key people were missing. One was Ericka Huggins. Once freed, she hadn't been inclined to spend much time in New Haven. The other was Kingman Brewster. Brewster died in 1988.

The local daily, the *New Haven Register*, editorialized that someone else was missing from the panel, too: writer David Horowitz, a white one-time far-left-wing Panther supporter who turned far-right-wing militant Panther critic. The *Register* editorial argued that Horowitz would have provided balance. It noted how the festival's events evoked "a time fondly embraced by the American left. The local nostalgia shouldn't gloss over the vicious crime at its heart."

Inside the church, a group of local high school students sat up front in reserved seats. Festival organizers wanted the Panther events to include a focus on what lessons young people could draw for the future. The thirteen students had spent months researching the Rackley case for a festival-sponsored oral history project.

Sam Chauncey, standing in for Kingman Brewster and Yale University, appealed to the students to follow the example of the Panthers.

"We have to have a revolution, and these people have to do it. We're too old," Chauncey said. He urged the students on to "revolutionary" action on the model of Bobby Seale.

Warren was startled. He spoke up right after Chauncey. He didn't want the youths to follow in the Panthers' footsteps.

Warren said, "I don't want you to pick up a gun like me. I want you to do this revolution by getting into Yale Law School and changing our country's law."

The same week, Warren and Nick opened up in a more intimate setting with the thirteen high schoolers. They met with the students in a conference room in the Arts & Ideas office high up in the New Haven Savings Bank tower overlooking the Green, a building that didn't exist in 1970. (In its stead stood the New Politics Corner, where a fire broke out over the May Day demonstration weekend.) The students had studied the case and debated issues of racism and protest then and now. And they interviewed key participants from the era.

"Why do you think that you were convicted, but others never were?" one student asked Warren.

Warren responded with a smile.

"Because I was guilty. I was the one who pulled the trigger, child," Warren said. "It was a sorry act. And once you pull that trigger, you never forget it one day in your life."

The room fell silent.

Warren pressed on. "Now some folks may not want to be in the room with someone who took someone's life. It wasn't a heroic deed."

Warren did not want the kids to view him as a hero. He also wanted them to know that *nobody* was very heroic back then, including the police.

He wondered aloud about the mysterious young man who lent the Panthers the tape recorder used in the interrogation of Alex Rackley. Warren never saw the man again. In retrospect, he told the children, he believed that evidence was being created with that tape recorder, evidence to be preserved for a trial.

"This was a stage. We were in a play. We didn't know what part we were playing. But we were in it," Warren told the students.

"When I look at it, when I go back and look at it and say, 'I was wiretapped, illegally or not,' if I was in law enforcement and somebody was spouting 'revolution' and all that stuff, I'd want to know what they were doing, too. But if I knew what they were doing, then I would want to prevent them from doing it—rather than have them do it and say, 'You see, I told you they were bad guys.'

"I think that's what happened in New Haven. They wanted to prove a point: 'The Panthers were bad guys. You see, I told you this all along.'"

Nick, too, was strikingly open and truthful with the students. Warren's openness challenged them to stare in the face of a human being they could no longer classify simply as "murderer" or "victim." Similarly, Nick's openness challenged them to see the case's lead police investigator as more than a "pig" or "protector." He still believed Bobby Seale was guilty. He also knew the police went too far. "We couldn't have been more oppressive," Nick acknowledged. Yes, he said, the government helped "create that paranoia." On the other hand, he spoke of how both sides hated each other, how the Panthers dehumanized all law enforcement by branding them "pigs," by calling on supporters to shoot them.

In that room, the students were challenged in a way missing from some of the public festival events, missing from the avalanche of books and movies spawned by the Panther era. The challenge was to view the Rackley murder, and the Panther era itself, as something other than a black-and-white tale, more complex than a cops-and-robbers movie with one-dimensional heroes and villains.

A student pressed Nick. "Do you understand why somebody would want to ambush cops," she pressed, "when the cops have been ambushing them?"

"It gets out of hand. There's no question about it," Nick responded. "It was like war. That's what it was. And you don't always play by the rules. Next question?"

As he did on the plane ride returning Bobby Seale to Connecticut in 1970, Nick made a plea to remember the spirit too often ignored in the attic of the ghosts of Panthers past. "Alex Rackley is just a lost name in all of this," Nick said, "a sacrificial lamb."

Epilogue

Ghosts of Panthers Past

Aᴌᴇx Rᴀᴄᴋᴌᴇʏ's sᴘɪʀɪᴛ visited Freddie and Sandra Rackley's modern living room in northern Jacksonville, Florida, one October evening in 2004. Freddie, the brother closest in age to Alex and now in his mid-fifties, gathered two of his siblings to share thoughts about their long-dead brother. It was a pleasant fall evening after a long work day for all of them. Velva still had on her grey work shirt with "Aramark" and "Velva" stenciled on it. Wayne's gray work shirt read "JEA" for the initials of the city sewage plant. Freddie, a local truck driver and a one-time state high-hurdling champ, had "Rackley" scripted onto his gray shirt.

On the surface, Jacksonville remains the conservative Southern city Alex Rackley fled in 1968. Christian sermonizing fills practically every other station on the radio dial. The editorials in the local daily *Times-Union* still run hard right. But closer inspection reveals that the civil rights movement's door of opportunity eventually swung open here as elsewhere. Freddie and Sandra live in a racially integrated, modern, clean, almost suburban-style subdivision; before the 1970s, blacks came to neighborhoods like this to clean houses, not to live. Decent-paying office jobs like the one Sandra has at Bell South were once off-limits to blacks. Alex Rackley's siblings had stable jobs, comfortable homes in which to raise their families.

Warm, open, easy to talk to, the Rackleys mined their memories for traces of Alex's life—what school he attended, when he dropped out, and any other milestones of his shortened life. Even when they retrieved information, they couldn't always agree on one version. It all seemed so long ago. They knew Alex loved their mother dearly. They knew he liked dancing, karate, and sharp clothes.

They knew even less about his death. Their memories of Alex basically end the day he left town in 1968. Over the years they would come across an occasional reference to Alex on Tom Joyner's syndicated radio program or in a magazine retrospective on Panther deaths. No one ever offered the family the full story. "We're getting more information [in this conversation] than we ever had," Freddie said. Only his wife Sandra has done research into the story. She sat with a pile of print-outs from Internet sites including articles about COINTELPRO.

"I always thought Bobby Seale killed my brother. That's what they told my mother," Velva said.

They'd heard that the Panthers considered Alex an informant. Freddie never could believe it. "I always thought about it. That was my big brother. I used to look to him. He kept people off my ass."

"We couldn't see the body. My mama couldn't see the body," Wayne recalled. He seemed sure that the wrong body was sent home the first time, delaying the funeral.

Miles away, Mixontown, the dusty Jacksonville neighborhood where the Rackleys grew up, remained run-down and poor, isolated by the crisscrossing interstates that carved up Jacksonville after Alex left town. The three-bedroom house on Watts Street where up to twenty Rackleys lived at a time had been demolished years ago. It became a vacant, overgrown, trash-strewn lot. Six other houses on the block were knocked down, too, and never replaced. The corner store long ago shut down. Even the drug dealers whose trade had ravaged the neighborhood a decade earlier weren't visible in 2004. Dominated by a barbed-wire-enclosed exterminator company and small, low tenant houses, Watts Street gives the feeling of the old rural South, not a modern city neighborhood.

One afternoon, also in October 2004, Carol Mercer sat on the chipped concrete stoop of 265 Watts Street, next to the land where the Rackley homestead stood. She wore a print cotton dress. Her legs were stitched from knee replacement surgery. Mercer was born at 265 Watts. She grew up with the Rackleys, played with the kids on the block.

"They weren't riffraff," Mercer said of the Rackleys. "They were just people trying to raise their children." Alex's late mother, Parlee, raised the kids with a "strict," "firm" hand, Mercer recalled. The same with Grandpa Isaac Rackley.

"It kind of surprised us. Alex? An informer? Against the Panthers? He grew up knowing not to tell on people. It totally floored us."

"There's not a year that doesn't pass that I don't think of him," Mercer said. For some reason—she doesn't know why—thinking of Alex always reminded her of the old hit "Grazin' in the Grass." (The Hugh Masekela song was a Top 20 hit the month Alex was killed.) Mercer recalled how Alex loved to dance. Then, amid the quiet, dusty abandon of Watts Street, smiling with a faraway look in her eye, Mercer started singing, in a soft, soulful voice. *So real, so real, so real. Can you dig it?*

THAT SAME FALL, Warren Kimbro thought about Alex Rackley, too, as he watched the sun rise from the backyard of his home on a hilly subdivision in suburban Hamden. Warren got out of bed at 5:30. He assumed his customary morning spot on a swing in the backyard, by the Brinkmann grill and the rock-lined miniature pond he put in. He said his morning prayers. That's when, almost every day, Alex Rackley visited Warren. Despite the revelations of police misconduct, despite all the explanations of how he hadn't been thinking straight in that Panther moment, how in the swamp he feared for his life and the life of his family, Warren never forgave himself for depriving Alex Rackley of sunrises. There may have been explanations, but there were no excuses.

Warren meditated a while, a practice he took up in prison. Then he scanned the morning paper. He looked at every section, ending with the funnies. Then he lay down the paper and rocked. He listened to the gurgling of the pond. It relaxed him, prepared him for the day.

He and Beverly had settled into the house fifteen years earlier, not long after Little Butch's death. Life assumed a rhythm. It hummed. On try number three, Warren had held onto a marriage for more than twenty years.

He'd held onto a job, too, a job that made a difference. Over seventy years old, Warren was still running Project MORE. He managed sixty full- and part-time workers. Under contract with the state corrections department that once held him prisoner, Warren oversaw halfway houses and day programs for mostly young people already saddled with prison records. He revised an aborted idea from his CPI days: He sought money for a halfway house connected to a factory where ex-cons could earn paychecks and develop skills needed for self-sufficiency.

It was harder to turn convicts into Warren Kimbros than it was in the days when a warden would allow a prisoner to split time between his cell and a college classroom, when pardons boards were open to giving murderers second chances rather than warehousing nonviolent drug offenders into their old age. Uphill all the while, Warren kept plugging. As in his days at the RYC, he was still the locus of activity, bursting with ideas, still trying to connect with everybody. He could finally sit through staff meetings without pumping his legs; otherwise he was the center of the room, as in the old days.

In one sense, Warren continued to live the life of "Super Chimp," as his prison mates dubbed him. At seventy-one, Warren could have long retired to the material comfort of bourgeois life. Instead, he continued devoting long days to helping the people, a majority of them black, stuck at the bottom rungs of the social ladder. He continued running Project MORE, a difficult job, steering ex-cons to stable lives outside of jail. True, Warren was a part of the prison-industrial complex. He was a pillar of the establishment. He worked with, not against, exploitive politicians and poverty-brokers to achieve his goals. But he remained committed to the dream. He represented the positive ideal embodied in DuBois's vision: a member of the "Talented Tenth" who remained engaged with the other nine-tenths.

Outside of work, Warren remained central to the lives of his extended family. He was the father figure for his daughter Veronica's five kids, whom she was raising to successful adulthoods. If you asked Warren, or anyone else, she was the real hero of the family.

He reconnected with Germano, who founded a program to help young fathers take more responsibility in their children's lives; through the relationships he forged, he participated in drafting a statewide prison reform program passed by the legislature. Germano's male-involvement program earned a national award, helping New Haven earn designation as an "All-American City." A framed full-page newspaper ad trumpeting the program hung in Germano's office. The headline—"Father of the year starts with a father who's here"—echoed with irony.

Warren was back in Germano's life. They talked all the time. At an event in 2005 to celebrate state certification of his program, Germano credited Warren publicly for being his role model to success. (Germano lost the job in 2006; he was managing sober houses for recovering addicts and looking for a new job at that point.)

The father-son relationship continues to have its tensions. In his mid-forties, Germano feels the sting of memories of losing his father at nine years old. He still wants Warren to fill the role he'd abandoned.

Weekends might find Germano and Warren on the golf course together, learning a new game. Their roles have reversed from the days when Warren was his young son's coach. Germano has worked hard on his swing, hoping to catch up with his peers who picked up the game years earlier. Warren has always taken the game more lightly, and his scores have shown it. "Dad," Germano continually implores Warren, "you've got to practice. You're not serious about this game. Remember what you told me when I was a kid? You've got to look at the ball. You can beat these kids."

THREE AND A half decades later, everyone touched by the Alex Rackley murder, directly or indirectly, seemed moored to that pivotal period. They continued to wrestle with unfinished business, with old ghosts. Until the second time he was interviewed for this book, Kelly Moye never told people about his role as a police informer when he lent the Panthers his car the night they killed Alex Rackley. More than three decades later, Moye still seemed nervous about how ex-Panthers would react. Moye did eventually become a full-fledged member of the New Haven Police Department. Then he lost his job, and went to prison, after being arrested on an arson charge. (He claimed to be innocent.) In 2005 Moye was living in the same house in the Hill neighborhood he did back in 1969, on a street that remained as run-down and crime-plagued as in the days before the Great Society promised better. As a neighborhood volunteer, Moye tries to help keep drug dealers off the block.

Nor has Rackley's ghost ever fled from George Sams, the crazed Panther who helped to orchestrate the torture and the murder. In April

2005, Sams had his own cell at the Riverside Correctional Facility in Ionia, Michigan. It was the third prison authorities shuttled him through in a three-month period. Since serving his time in the Rackley case, Sams continued committing violent felonies and landing in jail. Behind bars he got into fights. Even at a maximum-security jail, he was considered more dangerous than his peers. That's why he had his own cell. On a visiting day, the other inmates wore dark striped pants and colored shirts; Sams had on a special tan jumpsuit. One of his hands was manacled to a chain belt. None of the dozens of other inmates was restrained that way while meeting visitors. Sams had to meet his visitors in a glass-walled room with just one piece of furniture, an aluminum bench bolted to the floor. During an interview that lasted hours, Sams was forbidden to stand.

In conversation, Sams was courteous and intense. The intensity emanated not from his roving dark eyes, but from his taut, muscular frame. Every point he made with emphasis—and there were many—was accompanied by a clang of metal against the bench as he shifted his weight. His speech came in torrents, rough, punctuated by ubiquitous "motherfucker"s and fancier words like "dysfunctional" and "characterized." He hardly sounded like the near-retarded character portrayed by Panther partisans during the trial.

Alex Rackley? Sams claimed that he always knew Rackley was innocent. Rackley was a "cross-addicted" unfortunate who loved the party, who would do anything to remain part of it, even when facing fatal accusations.

Alex Rackley was a scapegoat, Sams said. And so, Sams said, was he.

Sams stood by his story that Bobby Seale ordered the murder. His contempt for Seale oozed from every reference as prodigiously as it had on the stand thirty-four years earlier. He continued to insist, as he did back then, that he never worked for the FBI or any other arm of law enforcement.

That accusation will dog Sams to the grave, perhaps even inter him prematurely. That accusation led to attempts on his life behind bars, Sams claimed. Several writers have stated as fact in print that Sams was an agent. They had no conclusive evidence, only the observation that Sams helped destroy the party with his actions, that he behaved like an agent provocateur, and that his actions resembled those of actual FBI plants in other party chapters. But the facts have always been a casualty of the Alex Rackley murder.

Warren Kimbro has also been accused of being an informer, based solely on the fact that he knew a lot of influential people who helped him earn his get-out-of-jail-practically-free card. Huey Newton's doctoral thesis vaguely cites the "extensive research" of playwright Donald Freed into the Seale-Huggins trial as proof of this claim. However, Freed's book offers no evidence; Newton's thesis was subsequently cited as "evidence" of Warren's supposed FBI involvement.

Everyone involved still speculates about who really were the agents and informers during that era. Senate investigations, declassified COINTELPRO documents, and numerous interviews have established beyond a doubt that the party teemed with such characters. Beyond Kelly Moye, who reported on Panther meetings to Nick Pastore and lent the group the car for the murder ride, and who finally came clean about his role in a 2005 conversation at his home, no other infiltrators have been definitively identified in New Haven.

No one can say definitively whether Alex Rackley was an informer. He most probably wasn't. No credible evidence exists to taint him. It all seems to have been a tragic mistake. No matter: once someone is accused, once the suggestion is planted, it's impossible to erase the last scintilla of doubt in people's minds. Such charges can't be disproven, only proven.

That appears to be one insidious, debilitating effect of efforts like COINTELPRO: widespread, irretrievable suspicion. It destroyed people's names. It ended people's lives. It rendered dysfunctional groups opposed to people in power. In New Haven, as elsewhere, one can reasonably argue that Panthers could have taken care of blowing themselves up without the FBI's help. They didn't get the chance, as COINTELPRO lit the fuse for them. It left government fingerprints alongside the Panthers' fingerprints on Alex Rackley's corpse.

George Edwards, the Panther who almost paid with his life after refusing to torture Alex Rackley, who himself was accused without evidence of being a government informant in the '60s, never stopped watching out for spies in New Haven. He has seen them everywhere. COINTELPRO messed up his life, continued to mess up his life, he said. It never killed his determination to fight back.

The government did pay George Edwards back for a fraction of what it took from him. In 1983 the city, under Mayor Biagio DiLieto, paid 1,238 targets of its illegal wiretapping operation damages as part of a $1.75 million settlement of a class-action lawsuit filed by civil rights attorney John R. Williams. The victims each received between $1,000 and $6,000, depending on how often the police eavesdropped on their private conversations. Edwards, of course, took home the full $6,000.

One afternoon in 2005, Edwards visited an artsy hangout on Audubon Street called "Koffee?". On the way, he suddenly crossed streets in midblock in order to throw off someone who was tailing him. He carefully selected a table. Before he finished his coffee, he moved to a different table to avoid spies he identified as having assumed places throughout the room.

A middle-aged man in a fishing jacket took Edwards's former seat. "U.S. military," Edwards whispered.

Edwards pointed to a long-haired local leftist who operated a radical bookstore. He's really a "pig," Edwards said. "He won't look at me. That's why his back is to me. He's looking through the glass," at Edwards's reflection.

Edwards's every step was haunted by phantom pigs. After coffee, Edwards strolled down Whitney Avenue. He berated a middle-aged man in business attire as he passed for violating Edwards's rights by spying on him. "He changes clothes three times a day," Edwards said in disgust, as the man crossed the street shaking his head.

When not identifying spooks, Edwards has been a fixture of the city's antiwar and civil rights protest campaigns. He still calls himself a Panther. A beloved, albeit idiosyncratic, figure in town, he took up the cause of individuals struggling with landlords or government bureaucracies. To reporters and friends, he regularly reveals conspiracies: that the CIA sent women to seduce him in order to steal documents, for instance. Or that George W. Bush made it rain on an antiwar protest to depress turnout.

TED GUNDERSON, LONG retired from the FBI and COINTELPRO, was still smoking out conspiracies as well. A private eye on the West Coast, he had traveled the country investigating and calling attention to ignored threats to the country's security and morals. He received some attention in 2005 by promoting the theory that Jeffrey Gannon, a right-wing operative exposed after attending White House press conferences under an assumed reporter's name, was actually a long-abducted paperboy named Johnny Gosch who subsequently became a member of a D.C. homosexual prostitution ring (linked to the White House) that had some kind of connection to the death of Hunter S. Thompson. Gunderson also kept tabs on Satanists known as the "Illuminati." He said the country didn't realize what a threat the group had become—just like in the late '60s, when J. Edgar Hoover labeled the Panthers America's number-one domestic threat.

As a result of his digging, Gunderson said, the Satanists had targeted him for reprisals. It reminded him of his New Haven days when Panther José Gonzalvez called for his head.

"They've come in my house at night," Gunderson said of the Satanists. "Somebody stole my car a few weeks ago. I said, 'God's paying me back for what I did to the Panthers!' It's payback time for Gunderson!" Then he burst out laughing.

Some players in the May Day drama moved on to careers in the American mainstream. Hillary Rodham became Hillary Rodham Clinton—a first lady, then a U.S. senator and potential presidential candidate. Tom Hayden moved from SDS to Democratic Party electoral politics; he won a seat in the California State Senate. Panther Doug Miranda took a job as a health outreach worker for a Boston clinic. Two of the black student leaders at Yale who helped keep the peace, Kurt Schmoke and William Farley, won Rhodes scholarships. In 1987, Schmoke was elected Baltimore's first black mayor; he served three terms. He became a senior fellow of the Yale Corporation. After earning his law degree, Farley worked as assistant corporation counsel to Chicago's first black mayor, Harold Washington. He has since run a start-up information technology company and practiced corporate and real estate law.

Judge Harold Mulvey died in 2000, the Rackley case following him to his grave as his signal achievement. The Panther he came to like, Bobby Seale, became a barbecue cookbook author. He continues to tour the country lecturing to large crowds of college students, who receive him warmly.

Life after May Day proved an anticlimax for Kingman Brewster, as it did for other central participants. He had won his battle to open up Yale;

he spent his subsequent time in office focused on less controversial fund-raising efforts. He resigned in 1977 to become President Carter's ambassador to England. That tenure proved uneventful, too, as did his return to New Haven in the early '80s to dabble in an ultimately uncompleted writing project and to serve as counsel to a New York law firm. That firm sent him back to England in 1984. In 1986 Oxford University named him master of its University College, and Brewster intended to "defend Oxford and University College from [Margaret] Thatcher's antiestablishment populism," as one biographer put it. A stroke soon after he took the job derailed those plans. He died two years later.

LIKE WARREN IN his sunrise meditations, some of the central characters in the Rackley case sought peaceful refuge rather than drama, with mixed results.

Nick Pastore watched swans flying over the reeds by the Connecticut River out the back window of his condo in the placid Connecticut town of Essex, an hour—and a world—away from New Haven. After revolutionizing New Haven's police force for the better, and emerging as a national spokesman for humane policing, Nick resigned as chief in 1997 amid scandal: he fathered a child with a drug-addicted prostitute, then denied paternity until the state's child-welfare agency did a DNA test. Nick proceeded to bring up his daughter, who was growing up into a beautiful, smart, engaged girl. The past continued to gnaw at Nick. He still believed that the police, although they overstepped boundaries in those days, needed to stop the Panthers, whom he considered thugs taking advantage of idealistic young Americans—blacks and whites. Nick didn't want to talk about it anymore. He wanted to let the past rest, even if others didn't.

Ericka Huggins sought her refuge in yoga. After leaving New Haven for Oakland, she stuck with the Panther cause during the party's sunset years. As Huey Newton used the party as cover to fuel his cocaine habit and create an underworld extortion and murder racket, Ericka remained aboveground, struggling to fulfill the promise of the ten-point plan. For eight years she ran the party's "Liberation School," a well-regarded alternative neighborhood school, many of whose students had parents who struggled with drug addiction. The school eventually shut down amid revelations of Newton's skimming public funds. She also trained prisoners and drug-rehab workers in relaxation breathing techniques. She assumed a leadership role in another idealistic, controversial organization, a yoga organization described by some former members as a cult. A lecturer and coordinator for the group's Oakland ashram, Ericka joined in seeking a restraining order against a former disciple who made public accusations of sexual harassment in the group.

Ericka sounded like the spiritually minded flower child, but she could still switch on a dime from sugar to steel. She declined to speak on the record for this book. In general she has declined to grant many interviews about her historic, turbulent days in New Haven; she has been working on her own memoirs and has remained a popular public speaker, admired, especially in the Bay Area, as a Panther heroine. Unlike some others in the pantheon, Ericka didn't try to sugarcoat the story. She didn't make excuses for the party's mistakes. She came off as proud of the party's original goals and accomplishments, and determined to learn from its mistakes. Ericka and Warren never spoke again, never saw each other again after Warren testified against her in 1971.

Thirty years after her husband's murder, Ericka returned to the UCLA campus where it happened. She spoke on a panel, entitled "Educate to Liberate," commemorating John Huggins's and Bunchy Carter's deaths.

"What killed the Black Panthers wasn't" the FBI's COINTELPRO, Ericka said. "It helped and did a good job of weakening it, but what hurt was the internal pettiness. There were personality struggles and just a lack of ability to fight one more day."

"The Panthers were perceived as violent, but what I participated in was bringing to the fore the violence of this country from slavery onwards," she told the BBC in 2003 in a program on activists' memories of the March on Washington. "We saw ourselves as people who wanted to dismantle oppression on various levels—one was police brutality and the other was a system of government that did not support human beings in living the quality of life that they deserved by right of their birth.

"There were a lot of mistakes and incredible flaws in what we did," she acknowledged. "But there were also many successful things, including community support and education programs as well as helping to change the way in which African-American people think and speak about themselves. Sadly, however, there is still so much to be done."

WARREN CAME TO the same conclusion. Like Ericka Huggins and Nick Pastore, Warren pressed ahead even as he wrestled with old ghosts. He continued to dream of a more just criminal justice system that would give other people the second chance he received. In 2005, Warren had another dream. Its roots extended further back in time than the Rackley case. They went back to the '30s and '40s, to a one-block street in New Haven where it seemed that an entire world of different people, of strivers and jivers and survivors, toiled, danced, fought, drank, and dreamed all together.

Today, you can find no trace of Spruce Street. In its place stand the shampoos and deodorants in the aisles of a Walgreen's pharmacy.

In Warren's dream, he wins the jackpot in Connecticut's lottery. He takes the proceeds and buys the land that once was Spruce Street. Down comes the Walgreen's. From its ashes rise apartment houses, where all kinds of families can afford to live in dignity.

Acknowledgments

The publication of this book depended on the invaluable help of so many colleagues and friends that we could fill the entire program of a rubber-chicken dinner with thank yous. Fortunately we'll spare everyone the rubber chicken and the speeches and simply acknowledge the guidance and vision of the world's best agent/coach/editor, Betsy Lerner; the careful and nurturing editing of the manuscript by Chris Greenberg and the support of the late Liz Maguire at Basic Books; the manifold improvements that resulted from detailed readings of various drafts and blunt feedback by Carole Bass, Norman Oder, Kica Matos, Henry Fernandez, Roger Vann, Judith Chevalier, Stan Gartska, Joseph LaPalombara, Robert Johnston, and Sharon Oster; the generous financial support of William Graustein; the essential research help and sign-pointing from Yohuru Williams, Kathleen Cleaver, John R. Williams, George Edwards, the dedicated staff at the Manuscript and Archives section of Yale's Sterling Memorial Library, and Walter Rochow; the inspired assistance, day in and day out, of Camille Costelli; the input and enthusiasm of the students in "Race and Violence in the American City"; and the office space and good vibes at the Yale School of Management. The book wouldn't have been possible if not for the fifty key participants in and witnesses to these events, from the spies to the spied-upon to the bystanders, who opened their memories, sometimes for the first time on the record; and above all the Rackley and Kimbro families, most of all Warren Kimbro, who had the courage to put the interest of the truth above self-aggrandizement.

Needless to say, none of the book's shortcomings are the faults of the above-mentioned individuals, but many of its virtues can be credited to them.

Chapter Notes

Note: Much of the material for this book was drawn from interviews with Warren Kimbro. Because twenty-nine interviews took place with Kimbro, and because information on a particular incident was often drawn from various sessions, the notes below do not specify the dates.

PROLOGUE: THE FIRST NEW HAVEN PIG TRIAL

This account is drawn from New Haven Colony Records, 1641, 62–73; and Alexandra Paxton, "Laws of God, Lives of Men: The Trial and Execution of George Spencer in New Haven Colony," unpublished paper written for the History of New Haven course at Yale Law School, December 1997.

CHAPTER 1: TRIGGER MAN

3   **Warren Kimbro sat nervously . . .** Warren Kimbro interviews.
3   **Maybe it was the pistol Sams always waved around . . .** Warren Kimbro interviews; John H. Bracey Jr. interview; Peggy Hudgins testimony, *State v. Seale and Huggins*, 279–80 in transcript; Shirley Wolterding testimony, *State v. Seale and Huggins*, 2639–42; Ericka Huggins testimony, *State v. Seale and Huggins*, 2901, Valerie White testimony, *State v. Seale and Huggins*, 2550; Joseph Lelyveld, "Panthers Feared Sams, Court Told," *New York Times*, July 17, 1970, 31.

271

3   **"I'm going for a ride"** . . . Peggy Hudgins testimony, *State v. Seale and Huggins*, 166; Lesley Oelsner, "Seale Jury Told of Murder Night," *New York Times*, March 20, 1971, 26.

4   **a call went to Kelly Moye** . . . Kelly Moye interviews, November 10, 2004, and March 14, 2005.

5   **Back in the Panther apartment** . . . Warren Kimbro testimony, *State v. Seale and Huggins*, 1026–1064; Kimbro interviews; Lesley Oelsner, "Prosecutor Jabs at Mrs. Huggins," *New York Times*, May 13, 1971, 38.

6   **The party combined socialist ideology with street credibility** . . . Seale, *Seize the Time*; Pearson, *The Shadow of the Panther*; Hilliard and Cole, *This Side of Glory*; Collier and Horowitz, *Destructive Generation*.

8   **Indeed, undercover police** . . . Police may have known that a major crime was in the works. Stephen F. Ahern, the police department's chief of detectives, reported receiving a call from Nicholas Pastore to that effect when he testified in the Bobby Seale/Ericka Huggins murder trial (Stephen Ahern testimony, *State v. Seale and Huggins*, 491). Pastore himself stated the same thing in a May 27, 1969, affidavit filed with the application for a bench warrant in the murder case. "The Proceedings in the Alex Rackley Murder Case: Preliminary Memorandum," Yale Trial Report Committee, found in 1970 May Day Strike Collection, Manuscripts and Archives, Yale University Library, Box 1.

8   **They followed—at first** . . . Ahern, *Police in Trouble*, 32–34.

9   **Sams ordered everyone out** . . . Sources for this account of the murder included FBI interview with Lonnie McLucas Jr. in Salt Lake County Jail, Utah, June 12, 1969; Joseph Lelyveld, "Panther Testifies He 'Assumed' Party Leaders Ordered Murder," *New York Times*, July 29, 1970, 34; Warren Kimbro interviews.

11   **Sams ordered her and some others to clean up** . . . Peggy Hudgins testimony, *State v. Seale and Huggins*, 279–84.

Chapter 2: Busted

13   **May 21, 1969, was a good day for a ride** . . . This account of the discovery of Alex Rackley's body was based on an interview with John Mroczka, November 30, 2004, and on State Trooper William Leonard's testimony, *State v. Seale and Huggins*, 347–58.

14   **the cops found a handwritten note . . .** Ericka Huggins testimony, *State v. Seale and Huggins*, 2915–17.

15   **Police in Bridgeport, a twenty-five-minute drive west, rounded up a woman named Frances Carter and brought her to New Haven . . .** Carter interview in Hilliard and Cole, *This Side of Glory*, 253–54.

16   **In Nick's view . . .** Pastore interview.

16   **As the police planned a raid . . .** This account of the New Haven police bust of the Panther headquarters is based on an interview with Nicholas Pastore, November 9, 2004; interview with Billy White, December 15, 2004; and Stephen Ahern testimony, *State v. Seale and Huggins*, 491–584.

16   **Warren arranged for the purchase . . .** Warren Kimbro interviews.

17   **Billy White and Warren had known each other for years . . .** Billy White and Warren Kimbro interviews.

17   **Sylvia recognized him . . .** On Sylvia Kimbro's arrest, Sylvia Kimbro interview, January 10, 2005; Stanley Lundgren testimony, *State v. Seale and Huggins*, 753.

18   **Germano and Veronica awoke . . .** Veronica Kimbro interview, April 3, 2005; Germano Kimbro interview, October 27, 2004.

19   **Ernie made the call . . .** Ernest Osborne interview, December 9, 2004.

19   **In straggled George Edwards . . .** Interviews with George Edwards, October 21, 2004, and Warren Kimbro; testimony, *State v. Seale and Huggins*.

20   **the Panthers sought Edwards to deliver the same brand of justice to him . . .** "Panther Files Guilty Plea to Lesser Counts," *Washington Post*, September 24, 1970, A-3.

20   **A friendly voice . . .** Warren Kimbro interviews.

20   **Sylvia, too, didn't know what to think . . .** Sylvia Kimbro interview.

CHAPTER 3: BURIAL OF A FOOTNOTE

22   **"8 Black Panthers Seized in Torture-Murder Case" . . .** John Darnton, *New York Times*, May 23, 1969, 24.

22   **"8 Panthers Held in Murder Plot" . . .** Charles J. Hines, *New Haven Register*, May 22, 1969, 1.

22   **less than two weeks shy of his twentieth birthday . . .** Certificate of Death, Alex Rackley, Middlefield, Connecticut.

23   **The *Hartford Courant* put Rackley's age at thirty-five . . .** "Body Suspected Slaying Victim," *Hartford Courant*, May 22, 1969, 1.

23   **An Associated Press dispatch referred to Jacksonville as "the major Florida city most deeply rooted in the old-style Dixie politics" . . .** "Negroes Rising Fast in State Politics," Associated Press dispatch appearing in *Jacksonville Times-Union*, May 25, 1969, B-4.

23   **"City police arrested a giant Negro" . . .** *Jacksonville Journal*, January 29, 1968, 17.

23   **Parlee . . . was a strong woman . . .** Interviews with Freddie, Wayne, and Velva Rackley (Alex's siblings) and Sandra Rackley (Freddie's wife), including a visit to Jacksonville, Florida, October 11–14, 2004.

24   **Alex grew up on a crowded block . . .** Carole Mercer Roberts interview, October 2004; Freddie, Wayne, and Velva Rackley interviews.

24   **The FBI noted . . .** John R. Williams Papers, Manuscripts and Archives, Yale University Library, Box 1.

25   **He hung around Panther headquarters . . .** On Rackley in New York City: interviews with former undercover New York cop Gene Roberts, January 31, 2005, and with New York Panther Rose Mary Byrd, October 27 and December 5, 2004; letters from and a jailhouse interview (April 8, 2005) with former Panther George Sams; e-mail correspondence with Panther Landon Williams (December 13, 2004); Shirley Wolterding testimony, *State v. Seale and Huggins*, 2642–43; George Sams testimony, *State v. Seale and Huggins*, 1772.

25   **On March 11, in a conversation secretly recorded by a police infiltrator . . .** Edith Evans Asbury, "Undercover Agent Recalls How Role Was Almost Discovered by Black Panthers," *New York Times*, December 2, 1970, 51.

26   **Sams called himself "Crazy George" . . .** George Sams testimony, *State v. Seale and Huggins*, 1894, 1780; George Sams interview, April 8, 2005; Ericka Huggins testimony, *State v. Seale and Huggins*, 2901; Kathleen Cleaver interview, October 20, 2004; tape of an interview conducted with Ericka Huggins by author Yohuru Williams, July 10, 1995.

27   **"*Please*, sister" . . .** Rose Mary Bird interview, October 27, 2004.

27   **Rackley's identity may have been confused with that of Alex McKiever . . .** George Sams testimony, *State v. Seale and Hug-*

*gins,*1713; Warren Kimbro interviews. Landon Williams denied this assertion in an e-mail to author, December 13, 2004.

27 **one of the women should seduce Rackley, then determine if he was an informer** . . . Maude Francis testimony, *State v. Seale and Huggins,* 1619–20; Ericka Huggins testimony, *State v. Seale and Huggins,* 2864–6; George Sams testimony, *State v. Seale and Huggins,* 1688; Warren Kimbro testimony, *State v. Seale and Huggins,* 408–10.

28 **Wake up! Ericka demanded** . . . The account of the events leading up to and including Rackley's tape-recorded "confession" and torture is based on Ericka Huggins testimony, *State v. Seale and Huggins,* 2872–92; George Sams testimony, *State v. Seale and Huggins,* 1690–704; Warren Kimbro interviews; FBI interview with Lonnie McLucas Jr. in Salt Lake County Jail, Utah, June 12, 1969; Warren Kimbro testimony, *State v. Seale and Huggins,* 413–57, 902–54; George Edwards interview, October 21, 2004.

30 **Upstairs, Warren's children** . . . Veronica Kimbro interview, April 3, 2005; Germano Kimbro, October 27, 2004.

30 **"Ericka Huggins," she announced** . . . Transcript of torture session. Alex Rackley FBI file, authors' collection; transcript, *State v. Seale and Huggins,* 895ff.

33 **Ahern would claim** . . . Ahern, *Police in Trouble,* 32–34.

33 **According to Nick Pastore** . . . Nick Pastore interview, November 9, 2004.

33 **Alex Rackley spoke up** . . . Joseph Lelyveld, "Kimbro Describes Panther Slaying," *New York Times,* July 24, 1970, 17.

34 **Alex Rackley's murder made the *New York Times*** . . . John Darnton, "8 Black Panthers Seized in Torture-Murder Case," May 23, 1969, 24.

34 **a one-paragraph death notice** . . . "In Memoriam" section, *Jacksonville Times-Union,* May 24, 1969.

34 **Parlee Rackley . . . learned the news from the police** . . . Rackley family interviews.

CHAPTER 4: JAILHOUSE DAYS

35 **Hoover's men now had a justification** . . . "Chicago F.B.I. Raids Offices of Panthers," *New York Times,* June 5, 1969, 94; Pearson, *Shadow of the Panther,* 208–9.

35   **he remained determined to maintain . . .** Warren Kimbro interviews.

35   **His employers . . . announced . . . that they were officially suspending him . . .** "CPI Suspends Suspect in Panther Murder," *New
Haven Journal-Courier*, May 23, 1969, 4.

36   **Ericka stopped right behind Roraback's back. . .** Catherine
Roraback interview, February 3, 2005.

37   **Warren and Eddie knew each other . . .** Warren Kimbro interviews.

38   **interrogating McLucas. . .** FBI interview with Lonnie McLucas Jr.
in Salt Lake County Jail, Utah, June 12, 1969.

38   **George Edwards . . . started hearing about. . .** George Edwards interview, December 22, 2004.

39   **McDougal looked at Warren . . .** Warren Kimbro interviews.

39   **Germano walked out . . .** Germano Kimbro interview, October 27,
2004.

CHAPTER 5: THE MAKING OF A PANTHER

41   **Then came Henry Karney . . .** Warren Kimbro interviews. The
anecdotes in this chapter about Kimbro's life up to the time of the
Rackley murder come from those interviews.

44   **Spruce Street stretched less than the length . . .** New Haven city
maps, Sterling Library, Yale University.

44   **Nearly a third of the neighborhood's families were first-
generation . . .** New Haven city directories, Sterling Library, Yale
University.

46   **New Haven received $745.38 per citizen . . .** Rae, *City*, 324.

47   **Warren thrust the knife into Overby's chest . . .** Field Sheet,
State of Connecticut department of Parole, No. 24835, in Warren
Kimbro Department of Corrections file.

49   **Malcolm would say . . .** Perry, *Malcolm X*.

49   **Malcolm X was having a similar effect . . .** Seale, *Seize the Time*;
Cleaver and Katsiaficas, *Liberation, Imagination, and the Black Panther Party*, 76.

50   **a macroeconomic tidal wave would wash away more than half of
the 33,000 factory jobs in town, more than half the local employers . . .** "New Haven Factories and Stores, totals 1899–1999,"
Historical New Haven Digital Collection, http://www.library

.yale.edu/thecitycourse/Data_Tables/Commerce/Factories and Stores _New_Haven_1899_1999.xls ; Rae, *City*, 362.

51   **the militant Hill Parents Association . . .** Rose Harris interview, October 20, 2004; Balzer, *Street Time*; "New Haven" excerpts, Hearings Before the National Commission on Urban Problems, May–June 1967.

51   **police, disconnected from neighborhood groups like the HPA . . .** Williams, *Black Politics / White Power*, 82–88; Powledge, *Model City*, 111–12.

52   **A federal government commission on urban riots reported . . .** The Report of the National Advisory Commission on Civil Disorders, page 197, quoted in memo from Patricia Dyer to Joel Cogen, New Haven Redevelopment Authority archives, Manuscripts and Archives, Yale University Library, Box 334.

52   **the Black Coalition . . . took charge . . .** Hugh Price interview, November 17, 2004.

52   **fifty-seven pages of his book . . .** The Will K. story appears in Goldenberg, *Build Me a Mountain*, 334–91.

55   **Later in his life, DuBois came to acknowledge . . .** Both DuBois's original essay and his later revisiting of the subject are reprinted in Gates and West, *The Future of the Race.*

56   **Ethan Gardens, a government-built complex . . .** Donald Dallas, "City Gets First 'Mixed' Income Cooperative: Model Program For Nation," *New Haven Register*, April 27, 1968, 36; Land Disposition Agreement, revised March 24, 1967, and Dwight Renewal and Redevelopment Project plan, 39–45, New Haven Redevelopment Authority archives, Manuscripts and Archives, Yale University Library, Box 241.

59   **Huggins was the son of a middle-class family . . .** Alice Mick, "John Huggins: The Beginning." This article appeared in an alternative or underground New Haven newspaper some time between 1969 and 1971; the exact source is unclear from the photocopy in the John Williams Papers collection in Manuscripts and Archives, Yale University Library, where it was found; Sam Negri, "Slain 'Panther' Active in Rights Drive Here Before Going to L.A.," *New Haven Register*, January 19, 1969, 1; "Rites Set Friday for Slain Student, John Huggins Jr.," *New Haven Register*, January 23, 1969, 25; Yohuru Williams interview with Ericka Huggins, July 10, 1995.

61   **More than fifty anticolonial uprisings . . .** The list includes Algeria, Barbados, Benin, Bhutan, Botswana, Burkina Faso, Burma, Burundi, Cambodia, Cameroon, Central African Republic, Chad, Congo, Cuba, Cyprus, Egypt, Equatorial Guinea, Gabon, Gambia, Ghana, Guinea, Guyana, India, Indonesia, Ireland, Jamaica, Jordan, Kenya, South Korea, Laos, Lesotho, Libya, Madagascar, Malawi, Malaysia, Mali, Malta, Mauritania, Mauritius, Morocco, Niger, Nigeria, Pakistan, Philippines, Senegal, Sierra Leone, Singapore, Somalia, Sri Lanka, Sudan, Swaziland, Tanzania, Togo, Tunisia, Uganda, and Vietnam.

63   **houseguests from hell . . .** Sylvia Kimbro interview, January 10, 2005.

Chapter 6: Five Hail Marys

66   **Maybelle coached Warren . . .** Prison stories are drawn from interviews with Warren Kimbro.

66   **Veronica had nightmares . . .** Veronica Kimbro interview, April 3, 2005.

66   **Lee reflected in his official two-page announcement . . .** Powledge, *Model City*, 12–13.

68   **police in Toronto . . .** FBI memo, August 7, 1969, John R. Williams Papers, Folder 11, Manuscripts and Archives, Yale University Library; "Detroit Panther Arraigned Here," *New Haven Register*, August 22, 1969; UPI dispatch, August 22, 1969.

68   **the Nixon Justice Department formed a special unit . . .** "Urgent" teletype to SAC (Special Agent in Charge), New Haven, from FBI Director, August 12, 1969, John R. Williams Papers, Folder 16.

69   **Nixon's assistant attorney general also directed the FBI to reinterview . . .** Memo from Assistant Attorney General, September 9, 1969, John R. Williams Papers, Folder 12.

69   **Chief Ahern would write . . .** Ahern, *Police in Trouble*, 34.

69   **For antigovernment protesters . . .** Earl Caldwell, "Declining Black Panthers Gather New Support from Repeated Clashes with Police," *New York Times*, 64; John Darnton, "Panther Hearing: A Trial Preview," *New York Times*, November 30, 1969, 59.

69   **Seale told a United Press International reporter . . .** "Seale Brands Conn. Murder Rap a Frame," UPI dispatch, August 23, 1969; published in *New York Daily News*, August 24, 1969, 52.

71   **Johnson didn't know** . . . George Johnson interview.

73   **wearing a gold tie** . . . Stan Simon, "Panther Enters Plea of Guilty in Slaying," *Hartford Courant*, January 17, 1970, 1; "A Panther Admits He Killed Another," *New York Times*, January 17, 1970, 1.

73   **The local Panthers held a press conference** . . . "Panthers Attack Methods Used In Kimbro Case," *New Haven Register*, February 6, 1970; "Policeman Denies Panthers' Charge," *New York Times*, February 8, 1970.

74   **In a book published three years later** . . . Freed, *Agony in New Haven*, 27.

74   **Betty and Ernie Osborne knew** . . . Ernest Osborne interview, December 9, 2004.

75   **Iannotti wasn't sure** . . . Larry Iannotti interview, November 16, 2004.

77   **"The only pressure"** . . . "Policeman Denies Panthers' Charge," *New York Times*, February 8, 1970.

CHAPTER 7: LEADING LADY

78   **At first the Panthers rationalized his guilty plea** . . . "Press Release: Why Warren Kimbro Pleaded Guilty," *People's News Service*, undated photocopy, John R. Williams Papers, Manuscripts and Archives, Yale University Library, Box 4, Folder 25; "Panthers Declare Kimbro Is Innocent," *The Crow*, no. 2, February 1970, 1.

78   **Niantic officials opened their mail** . . . Federal court complaint, *Bobby Seale and Ericka Huggins v. Ellis C. MacDougall, Commissioner of Corrections et al.*; Plaintiffs' exhibit 2–1, letter to Attorney Catherine G. Roraback from Ellis C. MacDougall, September 22, 1969; memorandum of decision, *Seale and Huggins v. Manson, Commissioner of Corrections et al.*, civil no. 14077, U.S. District Court.

79   **Elaine Brown found Ericka to be "very brave"** . . . Brown, *A Taste of Power*, 202–4.

79   **writing prison verses like these** . . . Freed, *Agony in New Haven*, 332.

80   **Behind bars, as in Panther houses, she was a natural leader** . . . Ericka Huggins interview with Yohuru Williams, July 10, 1995; Joelle Dominski, "The Panther Women," *Modern Times*, October 1, 1970, 8.

81 **Ericka's face popped up** . . . Henry Louis Gates Jr., "Are We Better Off?" http://www.pbs.org/wgbh/pages/frontline/shows/race/etc/gates .html.

81 **The "New Haven Women's Liberation Rock Band" enter-tained** . . . "'Watching Faces Smile': Women's Band Rocks Niantic Prison," *Modern Times*, January 15, 1971, 10; Freed, *Agony in New Haven*, 144–46.

81 **In an open letter** . . . "Cleaver to Ericka Huggins," *View from the Bottom*, August 21, 1969, microfilm, underground press archives, Sterling Memorial Library, Yale University.

82 **Growing up in the segregated southeast section** . . . Ericka Huggins testimony, *State v. Seale and Huggins*, 2808–21; Cozette Jenkins testimony, *State v. Seale and Huggins*, 2706–8; Huggins interview with Williams; BBC, "A Passion for Action," August 21, 2003, http://news.bbc.co.uk/2/hi/americas/3150491.stm.

83 **So Ericka and fellow Panther Elaine Brown wrote a tract on the subject** . . . On Ericka Huggins's reaction to sexism in the Black Panther Party: Huggins interview with Williams; Brown, *A Taste of Power*, 191–92.

84 **her husband was dead** . . . On the murder and the subsequent arrest: Ericka Huggins testimony, *State v. Seale and Huggins*, 2824–33; Senate Select Committee, *Book III: Final Report*, 188; Swearingen, *FBI Secrets*, 82–83; Elaine Brown testimony, *State v. Seale and Huggins*, 2720; Elaine Brown, *A Taste of Power*, 161–74; Catherine Roraback interview, February 3, 2005; UPI, "Black Militant Power Clash Probed in UCLA Slayings," in *New Haven Register*, January 19, 1969, 1; Huey P. Newton, *War Against the Panthers: A Study of Repression in America*, doctoral dissertation, University of California Santa Cruz, June 1980, 104–7.

84 **mired in grief** . . . Elizabeth Huggins testimony, *State v. Seale and Huggins*, 2701–2; Elaine Brown testimony, *State v. Seale and Huggins*, 2728.

84 **Gonzalvez, the "state captain," was** . . . Warren Kimbro interviews.

84 **He threatened the life** . . . "Black Panther Party, Racial Matters; Possible Assault on a Federal Agent," "urgent" teletype, February 19, 1969, to Director, FBI, and New Haven from Boston, John R. Williams Papers, Box 1; "Racial Matters—Possible Assault on a Federal Officer," March 11, 1969 memo from Director, FBI, to

SAC, New Haven, John R. Williams Papers, Box 1; Ted Gunderson interview, November 1, 2004; Domestic Intelligence Division, Informative Note, February 19, 1969, John R. Williams Papers.

85   **He wrote leaflets . . .** Reprinted in March 20, 1969, memo to SAC, New Haven, John R. Williams Papers, Folder 79. (The identity of the sender was blacked out by an FBI declassifier.)

85   **in one case they lifted . . .** "Counterintelligence Program Black Nationalist-Hate Groups," Memorandum from Director, FBI, to SAC, New Haven, April 28, 1969, authors' collection of declassified COINTELPRO documents.

85   **Warren responding to such "misinformation" . . .** "Misinformation Clouds Black Panthers' Role," *New Haven Journal-Courier,* March 18, 1969.

86   **Ericka's intimidation talents . . .** Richard Kaukas, "Black Panthers Outline Stand," *Hartford Courant,* April 1, 1969, 28.

86   **In later years . . .** Andy Shah, "'Educate to Liberate' Event Unites Student Activists, Former Black Panthers at UCLA," *Daily Bruin,* March 15, 1999.

87   **She and Warren did keep an eye on José Gonzalvez . . .** Warren Kimbro interviews; "Threats against José Rene Gonzalvez," FBI memo, December 9, 1969, John R. Williams Papers, Folder 17; "urgent" teletype from New Haven FBI office to Charlotte, Tampa, and San Francisco offices, May 22, 1969, John R. Williams Papers, Box 1; Airtel from SAC San Francisco to Director, FBI, May 14, 1969, John R. Williams Papers, Box 1; File # 100-19186, memo from New Haven FBI office, October 31, 1969, John R. Williams Papers, Folder 14; notes, April 11, 1969, "Central Staff Meeting" minutes, and memo to "Central Committee, Black Panther Party" from New Haven branch, both confiscated during the raid on Panther headquarters following the Rackley murder, photocopied by the FBI, and included in the John R. Williams Papers.

CHAPTER 8: WELCOME TO NEW HAVEN

88   **national dispatched a crew . . .** "Urgent teletype" from New Haven FBI office, September 25, 1969, John R. Williams Papers,

Manuscripts and Archives, Yale University Library, Folder 12; Charles "Cappy" Pinderhughes interview, October 19, 2004.

88 **Miranda's new assignment displeased Nick Pastore** . . . Nick Pastore interview, November 9, 2004.

88 **placed a call to Ted Gunderson** . . . Ted Gunderson interview, November 10, 2004.

89 **A "hard core"** . . . Airtel from SAC, New Haven, to Director, FBI, April 6, 1970, John R. Williams Papers, Folder 33.

89 **Spurlock's manifold alleged offenses** . . . Memo from a special agent in the New Haven FBI office (name blacked out by FBI declassifier), February 28, 1970, John R. Williams Papers, Folder 22.

89 **Ideology classes resumed** . . . FBI memo, John R. Williams Papers, Box 5.

89 **free breakfast program** . . . FBI memos and clippings, John R. Williams Papers, Folder 14; September 23, 1969, FBI memo, Folder 16.

89 **They launched** . . . "Free Health Clinic Opens," *Modern Times*, February 12, 1971, 12.

89 **One day in Boston** . . . Charles "Cappy" Pinderhughes interview.

89 **Yale debate over Marxism** . . . William H. Farley interview, January 4, 2005.

90 **wiretapped phone conversation** . . . Airtel from SAC, New Haven, to Director, FBI, February 19, 1970, John R. Williams Papers, Folder 21.

91 **That job fell to Charles** . . . Charles "Cappy" Pinderhughes interview.

91 **The paper reported** . . . Clips of articles from *The People's News Service*, photocopied by the FBI, collected in John R. Williams Papers, Folders 23, 25, and 30.

92 **Gallyot resented** . . . Michael Gallyot interview, November 5, 2004.

92 **words like these** . . . Michael Gallyot, "Revolution in Our Lifetime," *People's News Service*, undated FBI photocopy, John R. Williams Papers, Folder 23.

93 **Ericka wrote the following account** . . . "A Letter from Ericka Huggins," *People's News Service*, February 16, 1970.

95 **the FBI chief ordered the local office** . . . Memo from Director, FBI, to SAC, New Haven, March 8, 1970, John R. Williams Papers, Folder 23.

95   **The FBI considered the party's national newspaper "one of the [party's] most effective propaganda operations"** . . . The information in this paragraph all comes from Senate Select Committee, *Book III: Final Report*, 214–15.

95   **a chemical agent called "Skatol"** . . . Ibid., 214; Airtel from SAC, Newark, to Director, FBI, June 3, 1970, authors' collection.

95   **"Extreme caution must be exercised"** . . . Airtel to Director, FBI, from SAC, New Haven, January 28, 1970, John R. Williams Papers, Folder 19.

96   **"continuing to obtain weapons"** . . . FBI memo from New Haven Special Agent (name blacked out by FBI declassifier), February 23, 1970, John R. Williams Papers, Folder 22.

96   **When Cappy Pinderhughes exhorted an audience** . . . Memo from Hartford FBI office, January 8, 1970, John R. Williams Papers, Folder 20.

CHAPTER 9: PLANE RIDE FROM CALIFORNIA

97   **Nick Pastore was . . . on the phone** . . . Nick Pastore interview, November 9, 2004.

97   **"Today's pig is tomorrow's bacon!"** . . . The speech was transcribed by the New Haven FBI, document number NH 100-19186, authors' collection. Account of the event and audience reaction: Marvin Olasky, "Seale Roasts 'Pigs,' 'Hits Hogs,'" *Yale Daily News*, May 20, 1969, 1.

98   **To himself, Seale thought** . . . Bobby Seale interview, March 13, 2005.

98   **a pre-extradition interview** . . . "Bobby Seale Raps on the New Haven Panther Trial," *People's News Service*, March 21, 1970, John R. Williams Papers, Folder 30.

99   **a memo to J. Edgar Hoover** . . . Teletype from San Francisco FBI office to Director, FBI, March 13, 1970, John R. Williams Papers, Manuscripts and Archives, Yale University Library, Folder 25.

99   **Nick grew up** . . . Nick Pastore interview.

101   **People like Kelly Moye, whom Nick originally met on March 3, 1964** . . . Kelly Moye interview, November 10, 2004; Kelly Moye police personnel file.

102   **COINTELRPO . . . was FBI Director J. Edgar Hoover's pet project . . .** Senate Select Committee, *Book III: Final Report*, 3, 27, 187–223.

103   **Even before COINTELPRO, Hoover considered integrationists and black civil rights leaders as threats to the social order . . .** This conclusion is drawn from, among other sources, the analysis and documentation provided in Kornweibel, *Seeing Red*.

103   **His agents' duties . . .** Senate Select Committee, *Book III: Final Report*, 1–2, 7–11, and Chapter 4.

103   **five hundred such "black bag jobs" . . .** Swearingen, *FBI Secrets*, 165.

103   **The latter category of groups . . .** Senate Select Committee, *Book III: Final Report*, 20–22, 187.

103   **"the greatest threat" . . .** Ibid., 187.

104   **By the following January, when the FBI played at least an indirect role in John Huggins's murder . . .** Ibid., 188–90; Swearingen, *FBI Secrets*, 82–83.

104   **repeat itself in cities like San Diego, Chicago . . .** Senate Select Committee, *Book III: Final Report*, 194–95, 199.

104   **Hoover personally directed . . .** Airtel to SAC, New Haven, from Director, FBI, March 11, 1969, John R. Williams Papers, Box 1.

104   **Gunderson responded . . .** Ted Gunderson interview, November 1, 2004.

104   **"To date" . . .** Memo to SAC, New Haven, from Director, FBI, March 28, 1969, authors' collection.

Chapter 10: Super Chimp

This chapter's account of Warren Kimbro's switch to the Brooklyn, Connecticut, jail and his experiences there is drawn from interviews with Kimbro.

Chapter 11: Disorder in the Court

113   **Seale, in an olive windbreaker and blue shirt . . .** John Darnton, "Seale, Under Guard, Shows Up in New Haven Court in Slaying," *New York Times*, March 19, 1970, 36.

113 **A recent Yale Law School graduate** . . . David Rosen interview, September 28, 2004.

114 **Theodore Koskoff, Lonnie McLucas's lawyer, chaired** . . . Airtel to Director, FBI, from SAC, New Haven, March 12, 1970, John R. Williams Papers, Manuscripts and Archives, Yale University Library, Folder 25.

114 **Ericka's lawyer, Catherine Roraback** . . . Ibid.

115 **The glossary appeared** . . . Memo to Director, FBI, from SAC, New Haven, February 27, 1970, authors' collection.

115 **a point-by-point anonymous flyer** . . . Memo to Director, FBI, from SAC, New Haven, August 7, 1970, authors' collection.

115 **an attack on the Panthers by "A Concerned Merchant"** . . . Memo to Director, FBI, from SAC, New Haven, March 25, 1971, authors' collection.

115 **Another letter, supposedly from a Yale "alumnus"** . . . Memo to SAC, New Haven, from Director, FBI, August 25, 1969, authors' collection.

116 **like William F. Buckley** . . . Memo to Director, FBI, from SAC, New Haven, September 3, 1969, authors' collection.

116 **A Hoover-approved anonymous letter to national Panther headquarters** . . . To SAC, New Haven, from Director, FBI, March 13, 1970, authors' collection.

116 **"Not only will we burn buildings"** . . . FBI memo and transcript, March 30, 1970, John R. Williams Papers, Folder 31.

116 **forwarded . . . to . . . John Ehrlichman** . . . Note from "ERS" of the FBI to Ehrlichman, April 22, 1970, John R. Williams Papers, Folder 31.

116 **"A rumor is spreading in the ghetto area of New Haven"** . . . Memo from New Haven FBI office, March 31, 1970, John R. Williams Papers, Folder 28.

116 **From Washington came a summary** . . . Teletype from Director, FBI, to SAC, New Haven and San Francisco, April 8, 1970, John R. Williams Papers, Folder 29.

117 **As part of a $75,000 security upgrade** . . . FBI memo from "New Haven" to "Director," April 8, 1970, John R. Williams Papers, Folder 30.

117 **Yale students . . . filled Woolsey Hall** . . . Teletype to Director and San Francisco from New Haven, April 14, 1970, John R. Williams Papers, Folder 30; Taft, *May Day at Yale*, 19–20.

117   **"Hey, we've got a problem here!"** UPI, "Astronauts Battle for Life," *New Haven Register*, April 14, 1970, 1.

117   **The problems in New Haven began . . .** "Police Disperse Downtown Gangs Following Panther Trial Protests," *New Haven Register*, April 14, 1970, 1; "2 Top Panthers Jailed for Contempt," *New York Times*, April 15, 1970, 32; teletype from New Haven FBI office to Director and San Francisco office, April 14, 1970, John R. Williams Papers, Folder 30; Taft, *May Day at Yale*, 15–16.

119   **"As many as half a million persons" . . .** Teletype from New Haven FBI office to Director, FBI, April 14, 1970, John R. Williams Papers, Box 5.

119   **On April 15, in Cambridge, Massachusetts . . .** Donald Janson, "Damage Estimated at $100,000 after Harvard Riot," *New York Times*, April 17, 1970, 35.

119   **At the rally, Yippie leader Abbie Hoffman vowed . . .** Kabaservice, *The Guardians*, 405.

CHAPTER 12: THE MAGIC BUS

120   **Brewster and his young assistant, Henry "Sam" Chauncey . . .** This account of the picnic, the internal discussion involving Chauncey and Brewster, and the arrangements for the bus all come from an interview with Henry Chauncey, January 27, 2005; Brewster Papers, Manuscripts and Archives, Yale University Library, Box 1; Kabaservice, *The Guardians*, 404–11; Paul Bass, "The Magic Bus: How the 'Friendly Face of Authority' Really Kept the City Cool," *New Haven Advocate*, April 27, 1995, 10. Brewster, Guida, and Ahern are dead.

121   **The Ivy League represented the old East Coast establishment . . .** For an exhaustive treatment of Brewster's place in that establishment, and its battles with old Yale and Washington, see Kabaservice, *The Guardians*.

123   **Conservative Old Blue William F. Buckley . . .** William F. Buckley, "The Metamorphosis of Kingman Brewster," syndicated column May 3, 1970, in 1970 May Day collection, Manuscripts and Archives, Yale University Library, Box 2; Kabaservice, *The Guardians*, 333, 360–61, 414.

124   **Abbie Hoffman predicted the biggest riot in history in New Haven . . .** Greenfield, *No Peace, No Place*, 212.

CHAPTER 13: PANTHER, PANTHER . . . BOW, WOW, WOW!

127   **Miranda exhorted one gathering** . . . William H. Farley Jr. interview, January 4, 2005; William H. Farley Jr., "Amerikca the Ugly Spurs Revolutionary Reaction," *Yale Daily News*, "May Day: Five Years Later" issue, April 22, 1975, 1; Taft, *May Day at Yale*, 25.

128   **The young student had enrolled in Doug Miranda 101** . . . Farley interview.

128   **one of ninety-six black students** . . . Henry Louis Gates Jr., "Are We Better Off?" http://www.pbs.org/wgbh/pages/frontline/shows/race/etc/gates.html.

128   **They felt the pressure** . . . Ibid.

130   **Hersey wrote** . . . Hersey, *Letter to the Alumni*, 18

130   **The journalist Jeff Greenfield** . . . Greenfield, *No Peace, No Place*, 213.

131   **Martin Luther King was a "Negro"** . . . Freed, *Agony in New Haven*, 18–21.

131   **Michael Lerner did that** . . . Michael Lerner, "Respectable Bigotry," *The American Scholar*, 38, no. 4 (Autumn 1969).

132   **Doug Miranda . . . in a speech on Sunday night, April 19** . . . William Bulkeley, "Panther Leader Requests Strike," *Yale Daily News*, April 20, 1970, 1; Hersey, *Letter to the Alumni*, 80; Taft, *Mayday at Yale*, 35–36; "Chronology," Office of the Secretary, Yale University, mailing to alumni, May 4, 1970, Brewster Papers, Manuscripts and Archives, Yale University Library, Box 22.

133   **running off T-shirts with the Panther-Bulldog logo** . . . 1970 May Day Collection, Manuscripts and Archives, Yale University Library, Box 1.

133   **students formed a committee—cochaired by future first lady and U.S. senator Hillary Rodham (Clinton)** . . . *Strike Newspaper*, April 24–28, 1970, and "Position Paper of the Steering Committee," 1970 May Day collection. Rodham's law school committee voted, for instance, to "insist . . . that no coercion or extra-legal attempts to stop the trial should be tolerated" (*Strike Newspaper*, April 28, 1970, 2).

133   **De Jaager would remember Rodham** . . . Jerry de Jaager interview, January 2005.

134   **right-wingers would twist Rodham Clinton's role** . . . For a particularly egregious example of inventing facts to smear Clinton, see

http://www.trendmicro.com/vinfo/hoaxes/hoaxDetails.asp?HName
=Hillary+Clinton+and+the+Black+Panther+Trial&Page=1.

134 **She has also limited her public recollections . . .** For example, Clinton, *Living History*, 44–45. On Rodham Clinton at Yale Law: Carole Bass, "Rights of Passage," *Connecticut Law Tribune*, October 12, 1992, 1. Through her press secretary, Rodham Clinton declined to be interviewed for this book.

134 **Secretly, he met with Kingman Brewster . . .** William Farley interview.

134 **At a rally in New Haven's Beaver Pond Park . . .** Teletype from New Haven to Director, FBI, April 14, 1970, John R. Williams Papers, Manuscripts and Archives, Yale University Library, Box 5. [According to the memo, Panthers distributed a bulletin at the event showing Police Chief James Ahern's face and the title "Wanted Dead."]

134 **On April 20, at the University of Connecticut, pro-Panther students beat another student . . .** Ibid.

135 **Bobby Seale told the judge . . .** Taft, *Mayday at Yale*, 50–51.

135 **It was a turning point . . .** David Rosen interview, September 28, 2004.

135 **In front of the 4,500 to 5,000 people . . .** Taft, *Mayday at Yale*, 55–65; *Bright College Years* (film), Peter Rosen Productions, Avco Embassy Pictures, 1970, Manuscripts and Archives, Yale University Library; Hersey, *Letter to the Alumni*, 82–83.

137 **Brewster and Chauncey—heeding Archie Cox's advice . . .** Henry Chauncey interview.

CHAPTER 14: CALLING THE QUESTION

139 **The faculty meeting took place . . .** "Chronology," Office of the Secretary, Yale University, mailing to alumni, May 4, 1970, Brewster Papers, Manuscripts and Archives, Yale University Library, Box 22, p. 5.

139 **Brewster spoke next, from a prepared text . . .** "Statement by Kingman Brewster, Jr. at meeting of the Faculty of Yale College, April 23, 1970," Brewster Papers, Box 21; Taft, *Mayday at Yale*, 82–97; Hersey, *Letter to the Alumni*, 86–90.

140 **Later that night, Yale released a text of Brewster's remarks . . .** "Chronology," 5.

140   declared a prominent judge, Herbert S. MacDonald . . . "Judge Hits Statements by Brewster," *New Haven Register*, April 25, 1970.

140   "Dear Hub" . . . Letter from Kingman Brewster to Honorable Herbert S. MacDonald, April 25, 1970, Brewster Papers, Box 21.

141   "The Metamorphosis of Kingman Brewster" . . . William F. Buckley, syndicated column May 3, 1970, in 1970 May Day Collection, Manuscripts and Archives, Yale University Library, Box 2.

141   U.S. senator Thomas J. Dodd of Connecticut also attacked Yale's administration . . . "Chronology," 11; Taft, *Mayday at Yale*, 117; Hersey, *Letter to the Alumni*, 96.

141   A New Haven politician named Ed Marcus . . . Letter and press release, May Day Collection, Box 2; "Marcus Calls for Poll on Ouster of Brewster," *New Haven Register*, April 27, 1970.

142   Vice President Spiro Agnew . . . made a speech . . . Taft, *Mayday at Yale*, 117.

142   1,500 students signed . . . "Chronology," 10–12.

142   Agnew's salvo also bombed with some influential editorial writers . . . Brewster Papers, Box 22.

143   Some letter writers asked . . . Brewster Papers, Box 21.

143   a well-publicized speech Brewster had given to newspaper publishers convening in New York . . . "Supplementary Introductory Remarks by Kingman Brewster, Jr. to American Newspaper Publishers Association Speech, April 21, 1970," Brewster Papers, Box 21.

CHAPTER 15: BALL OF CONFUSION

144   A bank of black rotary telephones . . . Henry Chauncey interview, January 27, 2005; Taft, *Mayday at Yale*, 143.

144   President Johnson named Vance . . . Taft, *Mayday at Yale*, 129.

145   the White House was dispatching . . . Ahern, *Police in Trouble*, 48–60; "Chronology," Office of the Secretary, Yale University, mailing to alumni, May 4, 1970, Brewster Papers, Manuscripts and Archives, Yale University Library, Box 22, 12.

145   Ahern battled . . . Ahern, *Police in Trouble*, 57.

145   He had sent teams to Chicago . . . Ibid, 36–37, 41–42, 63–64.

145   Ahern struggled to dampen the hysteria generated by the FBI . . . Ahern, *Police in Trouble*, 49–55.

145   **Hoover had instructed** . . . Teletype to SAC, New Haven, from Director, New Haven, April 24, 1970.

146   **"Consciously or unconsciously"** . . . Ahern, *Police in Trouble*, 54.

146   **the theft of eighteen rifles** . . . the theft of hundreds of bayonet-mounted guns . . . 140 pounds of explosive mercury fulminate . . . a suspicious fire in the Yale law school library's basement . . . U.S. Government memorandum to Mr. DeLoach from A. Rosen, April 30, 1970, John R. Williams Papers, Manuscripts and Archives, Yale University Library, Folder 33; Williams Papers, Box 5; Taft, *Mayday at Yale*, 107; Hersey, *Letter to the Alumni*, 95.

146   **"The current situation at New Haven is extremely volatile"** . . . Airtel to "All SACs (except Anchorage, Honolulu and San Juan)" from Director, FBI, April 24, 1970, John R. Williams Papers, Folder 33.

147   **The Black Coalition** . . . attack on "so-called allies of the oppressed" . . . 1970 May Day Collection, Manuscripts and Archives, Yale University Library, Box 3.

147   **the Black and Spanish Community Control Network** . . . 1970 May Day Collection, Box 1.

148   **Black Coalition organizers hoped** . . . Hugh Price interview, November 17, 2005.

148   **Sheldon Rhinehart** . . . Sheldon Rhinehart interview, January 7, 2005.

149   **riots erupted at Ohio State** . . . "New Clash Erupts at Ohio State U.," *New York Times*, May 1, 1970.

149   **"My fellow Americans"** . . . *Mayday*, 1970 film by Jericho Pictures, Manuscripts and Archives, Yale University Library.

149   **Behind the scenes** . . . Bob Woodward, "How Mark Felt Became 'Deep Throat,'" *Washington Post*, June 2, 2005.

150   **Brewster and Chauncey heard** . . . Henry Chauncey interview.

150   **Chief Ahern reasoned** . . . Ahern, *Police in Trouble*, 56.

150   **he had reason to anticipate one** . . . "May Day: Five Years Later," *Yale Daily News*, April 22, 1975, 1.

150   **Guardsmen had been told that, if they had to shoot** . . . "Guardsman Speaks: 'These Are My Friends,'" *Modern Times*, May 15, 1970.

150   **More than six hundred reporters** . . . Ahern, *Police in Trouble*, 70.

150   **He told Sam Chauncey** . . . Henry Chauncey interview.

CHAPTER 16: TWO DAYS IN MAY

151   **furtive get-togethers** . . . Henry Chauncey interview; Taft, *Mayday at Yale*, 129.

152   **Slogans screamed from banners** . . . Greenfield, *No Peace, No Place*, 243.

152   **The First Battalion of the 102nd infantry** . . . Press release, Connecticut Army National Guard, May 1, 1970, 1970 May Day Collection, Manuscripts and Archives, Yale University Library, Box 3.

152   **At a battalion meeting at the Goffe Street Armory** . . . "Guardsman Speaks: 'These Are My Friends,'" *Modern Times*, May 15, 1970.

152   **"Fuck Kingston Brewer!"** . . . Taft, *Mayday at Yale*, 135–36; *Strike Newspaper*, May 2, 1970, 4, 1970 May Day Collection, Box 1; Hersey, *Letter to the Alumni*, 98–99.

153   **for New Haven's white radicals** . . . Paul Bass, "Then and Now: New Haveners Recall How Mayday Reached into Their Lives—and What It Means Today," *New Haven Advocate*, April 27, 1995, 15; Hersey, *Letter to the Alumni*, 99; Taft, *Mayday at Yale*, 152.

153   **Local COINTELPRO chief Ted Gunderson** . . . Ted Gunderson interview, November 1, 2004.

154   **Facts mingled with rumors** . . . Teletypes, May 1 and 2, 1970, from Hoover to the offices of the president, vice president, CIA director, and attorney general, John R. Williams Papers, Manuscripts and Archives, Yale University Library, Folder 33.

154   **Warren Kimbro watched all of the demonstrations** . . . Warren Kimbro interview.

155   **"We're more oppressed than you are"** . . . Taft, *Mayday at Yale*, 151.

156   **Lee Weiner addressed sixty people** . . . *Strike Newspaper*, May 2, 1970, 4, 1970 May Day Collection, Box 1.

156   **Allen Ginsberg recited a poem** . . . *Strike Newspaper*, May 2, 1970, 4, 1970 May Day Collection, Box 1.

157   **the fragile peace was broken** . . . This account of the Friday night confrontation with the guard and the cops was based on *Strike Newspaper* accounts, May 2, 1970, Box 1; press release, Chief James F. Ahern, Department of Police Service, New Haven, May 2, 1970, May Day Collection; William H. Farley Jr. interview, January 4, 2005; Henry Chauncey interview; Greenfield, *No Peace, No Place*,

260–63; Taft, *Mayday at Yale*, 144–49; Hersey, *Letter to the Alumni*, 100–102.

158 **Ommmmmm . . .** Hersey, *Letter to the Alumni*, 101; Greenfield, *No Peace, No Place*, 62.

159 **He called the news desk . . .** Henry Chauncey interview.

160 **Citywide, police made only twenty-one arrests all day . . .** Press release, Chief James F. Ahern, Department of Police Service, New Haven, May 2, 1970, May Day Collection.

160 **Keefe represented . . .** Hugh Keefe interview, March 3, 2005.

161 **"Fuck Kingman Brewer" . . .** *Strike Newspaper*, May 3, 1970, 3.

161 **"Fuck Jerry Rubin!" . . .** Bass, "Then and Now," 15.

161 **" . . . all power to the good shooters!" . . .** *Mayday*, 1970 film by Jericho Pictures, Manuscripts and Archives, Yale University Library.

161 **"Facts are as irrelevant . . . "** Taft, *Mayday at Yale*, 154.

162 **Even John Dean had seen all he needed to see . . .** Letter by fax, John Dean to Paul Bass, April 21, 1995; Paul Bass, "Brewster's Dean List: Yale's Prez Saw Nixon 'Trickster's' Hand in Bombing," *New Haven Advocate*, April 27, 1995; John W. Dean III, *Blind Ambition: The White House Years* (New York: Simon & Schuster, 1976), 364.

162 **New Politics Corner . . .** News release, Chief James F. Ahern, Department of Police Service, New Haven, May 3, 1970, May Day Collection; "Visitors Find N.H. a Gas," *Strike Newspaper*, May 3, 1970, 1.

162 **"Send them back to Africa" . . .** "Guardsman Speaks: 'These Are My Friends,'" *Modern Times*, May 15, 1970.

CHAPTER 17: TAKING THE STAND

165 **Warren didn't want to see either of them die . . .** The account of Warren Kimbro's state of mind and actions leading up to this testimony comes from interviews with Kimbro.

166 **the longest deliberation in state history . . .** "Verdict in New Haven," *Newsweek*, July 27, 1970, 34.

166 **Warren had pulled back from identifying Ericka . . .** Kimbro's initial testimony in the trial: *State v. Seale and Huggins*, 365–444.

168 **The Las Vegas memo . . .** Response by Hoover: Airtel to SAC, Las Vegas, from Director, FBI, April 22, 1971, authors' collection.

168 **Though similar tactics had been used all over the country . . .** Airtel to SAC, New Haven, from Director, FBI, February 17, 1971, authors' collection; Senate Select Committee, *Book III: Final Report*, 1–2, 185–224.

169 **At one point the New Haven office sent the San Francisco office . . .** Airtel to SACs, New Haven, San Francisco, from Director, FBI, October 10, 1970, authors' collection.

169 **anonymous letter to Eldridge Cleaver in Algiers . . .** Airtel to SAC, New Haven, from Director, FBI, February 17, 1971, authors' collection.

170 **set a trap . . .** Secret testimony, Nicholas Pastore, before the New Haven Board of Police Commissioners, March 23, 1977, 76–79, authors' collection. Afterward, a high-ranking Irish-American cop proclaimed, "We got him now" (secret testimony, Pasquale Carrieri, before the New Haven Board of Police Commissioners, March 15, 1977, 56–57).

171 **DiLieto summoned Nick to Kaysey's restaurant . . .** Secret testimony, Nicholas Pastore, before the New Haven Board of Police Commissioners, March 23, 1977, 83–86; Charles Kochaikan, "Probe Told Ahern Threatened to Reveal DiLieto Wiretapping," and Stanley J. Venoit, "DeRosa's Tap Testimony 'Vicious Lies'— DiLieto," *New Haven Register*, June 24, 1977, 1. Biagio DiLieto is dead.

171 **both sides rested . . .** Edith Evans Asbury, "Both Sides Rest in Trial . . . ," *New York Times*, April 15, 1971, 51.

171 **1,034 potential jurors . . .** Stan Simon, "Court-Ordered Gag Irked Seale Lawyer," *Hartford Courant*, December 12, 1971, 1.

172 **Judge Mulvey insisted . . .** Stan Simon, "Judge Who Freed Bobby Seale Believed Him Guilty," *Hartford Courant*, November 21, 1971, 1.

172 **Mulvey thought he had a guarantee of anonymity . . .** Ibid.; "Calm New Haven Judge," *New York Times*, September 1, 1970, 24.

173 **As a writer put it . . .** Joelle Dominski, "Panther Judge Interview Raises Doubts of Fitness," *Modern Times*, June 15–30, 1970, 1.

173 **telegram to President Nixon supporting Lieutenant William Calley . . .** Simon, "Judge Who Freed Bobby Seale Believed Him Guilty," 1.

173 **"Judge Mulvey! Judge Mulvey!" Seale hollered . . .** Bobby Seale interview, March 13, 2005.

174   **The pugnacious prosecutor, Markle** . . . Julie Ellison, "Markle: A Fanatic Sways the Court," *Modern Times*, December 15, 1970, 2; Stan Simon, "'Simmering Anger' Shatters Judge-Prosecutor Alliance," *Hartford Courant*, November 28, 1971, 1.

174   **Charles Garry, the flamboyant, jet-setting, West Coast Panther lawyer** . . . Simon, "Court-Ordered Gag Irked Seale Lawyer."

174   **he left the real work** . . . David Rosen interview, September 28, 2004.

174   **She found Garry to be a male chauvinist who disregarded Ericka's interest as he pressed Seale's case** . . . Catherine Roraback interview February 3, 2005; David Rosen interview.

174   **Behind the scenes, Rosen would have to mediate between the two** . . . David Rosen interview.

CHAPTER 18: BETRAYAL

175   **He wanted to look Ericka in the eye** . . . Warren Kimbro interview.

175   **To the outrage of Panther supporters** . . . Jan Von Flatern, "Panther Trial Squeezes Out Public," *Modern Times*, April 1, 1971, 2.

175   **Mulvey didn't allow his friends to pull strings** . . . Jack Keyes interview, January 11, 2005.

176   **The jurors would get to hear the tape** . . . *State v. Seale and Huggins*, 882ff.

176   **her harsh rebukes flew at the ghost** . . . *State v. Seale and Huggins*, 895ff.

176   **"Another defeated black man in a suit and tie"** . . . Freed, *Agony in New Haven*, 225.

176   **the name "Landon" kept appearing** . . . *State v. Seale and Huggins*, 408–10, 972–79, 1036–37, 1059–64.

177   **"I should pick this up"** . . . Kimbro interview.

177   **"We said right on"** . . . *State v. Seale and Huggins*, 1064.

178   **Roraback couldn't believe what she was watching** . . . Roraback interview.

178   **so I called to get another car** . . . *State v. Seale and Huggins*, 1184–85.

179   **Roraback would stop talking to Garry—again** . . . Roraback interview; Stan Simon, "Atty. Roraback Angered by Co-Counsel," *Hartford Courant*, December 19, 1971, 1.

180   "And adding and adding and adding and adding and adding?" . . . *State v. Seale and Huggins*, 1381–82.

180   **it had deleted Warren from the "Agitator Index"** . . . Memo to Director, FBI, from SAC, New Haven, May 12, 1971, authors' collection.

180   **George Sams confronted Warren** . . . Kimbro interview.

CHAPTER 19: THE UNRAVELING OF DINGEE SWAHOO

181   **"Dingee Swahoo . . . Rats, Snitch"** . . . *State v. Seale and Huggins*, 1894.

182   **It was Williams** . . . Ibid., 1688, 1698, 1713, 1772.

183   **"Sister Ericka . . . asked her to check Brother Alex out, and to seduce him".** . . Ibid., 1688–90.

183   **"Ericka brought down the first bucket of hot water"** . . . Ibid., 1696.

183   **Sams's account of what happened when Seale briefly stopped by** . . . Ibid., 1721–23.

184   **Seale once kicked him out** . . . Ibid., 1780.

184   **"Cutty Sauce" (and subsequent tirade)** . . . Ibid., 1911–16.

187   **"Your Honor," Roraback interjected, "I object"** . . . Ibid., 1916.

187   **"3,000 motherfucking times"** . . . Ibid., 1964.

188   **"I have no other questions"** . . . Ibid., 2133.

CHAPTER 20: ERICKA'S GAMBLE

189   **"My advice to black students"** . . . Quoted in Freed, *Agony in New Haven*, 148.

189   **Some days, she might have** . . . Ibid., 234, 288.

189   **Upon his daily entrance, Bobby Seale** . . . Ibid., 235.

189   **On his way to his seat at the defense table** . . . Walter Rochow interview, October 22, 2004.

190   **Roraback and Ericka decided** . . . Catherine Roraback interview, February 3, 2005; Stan Simon, "Atty. Roraback Angered by Co-Counsel," *Hartford Courant*, December 19, 1971, 1.

190   **Roraback discovered Hithe's presence** . . . Roraback interview; Simon, "Atty. Roraback Angered by Co-Counsel."

191   **She penned a tribute** . . . Freed, *Agony in New Haven*, 143.

191   **The captured escapee contacted** . . . Roraback interview. Also, news item about the arrest of the woman from Boston, headed "Conn.," *View from the Bottom*, September 4, 1969.

192   **The police had shot Chicago Panther leader Fred Hampton** . . . Senate Select Committee, *Book III: Final Report*, 223; Swearingen, *FBI Secrets*, 88–89.

192   **Ericka "could have been Pakistani"** . . . Freed, *Agony in New Haven*, 288.

192   **Ericka followed the lead** . . . *State v. Seale and Huggins*, 2808ff.; Lesley Oelsner, "Mrs. Huggins, on Witness Stand, Protests Innocence," *New York Times*, May 12, 1971, 38; Simon, "Atty. Roraback Angered by Co-Counsel."

192   **Judge Mulvey beckoned Roraback to the bench** . . . Roraback interview.

192   **"slowly and calmly, her tall thin frame almost motionless."** . . . **Ericka did raise her voice** . . . Oelsner, "Mrs. Huggins, on Witness Stand."

193   **Sams did order her** . . . *State v. Seale and Huggins*, 2864–66.

193   **She "gave" it to him** . . . Ibid., 2872.

193   **horror stories of her time with George Sams** . . . Ibid., 2900ff.

193   **Shirley Wolterding** . . . Ibid., 2639.

193   **she had met Bobby Seale "just once"** . . . Ibid., 2905.

194   **"Why did all that have to happen?"** . . . Ibid., 2892.

CHAPTER 21: THE CUT-OFF

196   **"That's the way George Sams felt about it"** . . . *State v. Seale and Huggins*, 3058–59.

196   **Ericka "never flustered"** . . . Stan Simon, "Atty. Roraback Angered by Co-Counsel," *Hartford Courant*, December 19, 1971, 1.

197   **"it's very hard, first of all, for a woman to be heard by men"** . . . *State v. Seale and Huggins*, 3158ff.

197   **The moment Roraback had hoped for** . . . Catherine Roraback interview, February 3, 2005; Simon, "Atty. Roraback Angered by Co-Counsel."

199   **In his appeal to the jurors** . . . *State v. Seale and Huggins*, 3443ff.

200   **"Warren Kimbro"** . . . Ibid., 3496ff.
201   **"Even animals don't treat their own like that"** . . . Ibid., 3578ff.

CHAPTER 22: DAYS OF DECISION

202   **It was unanimous** . . . Stan Simon, "Partisans on Seale Jury?" *Hartford Courant*, December 26, 1971, 1. Most of the behind-the-scenes material here about the jurors' deliberations is drawn from this article.
202   **Ericka had sensed it** . . . Stan Simon, "Atty. Roraback Angered by Co-Counsel," *Hartford Courant*, December 19, 1971, 1.
203   **Mulvey declared mistrials** . . . *State v. Seale and Huggins*, 2797.
204   **the next afternoon's meeting in Judge Mulvey's chambers** . . . Catherine Roraback interview, February 3, 2005; David Rosen interview, September 28, 2004.
204   **Mulvey allowed Markle to go first** . . . *State v. Seale and Huggins*, 3804ff.
205   **praise the defendants** . . . Ibid., 3816.
205   **the judge later revealed** . . . Stan Simon, "Judge Who Freed Bobby Seale Believed Him Guilty," *Hartford Courant*, November 21, 1971, 1.
206   **Bobby Seale was ecstatic** . . . Bobby Seale interview, March 13, 2005.
206   **Seale clasped their hands warmly** . . . Walter Rochow interview, October 22, 2004.
206   **supporters prepared to usher her through the crowded hallway onto the Green** . . . Freed, *Agony in New Haven*, 321.
206   **On her way out** . . . Rochow interview.

CHAPTER 23: TIME OUT

209   **A letter pleading Warren's case** . . . Letters to Leonard Russman, Department of Adult Probation, from I. Ira Goldenberg (November 24, 1970), Leander C. Gray (November 24, 1970), Joseph E. Downey (December 3, 1970), Frederic Osborne (December 18, 1970), Milton A. Brown (December 9, 1970), Wesley T. Forbes (December 17, 1970), Michael S. Fuoco (December 14, 1970), the Rev. John P.

Cook (December 1, 1970); all in the Connecticut Department of Corrections file of Warren Aloysious Kimbro, authors' collection.

209 **Making his pitch . . .** Court transcript of Warren Kimbro's sentencing before Judge Harold M. Mulvey, June 23, 1971.

210 **McLucas's lawyer had a plan . . .** Michael Koskoff interview.

211 **The trial produced revelations . . .** Edith Evans Asbury, "Police Agent in Panther Case a Boyhood Friend of Defendant," *New York Times*, December 3, 1970, 32; Asbury, "Undercover Agent Recalls How Role Was Almost Discovered by Black Panthers," *New York Times*, December 2, 1970, 51; Asbury, "Undercover Agent Tells of Panther Drills and Plots," *New York Times*, November 11, 1970, 39; Asbury, "Black Panther Defense Finishes Cross-Examining of Infiltrator," *New York Times*, December 22, 1970, 43; Asbury, "Undercover Agent in Panthers 'Feared' the Police," *New York Times*, December 4, 1970, 38.

211 **Loyalists to Huey Newton gathered in Oakland to remold the party . . .** Pearson, *The Shadow of the Panther*, 234–68.

211 **When they appeared in court on November 19 . . .** Hugh Keefe interview, March 3, 2005.

212 **Warren walked through prison hallways . . .** Accounts in this chapter of Warren Kimbro's prison experiences are drawn largely from Warren Kimbro interviews.

214 **J.J. was flattered . . .** E-mail from Janice (J.J.) to author, April 25, 2005.

214 **Warren belonged in this Harvard program . . .** I. Ira Goldenberg interview, March 22, 2005.

214 **. . . the New Haven office informed J. Edgar Hoover that it was deleting Warren from its "Agitator Index". . .** Memo to Director, FBI, from SAC, New Haven, May 12, 1971, authors' collection.

214 **As a memo four days earlier noted . . .** Memo to Director, FBI, from SAC, New Haven, May 8, 1972.

215 **Iannotti . . . appeared before Superior Court Judge Anthony E. Grillo . . .** Larry Iannotti interview, November 16, 2004.

215 **"Panther Sues to Leave Prison for Harvard" . . .** *Washington Post*, June 8, 1972; memo to Director, FBI, from SAC, New Haven, July 12, 1972, FBI file of Warren Aloysious Kimbro, authors' collection.

215 **They invited Warren to appear on Susskind's syndicated show . . .** Warren Kimbro interviews.

217 **"I miss you precious"** . . . Notes in possession of Warren Kimbro.

217 **"Murderer in 1969, Counselor Today"** . . . Michael Knight, *New York Times*, September 14, 1973, 41.

218 **Hills recommended Warren** . . . Outstandingly Meritorious Performance Award Request, Brooklyn Division, in Warren Kimbro's Connecticut Department of Corrections file, authors' collection.

219 **Corrections Commissioner Manson granted** . . . Letter, Commissioner John R. Manson to Warren A. Kimbro, January 11, 1973, Department of Corrections file.

CHAPTER 24: BMOC

219 **an Ivy Leaguer now** . . . Except where noted, this account of Warren Kimbro's Harvard experiences is drawn from interviews with Kimbro.

219 **Dr. Willie . . . noticed** . . . Charles V. Willie interview, March 21, 2005.

220 **Dr. Willie's course** . . . Willie included a chapter written by Warren in one of his books. Warren Kimbro, "The Smith Family," in Charles Vert Willie, *Black and White Families: A Study in Complementarity* (Dix Hills, N.Y.: General Hall, 1985), 222–26.

221 **A smiling Warren grabs a rope** . . . Marsha R. Cochran, "A Black Panther Who Murdered Salvages His Life and Becomes a College Dean," *People*, November 24, 1975, 64.

222 **his brand of advice initially disappointed student body president Joel Ide** . . . Joel Ide interview, March 18, 2005.

222 **Veronica came up for the fall of '75** . . . The account of Veronica Kimbro's experiences in Willimantic is based on interviews with Veronica Kimbro (April 3, 2005) and Warren Kimbro.

223 **J.J. watched, horrified** . . . E-mail from Janice to author, April 26, 2005.

234 **Germano had fallen into deeper trouble** . . . Interview with Germano Kimbro, November 3, 2004.

226 **commencement exercises at Fitch High School** . . . Associated Press, "Parents Scorn Former Panther as School Graduation Speaker," *Manchester Journal-Inquirer*, June 15, 1976, 7; Warren Kimbro interview.

CHAPTER 25: COMING HOME

228   **To his friends . . .** Wesley Forbes interview, March 24, 2005.

228   **In prison, he had written to J.J. . . .** Notes in possession of Warren Kimbro.

229   **J.J. watched the gentle Warren . . . turn into a violent control freak . . .** The account of violence between Warren Kimbro and J.J. is drawn from Warren Kimbro interviews and from e-mail messages from Janice to author.

229   **Goldenberg launched yet another idealistic . . .** I. Ira Goldenberg interview, March 22, 2005.

230   **The parole board decided to end Warren's parole early . . .** Certificate of Discharge, Board of Parole, Department of Correction, State of Connecticut, in the Connecticut Department of Corrections file of Warren Aloysious Kimbro, authors' collection.

230   **Beverly glanced out the window . . .** This account of Warren and Beverly's courtship is based on interviews with Beverly Kimbro (March 30, 2005) and Warren Kimbro.

233   **Warren began drawing closer again to his daughter, Veronica . . .** Veronica Kimbro interview; Warren Kimbro interviews.

234   **they agreed they should part professional ways . . .** I. Ira Goldenberg interview; Warren Kimbro interviews.

235   **The majority of these inmates were blacks and Latinos under forty . . .** Bruce Western, "Incarceration, Employment and Public Policy," Prepared for the New Jersey Reentry Roundtable, Session Three, New Jersey Institute for Social Justice, April 2003; Western, "The Prison Boom and Labor Market Inequality," presentation based on research funded by the National Science Foundation and the Russell Sage Foundation, December 2004.

235   **Warren built a staff in the image . . .** Interviews with Gaspar Ortega (March 30, 2005), Joseph Caccone (April 4, 2005), and Warren Kimbro.

CHAPTER 26: FOOTSTEPS

The material in this chapter is based on interviews with Germano Kimbro and Warren Kimbro.

Chapter 27: Second Chances

242 **Beverly's boy, Arthur, aka "Little Butch" . . .** The story about Butch is based on interviews with Beverly Kimbro and Warren Kimbro.

246 **Peter Cox called him "Pop" . . .** Peter Cox interview, June 7, 2005.

247 **testifying during hearings of a government investigatory commission . . .** *Interim Report of the Board of Police Commissioners of the City of New Haven on Its Investigation of Illegal Wiretapping*, vol. 1, January 1978 secret testimony, Nicholas Pastore, before the New Haven Board of Police Commissioners, March 23, 1977, authors' collection.

247 **A vanload of cops known as the "Beat-Down Posse" . . .** Paul Bass, "Fury on the Front Lines: On New Haven's Streets, 'Drug War' Tensions Pose Civil-Rights Problems," *New Haven Advocate*, January 22, 1990, 1.

248 **Nick proceeded to turn the department upside down . . .** Paul Bass, "Saint Nick: The Other Side of the Pastore Furor," *New Haven Advocate*, December 22, 1994, 1.

248 **Nick joined with Yale to develop a program . . .** Nicholas Pastore, "Alternatives to 'Surgery': In the World of Community Policing, an Arrest Is the Last Thing Police Want," *Yale Medicine*, November 15, 1995, 16.

249 **at the top of the front page . . .** Joseph Brady, "Former Foes Join Forces to Push Alternative to Jail Project," *New Haven Register*, February 25, 1990.

249 **Warren held no grudge . . .** Warren Kimbro interviews.

Chapter 28: Arts & Ideas

251 **the emergence of "million-dollar blocks" . . .** Jennifer Gonnerman, "Million-Dollar Blocks: The Neighborhood Costs of America's Prison Boom," *Village Voice*, November 16, 2004.

252 **One young woman, a pacifist . . .** Paul Bass, "The Nonsense Police: New Haven Still Defers to Black Panther Bullying and Ego-Tripping," *New Haven Advocate*, June 28, 2001.

252 **Another evening, Bobby Seale himself arrived . . .** Randall Beach, "Passing the Torch," *New Haven Register*, May 22, 2001, 1; author's observation of event; Warren Kimbro interview.

253   **The local daily . . . editorialized . . .** "Grisly Crime Led to May Day: A Moment of Glory for the Left Began with a Murder," *New Haven Register*, May 20, 2001.

253   **Warren and Nick opened up in a more intimate setting . . .** *Next Question: The May Day 1970 Oral History Project*, film by American Beat and International Festival of Arts & Ideas, directed and edited by Elena Oxman and Elihu Rubin, 2003, Yale Digital Media Archives.

Epilogue: Ghosts of Panthers Past

257   **Freddie and Sandra Rackley's modern living room . . .** Rackley family interview with author, October 2004.

259   **"They weren't riffraff" . . .** Carole Mercer Roberts interview, October 2004.

259   **Warren Kimbro thought about Alex Rackley, too . . .** Warren Kimbro interview.

260   **Germano, who founded a program . . .** Germano Kimbro and Warren Kimbro interviews.

261   **Moye still seemed nervous . . .** Kelly Moye interviews, November 10, 2004, and March 14, 2005.

261   **Nor has Rackley's ghost ever fled from George Sams . . .** Prison interview, April 8, 2005; letters from Sams to author, November 17, 2004, and January 9, 2005.

264   **the city . . . paid 1,238 targets . . .** Carole and Paul Bass, "A City Bugged," *Connecticut* magazine, September 1984, 75; Paul Bass, "Wiretap Suit Stirs New Haven Dispute," *New York Times*, Connecticut Weekly section, February 13, 1983, 1.

264   **Edwards visited an artsy hangout . . .** George Edwards interview, January 4, 2005.

264   **He received some attention in 2005 . . .** Erin Crawford, "Is He Johnny Gosch?" *Des Moines Register*, April 5, 2005; Tim White, "100% Confirmation Gannon/Guckert Is Johnny Gosch," http://www.rense.com/general63/100.htm; "Ex FBI Ted Gunderson: Jeff Gannon Is Johnny Gosch," http://www.conspiracyplanet.com/channel.cfm?channelid=2&contentid=1995.

265   **the Satanists had targeted him . . .** Ted Gunderson interview, November 1, 2004.

265   **After earning his law degree . . .** William H. Farley Jr. interview, January 4, 2005.

266   **Nick Pastore watched swans . . .** Nick Pastore interview, November 9, 2004.

266   **he fathered a child . . .** David McClendon, "Pastore Says He Fathered Tot Now in Foster Care," *New Haven Register*, February 5, 1997, 1; Dave Altimari and Karla Schuster, "Mother of Pastore's Baby Has Record," *New Haven Register*, February 6, 1997, 3; Nicholas Pastore as told to Paul Bass, "The Confessions of St. Nick," *New Haven Advocate*, February 13, 1997, 1.

266   **Ericka Huggins sought her refuge . . .** Ericka Huggins interview with Yohuru Williams, July 10, 1995; Will Harper, "Pursuing SYDA: The International Yoga Organization—Some Consider It a Cult—Takes to Court an Ex-Member Bent on Airing Sexual Allegations," *East Bay Express*, January 14, 2004; "The No on Measure Y Campaign," October 5, 2004, http://bayarea.indymedia.org/news/2004/10/1697902.php; Brown, *A Taste of Power*, 408–14.

266   **well-regarded alternative neighborhood school . . .** Pearson, *The Shadow of the Panther*, 261, 282, 297; Brown, *A Taste of Power*, 362, 434; S. Smith, "Former Black Panther Members Recall Struggle," *Oakland Post*, February 27, 1994; Horowitz, *Radical Son*, 240–41.

267   **her own memoirs . . .** Bob Jackson, "Panther Founders Penning Books," *Rocky Mountain News*, September 28, 2000. In a 2004 telephone conversation with the author, Huggins offered the pending memoirs as one of several reasons she wished not to be interviewed on the record for this book.

267   **"What killed the Black Panthers" . . .** Andy Shah, "'Educate to Liberate' Event Unites Student Activists, Former Black Panthers at UCLA," *Daily Bruin*, March 15, 1999.

Bibliography

Ahern, James. *Police in Trouble: Our Frightening Crisis in Law Enforcement.* New York: Hawthorn Books, 1972.

Baldwin, James. *Go Tell It on the Mountain.* New York: Random House, 1953.

Balzer, Richard. *Street Time.* New York: Grossman, 1972.

Bass, Paul. Articles, *New Haven Advocate*, 1990–2004. Collected in Paul Joseph Bass Papers, Manuscript Group 1826, Manuscripts and Archives, Yale University Library.

Brown, Elaine. *A Taste of Power: A Black Woman's Story.* New York: Pantheon Books, 1992.

Cleaver, Kathleen, and George Katsiaficas, eds. *Liberation, Imagination, and the Black Panther Party: A New Look at the Panthers and Their Legacy.* New York: Routledge, 2001.

Clinton, Hillary Rodham. *Living History.* New York: Simon & Schuster, 2003.

Collier, Peter, and David Horowitz. *Destructive Generation: Second Thoughts About the Sixties.* New York: Summit, 1989.

Elkins, Caroline. *Imperial Reckoning: The Untold Story of Britain's Gulag in Kenya.* New York: Henry Holt, 2005.

Epstein, Edward J. "A Reporter at Large: The Panthers and the Police: A Pattern of Genocide?" *The New Yorker*, February 13, 1971.

Freed, Donald. *Agony in New Haven: The Trial of Bobby Seale, Ericka Huggins, and the Black Panther Party.* New York: Simon & Schuster, 1973.

Fullilove, Mindy Thompson. *Root Shock: How Tearing Up City Neighborhoods Hurts America, and What We Can Do About It.* New York: One World/Ballantine Books, 2004.

Gates, Henry Louis, Jr., and Cornel West. *The Future of the Race*. New York: Alfred A. Knopf, 1996.

Goldenberg, I. Ira. *Build Me a Mountain: Youth, Poverty, and the Creation of New Settings*. Cambridge, Mass.: MIT Press, 1971.

Golding, William. *Lord of the Flies: A Novel*. London: Faber & Faber, 1954.

Goldstein, Warren. *William Sloane Coffin Jr.: A Holy Impatience*. New Haven: Yale University Press, 2004.

Greenfield, Jeff. *No Peace, No Place: Excavations Along the Generational Fault*. Garden, City, N.Y.: Doubleday, 1973.

Hersey, John. *Letter to the Alumni*. New York: Knopf, 1970.

Hilliard, David, and Lewis Cole. *This Side of Glory: The Autobiography of David Hilliard and the Story of the Black Panther Party*. Boston: Little, Brown, 1993.

Horowitz, David. *Radical Son: A Generational Odyssey*. New York: Simon & Schuster, 1997.

Jones, Thai. *A Radical Line: From the Labor Movement to the Weather Underground, One Family's Century of Conscience*. New York: Free Press, 2004.

Kabaservice, Geoffrey. *The Guardians: Kingman Brewster, His Circle, and the Rise of the Liberal Establishment*. New York: Henry Holt, 2004.

Kopkind, Andrew. *The Thirty Years' Wars: Dispatches and Diversions of a Radical Journalist, 1965–1994*. London: Verso, 1995.

Kornweibel, Theodore, Jr. *Seeing Red: Federal Campaigns Against Black Militancy 1919–1925*. Bloomington: Indiana University Press, 1998.

McAleer, Dave. *The All Music Book of Hit Singles: Top Twenty Charts from 1954 to the Present Day*. London: Carlton Books, 1994.

Pearson, Hugh. *The Shadow of the Panther: Huey Newton and the Price of Power in America*. Reading, Mass.: Addison-Wesley, 1994.

Peck, Abe. *Uncovering the Sixties: The Life and Times of the Underground Press*. New York: Pantheon Books. 1985.

Perry, Bruce, ed. *Malcolm X: The Last Speeches*. New York: Pathfinder, 1989.

Powledge, Fred. *Model City: A Test of American Liberalism: One Town's Efforts to Rebuild Itself*. New York: Simon and Schuster, 1970.

Rae, Douglas W. *City: Urbanism and Its End*. New Haven: Yale University Press, 2003.

Seale, Bobby. *Seize the Time: The Story of the Black Panther Party and Huey P. Newton*. New York: Random House, 1970.

Sheehy, Gail. *Panthermania: The Clash of Black and Black in One American City*. New York: Harper & Row, 1971.

Siegel, Fred. *The Future Once Happened Here: New York, D.C., L.A., and the Fate of America's Big Cities*. New York: Free Press, 1997.

State v. Ericka Huggins; State v. Bobby G. Seale. Trial transcript.

Swearingen, M. Wesley. *FBI Secrets: An Agent's Exposé*. Boston: South End, 1995.

Taft, John. *Mayday at Yale: A Case Study in Student Radicalism*. Boulder, Colo.: Westview, 1976.

Trickett, Edison J. *Living an Idea: Empowerment and the Evolution of an Alternative High School*. Brookline, Mass.: Brookline Books, 1991.

Tyson, Timothy B. *Radio Free Dixie: Robert F. Williams and the Roots of Black Power*. Chapel Hill: University of North Carolina Press, 1999.

U.S. Congress. Senate. Select Committee to Study Governmental Operations with Respect to Intelligence Activities. *Supplementary Detailed Staff Reports on Intelligence Activities and the Rights of Americans, Book III: Final Report*. 94th Cong., 2nd sess., 1976.

Williams, Yohuru. *Black Politics / White Power: Civil Rights, Black Power, and the Black Panthers in New Haven*. St. James, N.Y.: Brandywine, 2000.

Index